CAPTURED

CAPTURED

The Corporate Infiltration
of American Democracy

Senator Sheldon Whitehouse

with Melanie Wachtell Stinnett

THE NEW PRESS

25 YEARS

NEW YORK
LONDON

Requests for permission to reproduce selections from this
book should be mailed to: Permissions Department,
The New Press, 120 Wall Street, 31st floor, New York, NY 10005.

Published in the United States by The New Press, New York, 2017
Distributed by Perseus Distribution

ISBN 978-1-62097-207-6 (hc)
ISBN 978-1-62097-208-3 (e-book)
CIP data available

The New Press publishes books that promote and enrich public discussion and
understanding of the issues vital to our democracy and to a more equitable world.
These books are made possible by the enthusiasm of our readers; the support of a
committed group of donors, large and small; the collaboration of our many partners in
the independent media and the not-for-profit sector; booksellers, who often hand-sell
New Press books; librarians; and above all by our authors.

www.thenewpress.com

Composition by dix!
This book was set in Electra

Printed in the United States of America

2   4   6   8   10   9   7   5   3   1

To my family. Please know how grateful I am to you for putting up with my choices, for standing by me through the ups and downs, and for always being there when I needed you. In particular, you've helped me keep my head on straight with your irreverence and good humor about my foibles. Such humility as I have is thanks to you.
I love you, and I am grateful.

—S.W.

To my husband and my daughter: thank you.

—M.W.S.

There are more instances of the abridgement of the freedom of the people by gradual and silent encroachments of those in power than by violent and sudden usurpations.

—JAMES MADISON

Contents

Author's Note

THIS BOOK IS ROOTED IN MY LIFELONG EXPERIENCE in government and politics. Without that experience, there'd be no book. More than anyone, I want to dedicate this book to my family—to Sandra and Molly and Alexander—and to acknowledge what they did to make this book possible.

A life in government and politics has its joys and it has its woes. The problem for families is that those joys and woes are not fairly distributed between the politician and his family. I got more of the joys; they got more of the woes. I got the feelings of accomplishment at things done well. I got the camaraderie of politics. I got the exposure to people I might not otherwise have known, and ideas I might not otherwise have considered. I got the attention. They didn't get as much of any of that.

Whether I would have made more money had I pursued a more lucrative career is an unknown. What is a known is that I didn't.

Another known is the time my work in government has required. There were many years of very long hours away from home. Often being home meant bringing work home. Sometimes there were surges of effort where I barely saw my family at all. At one point I was going to work so early and coming home so late that all I could do was kiss my little daughter while she was sleeping. I was in the press a lot at the time, and one evening when she saw me on the news, she asked my wife why I had gone away to the TV, and would I come back.

They have had to endure my defeats and failures, many of which were very public. They have had to console me and buck me up and keep a brave face through their own disappointment for me. They have had to endure harsh political criticisms of me. We all went without TV for a while because the political attack ads against me on the television were so unpleasant, and it wasn't worth explaining it to the kids. Thank goodness it was the time of the VCR—we watched lots of movies. They had to cope with the uncertainty and stress of campaigning, of press attention, of debates, and of election night. They showed amazing resilience: my son kept his close friendship with the son of a political opponent all the way through our demanding race, and they have remained close friends to this day. I'm proud of him for that.

My family members have often lost the chance to make a clean first impression with people, bearing whatever impression their relation with me imposes. Some of their friends may not like my politics, and that can shadow their friendship. Some people may not want to be friends of theirs at all, just for that reason. And it's not offset by the people who want to be their friends just because of my position—those are never real friends.

My family's mistakes have been amplified, and their achievements have been diminished, as a result of my career. My wife is a published, Ivy League–educated doctor of marine science, with a specialty in coastal biology; her appointment as an unpaid board member to our state coastal resources agency was announced by the local newspaper with the headline "Wife of Aide Gets Job." Other staffers in that administration years ago have the right to this day to refer to Sandra as "Wife of Aide"; it was so unfair, it became a thing among us all—a wry, New England way of bonding and standing with her.

I have been really stressed at times. I've tried my best to be a good husband and father, but all that stress couldn't have helped. At one point, after a particularly strenuous ordeal, I went to my doctor for a checkup, and he gave me a surprising diagnosis. Evidently, when one is under a lot of stress, the digestive process can slow down. That produced the memorable diagnosis (which had to be a joyous opportunity for a doctor to deliver, speaking to a politician): "Well, Sheldon, I can tell you that as a medical matter, you are officially F.O.S." I was not too stressed to figure out what that stood for. To those readers who may suspect this of me already—well, you have at least one medical diagnosis in your corner.

The upshot of all of this is that my family has put up with a lot. I expect most political and government families have to put up with a lot. It's not really their fault that they got dragged into this life. So reader, be kind, if you can, to the families.

Acknowledgments

DIANE WACHTELL APPROACHED ME ABOUT WRITING A BOOK, and that invitation launched the thought process about how disparate issues I was working on shared a common theme. I am grateful for her confidence and guidance, and glad that The New Press exists to make this kind of book happen. Melanie Wachtell Stinnett played an important role in this book. She ran down innumerable sources, edited choppy or turgid parts of the book, added additional research and text in various areas, kept me on schedule, patiently coped with my edits, re-edits, and re-re-edits, and organized reviews of drafts by other talented people who all helped make this a better book. My only other book was an assembly of quotations, so this was the first book I have written rather than just compiled. This was Melanie's first effort as a co-author/editor /researcher. It was a pleasure to learn from each other.

—S.W.

THIS BOOK WOULD NOT BE POSSIBLE WITHOUT THE dedicated efforts of The New Press's editors and staff, particularly Carl Bromley, Jed Bickman, and Maury Botton. We are grateful to the whole New Press team. We would also like to thank those who reviewed early drafts of the manuscript: Bill Novak, Trevor Potter, Steven Nightingale, Sabeel Rahman, and Tom Goldstein.

—S.W. & M.W.S.

Introduction

IN THE SENATE, I SEE EVERY DAY how power works in the political sphere. I see who's got it. I see who uses it. I see how they use it. I see the devices by which that power is applied. I see the schemes used to obscure who's pulling the strings. I see the smokescreens put up to distract people so they don't notice the string-pulling. This is my world; it is the ecosystem I inhabit as a United States senator.

The legendary, Pulitzer Prize–winning author William S. White observed, "A senator of the United States is an ambulant converging point for pressures and counter-pressures of high, medium and low purposes."[1] What I see all around me these days is immense pressure deployed by the corporate sector in our government. Some of this corporate power is deployed in traditional ways. For as long as there has been government, there have been efforts by powerful forces to bend government to their private advantage, and to evade or prevent government oversight. For as long as there have been legislatures, there have been efforts to acquire influence over them. For as long as there has been regulation of industries, there have been efforts to control the regulators and to condition them to the interests of the industries they are designed to regulate.

But some of what I see is new. I've had a close-up look at government—as a prosecutor, as a regulator, as a government staffer, as a reformer, as a candidate, and as an elected official. Never in my life have I seen such influence in our elections from corporations and their managers and billionaire owners. Their presence in American elections has exploded, indeed become dominant, as the campaign finance world has become virtually lawless.

Never in my life have I seen such a complex web of front groups sowing deliberate deceit to create public confusion about issues that should be clear. The corporate propaganda machinery is of unprecedented size and sophistication.

Never in my life have I seen our third branch of government, our courts, the place in our governmental system that is supposed to be most immune from politics, under such political sway. The track record of the Supreme Court in particular shows patterns that are completely inconsistent with disinterested neutrality.

It's always been tough to go up against the big guys. But for most of my life I felt we had a fighting chance. American politics has deep traditions of honor. There were always pockets of government that could be counted on to do the right thing. And there was such wisdom and safety in our American system of separated powers that corrupting influences could never take over completely. As a lawyer, and as a student of our Constitution, I believed that our American system would always protect us—maybe not right away, maybe not every time, but ultimately and for sure.

I'm no longer so sure.

Huge segments of the American public think things have gone badly wrong. Indeed, nearly three of every four Americans—71 percent—reported in a February 2016 poll that they were "dissatisfied with the way things are going in the United States at this time."[2] We see these numbers in action as voters across the political spectrum offer enthusiastic support to candidates pledging to change the status quo.

How could this be? We've persevered through a revolutionary war, a civil war, and two world wars. We've endured massive expansions and great depressions. We've overturned slavery, brought women well toward full equality, pushed racism back, and recognized gay relationships. We invented automobiles, airplanes, telephones, TV, the atom bomb, and the Internet. Ours has been a tumultuous 240 years. What now, after all that tumult, has gone wrong?

Abraham Lincoln reminded us at Gettysburg, over a field that covered the decaying remains of thousands of soldiers, both Union and Confederate, that it was our American destiny, and the prize of our Civil War sacrifice, that "government of the people, by the people, and for the people shall not perish from this earth."[3] The thing that has changed the most in our government, and the thing that to me best explains what has gone wrong, is that our politics is no longer "of the people, by the people, and for the people."

Corporations of vast wealth and remorseless staying power have moved into our politics, to seize for themselves advantages that can be seized only by control over government. Organizations of mysterious identity have moved into our politics, as screens for the anonymous power and "dark money" behind them. Political campaigns are now run by new and alien organizations, super PACs and 501(c)(4)s, bizarre creatures unknown to our politics until recently.

When I speak of corporate power in politics, let me be very clear: I do not mean just the activities of the incorporated entities themselves. The billionaire owners of corporations are often actively engaged in battle to expand the influence of the corporations that give them their power and their wealth. Front groups and lobbying groups are often the ground troops when corporate powers don't want to get their own hands dirty or when they want to institutionalize their influence. So-called philanthropic foundations are often the proxies for billionaire families who want influence and who launch these tools to professionalize their influence-seeking.

I count them all as faces of corporate power—just as they do themselves. The internal coordination behind the scenes between the politically active corporate entities, the billionaire funders, the right-wing "philanthropies," the front groups, and the lobbying organizations is constant. The structure of this enterprise, with common funders, interlocking directorates, and overlapping staff, is emerging as a result of academic and investigative studies. From my perch in the Senate, I see it all as one coordinated beast. That is how it behaves, and that is how I'm going to treat it in this book. This apparatus may seem like a very complicated and unwieldy way for corporations to exert influence, but it allows them to give the public the old razzle-dazzle, running intricate plays with what appear to be many independent voices. It's smart strategy.

These forces are everywhere, and they are dominant in every area where their influence on government can be brought to bear. They are right now, as a practical matter, our unseen ruling class. When you

are running for office, they can quietly back you—or your opponent—
with literally unlimited funds, depending on how comfortable they
are with how you'll vote. (The cudgel of secret spending need not
even be swung to have its desired effect; merely brandishing it can
be enough to get the attention, and obedience, of a politician.) Once
you're elected and in office, corporate influence comes in the form of
corporate lobbying—the behemoth on the legislative stage, drowning
out all other lobbying competition by a spending ratio of more than
thirty to one.[4]

As a bill moves through Congress, corporate lobbyists exploit procedural opportunities to accomplish the industry's purposes out of view
of the public. Once a bill becomes law, relentless industry pressure is
brought to bear on the agencies charged with enforcement: appointment of industry-friendly administrators; visible industry "caretaking"
of friendly administrators when they depart their posts (and visible
"freezes" on those who weren't so friendly); heavy lawyering of the
rulemaking and enforcement processes, often as simple brute pressure
to cause delay and cost; and sometimes direct kickbacks. All these avenues give special interests undue influence over administrative agencies, to the point of outright capture of the agency.

When there is a legal challenge to corporate behavior, or a legal
challenge to the way a law is administered, having business-friendly
courts to hear the case becomes important. Here corporate influence
in the selection of judges is brought to bear, business-friendly "train-
ing" for judges at luxurious resorts is offered, and corporate-funded
entities that are not traditional litigants appear in court, sometimes
in flocks, to amplify the corporate message. The Supreme Court can
do more than tilt the balance in business-related cases: the Court can
change the very ground rules of democracy in favor of corporate interests. And corporate forces are hard at work using their power to fix the
judicial system to seize more power.

Civil juries, the Constitution's designated check on outsized power
in the private sphere, have had their place in government shrunk to a
vestige of their intended role, leaving corporate forces free to wheel
and deal with the established, repeat players in government who are
most amenable to their influence.

Meanwhile, a vast corporate enterprise is busy constructing and

marketing a pro-corporate "alternate reality": climate change is an il-
lusion; tobacco is not really that bad for you; lead paint only hurts poor
children with negligent mothers; the ozone hole isn't being caused
by chemicals; various products' association with cancer is unproven;
pollution controls will cost way too much and hurt the economy; consumers should be free not to live in a "nanny state." Corporations have
become less willing to say these things themselves, so over the years
they have outsourced the crafting and selling of this alternate reality to
an array of dozens of front groups with innocent-seeming, respectable-
sounding names.

And corporate forces have acquired influence in an increasingly
compliant and even corporate-owned media. What better way to pro-
pagandize the American public than through the "news"?

It all adds up to massive tentacles of corporate power—particularly
emanating from a few highly regulated sectors, including finance and
fossil fuels—that are usually invisible or obscured but which are quietly and steadily having their way with government. Small wonder
people are angry about a nonresponsive democracy. Contrary to the
popular sentiment that government isn't working anymore, government is working fine; it's just working for the corporations.

Congress today is working great at helping polluters; it's working
great at protecting hedge fund billionaires' low tax rates; it's working
great at helping corporations offshore jobs, at letting chemicals and ge-
netically modified stuff into your food, at creating tax and safety loopholes for industry. Congress is also working great at ignoring corporate
misbehavior—until after a crisis has hurt or killed a lot of people. Even
then, Congress has worked great at having taxpayers bail out the industry that caused the harm.

And worst of all, government is now working great, in a vicious
cycle, to change its own ground rules and lock in the control over
government by big special-influence operators.

People can feel like they are in a car that won't respond to them,
that the car is dangerously out of control, that the car is broken. But
the problem isn't the car; the problem is who's now driving it. Regular
people are no longer in the driver's seat of American democracy.

A corporation is not an inherently bad thing. In proper circumstances and within proper bounds, the corporate form is an immensely

valuable proposition. But the economic ability to amass money can spawn a political desire to amass power. And at a certain level of political power, corporate forces can upshift into political overdrive and use their power to change the political system itself. Beyond just improving outcomes for their industry from the political system, they can make changes to the political system itself that lock in lasting advantages for them and protect their dominance. That overdrive is the most worrisome use of power. That's where I believe we are now, and why I'm writing this book.

Today there is virtually no element of the political landscape into which corporate influence has not intruded, and it is usually the strongest political force arrayed in any part of that landscape. You may not see it, because it is bad strategy for the purveyors of corporate influence to herald their victories; they are better off quietly pocketing their winnings than bragging about them, and they'd rather you not know how effectively they have rigged the game. But, visibly or not, our government has been captured. The "gradual and silent encroachments" that James Madison warned of have come in a corporate guise that Madison and his compatriots did not foresee and were not able to preempt.[5]

The big corporate interests now in control would like you to give up on government. The better solution is not to give up on the American government that generations of Americans fought, bled, and died to leave to us. The better solution is to take it back and put it to work for us. It will be a battle. Even if you do not now see a clean path to victory, remember the admonition of Rabbi Tarfon: "It may not be up to us to complete the work, but neither are we free to desist from it." As citizens, this must be our work.

CAPTURED

CHAPTER ONE

The Constitution's Blind Spot

AMERICA WAS FOUNDED AS AN EXPERIMENT. It was not an easy one. No one anywhere had successfully created our dream: a popular government, without kings and crowns, without aristocracy and class privileges, and safe from military rule by force of arms. Trusting common people with uncommon power—the power to govern themselves—was the great cause of our liberty.

The Founders knew the threats that they were up against. Experienced politicians, they had a keen sense of how easily things could go wrong. They had seen how selfish pressures and popular passions could overwhelm a government, and they knew government power could be captured or perverted to a wrongful purpose. Protecting against these threats, so that a popular government could prevail against them, was the great task of the Constitution. We are all familiar with the renowned system of "checks and balances" the Founders created to preempt the threat that any one branch of government would become too powerful. Yet even with all of the Constitution's precautions, there was at least one major threat that the Founders failed to foresee.

The Founding Fathers were learning on the fly—this truly was an experiment. They had Locke and Montesquieu and other Enlightenment thinkers to give them a general conceptual structure, but their experiment was a more challenging task than penning philosophical principles. They had to adapt those high-minded principles to the pressures of politics and the practicalities of governing. They had to make the theories work amid the dust and drama and passion of real-life politics. This was a new frontier.

The Founders' first effort at a constitution was designed to address the threats to democracy that they perceived. We know what those threats were, because they were the topic of the Federalist Papers. Published in various newspapers in 1787 and 1788 under the pen name "Publius," the Federalist Papers were written by Alexander Hamilton, James Madison, and John Jay to sell the new constitution to skeptical voters across the colonies. The arguments in the Federalist Papers signal to us the concerns of the time.

The predominant concerns were these: how the Constitution would protect the individual from the power of government, how it would protect society from the dangers of faction, and how it would protect the new democracy against the emergence of a new aristocracy or a new royalty. When it came into effect in 1789, the Constitution erected its defense against these threats primarily through its careful separation of powers.

But the Constitution wasn't enough. The American people were not satisfied. They wanted still more assurances about their role and rights as citizens of this new Republic. So the Founders went back and drew up the Bill of Rights. The Bill of Rights did two key things: it buttressed the public rights of the Constitution with an array of hard-and-fast individual rights, and it provided specific defenses of those rights in areas such as free speech, criminal process, and access to a jury.

Getting this done was a long and exhausting process. The Declaration of Independence was signed in 1776; the Bill of Rights wasn't adopted until 1791. A passionate running dialogue lit up that fifteen-year period—a dialogue among brilliant individual Founders, between rival states, between federalists and anti-federalists, and throughout a new American citizenry. They thought deeply and argued fiercely about this new democratic form of government.

And they were proud. Their American achievement reverberated throughout the world. The revolutionary Americans who had pledged "our lives, our fortunes and our sacred honor" to the cause yearned to prove that this experiment was worth all their blood and hope and sacrifice.[1] They felt a keen obligation to history to get this right, and getting it right meant building into this new Constitution defenses against all the threats they perceived. They threw their hearts and souls into building those defenses.

But they overlooked one threat. They overlooked the corporation.

At the time, they overlooked it with reason. The first corporations in America bore no resemblance to big, modern, for-profit entities. Originally, incorporated entities were mostly cities, schools, and charities. They usually had a public purpose or carried out quasi-governmental tasks. By the 1790s, business corporations began to emerge in America, but at the outset they were few. These corporations were usually specific in purpose, and the business purpose was still usually quasi-governmental—to build a toll road or a canal, for instance. They were often given a temporary monopoly, and they often closed up once the corporate purpose was achieved.[2]

The few corporations that existed were fully the legal creatures of state legislatures, and they existed under close local political control. A specific legislative charter spelled out everything from the corporation's capitalization and life span to its functions and operations. If a corporation in some way misbehaved or became politically aggressive, its charter could be revoked or modified, and that ended that. Nothing about corporations looked like a threat. No American mega-corporation marauded through the Founders' political landscape.

On our American continent, the big British corporations threatened no harm. The Hudson's Bay Company (or, more formally, the Governor and Company of Adventurers of England Trading into Hudson's Bay) was operating far away in Canada and not interfering in the American colonies.[3] The Massachusetts Bay Company was long gone; in fact, it had lost its charter even before the colony it founded fought its way to independence.[4]

Had the Founders given more attention to corporations, and foreseen that corporations might slip their bounds of public purpose and public control, every indication is that they would have been skeptical and suspicious of a political role for them. The experience of the great British corporations in the mother country would have been cautionary. The British East India Company notoriously corrupted the English Parliament and foreign governments; its "nabobs" were officers who had enriched themselves enormously in India, returned to

England, and bought themselves seats in Parliament, threatening to turn England into "a sink of Indian wealth."[5] The South Sea Company collapsed in a spectacular bubble, in a rancid combination of what Sir Isaac Newton reportedly called "the madness of a multitude"[6] and what parliamentary investigation called the "most notorious, dangerous and infamous corruption."[7]

The Founders may have thought that determining a political role for corporations was an issue for another day. Were Congress ever to charter a national corporation, safety measures could then be addressed in the charter. (When Congress did charter a national bank in 1791, the debate agitated our politics for fifty years.)[8] They may have attributed the power of those English corporations to the rotten political system in England, which the Founders were rejecting to build a better world. In any event, these scandals were far enough away that they did not provoke the Founders' concern and caution in the drafting of the Constitution.

The Founding Fathers saw no specific threat to our government from corporate entities, so they built in no specific defenses to protect against them. Nowhere in our Constitution or in our Bill of Rights does the word "corporation" even appear. In the eighty-five lengthy articles that together constituted the Federalist Papers, the word "corporation" appeared only three times, one of those times referring to municipal corporations.[9]

We have one pretty solid way to deduce how the Founders would have felt about a political role for corporate entities, had they considered that at the Founding: we know what two of the principal Founders said and wrote about corporations afterward. The genius of the Founding Fathers was perhaps most concentrated in the tiny form of James Madison and in the lanky frame of Thomas Jefferson, and their views are likely illustrative of what might have happened had the Constitution addressed the problem of corporations in our politics.

James Madison grew to see the dangers of corporations by 1817. That was far too late for our Constitution, but Madison's warning of two hundred years ago is plain: "There is an evil which ought to be guarded against in the indefinite accumulation of property from the capacity of holding it in perpetuity by ecclesiastical corporations. The power of all corporations ought to be limited in this respect. The growing wealth acquired by them never fails to be a source of abuses." [10] Similarly, in 1816, Thomas Jefferson had urged that we "crush in its birth the aristocracy of our monied corporations which dare already to challenge our government to a trial of strength, and bid defiance to the laws of our country." [11]

Twenty-five years earlier, when our great American constitutional effort concluded with the Bill of Rights, that threat to our country of a "trial of strength" was not yet present. As corporations blossomed in the booming 1790s, the traditional road, bridge, and canal monopolies remained of little concern. [12] But the 1790s also brought banking corporations. [13] These new entities caused new concerns, and the Founders' worries about them are instructive. Banking corporations were beyond the familiar mold for American corporations. They had no fixed, tangible purpose, and there were no obvious limits to their wealth or power, their reach, or their duration—they had no natural end. These characteristics rang alarm bells in the Founders' minds.

Looking back on this time through the lens of scholarly history, Supreme Court justice John Paul Stevens summed up the Founders' dim view of the corporation: "Members of the founding generation held a cautious view of corporate power and a narrow view of corporate rights." [14] And it was not just the Founders who came to see these new, emboldened corporations as a threat to popular self-governance if unleashed in the political arena. The American people long have as well. As Justice Stevens wrote, Americans "have recognized a need to prevent corporations from undermining self-government since the founding" and "have fought against the distinctive corrupting potential of corporate electioneering since the days of Theodore Roosevelt." [15] Indeed, at the Founding, most states prohibited any political contribution by a corporation, and punished it as a criminal offense. [16] The early restrictions on corporations in the nineteenth century were so limiting that building major enterprises such as Standard Oil required quite a bit of lawyerly ingenuity. The Rockefeller trust, for example, was created to work around laws restricting corporations from holding stock in other entities. That's why it was "trusts" that had to be busted. [17]

Economically, a corporation can be a great boon. The business corporation aggregates capital with unprecedented efficiency of both cost and purpose. Neither death nor illness interrupts it. It allocates liability and risk in ways that encourage investment. It is probably safe to say that the corporate form has allowed the creation of more wealth than any other invention. As an economic actor, it is without peer.

As a political actor, however, the corporation is a dangerous entity. The valuable characteristics of the corporate form as an economic tool are dangerous when pitted against humans in the political sphere. It was these characteristics of a modern for-profit corporation that members of the Founding generation came to perceive with such distress.

First, for-profit corporations are dedicated exclusively to profit-making, by law. That is their solemn and *sole* duty to their shareholders.[18] In business, this is an estimable characteristic, ensuring loyalty and diligence. In politics, where moral issues and public goods are so often at stake, such single-mindedness is a flaw.

Second, corporations have no soul or conscience. Courts have said they "have no personal attributes"[19]; a corporation is "without either mental or moral powers,"[20] is "without power to think, speak, or act, except as live sentient human beings may think, speak, and act for it,"[21] and "lacks capacity for numerous abilities of a natural person."[22] An artificial being without conscience or remorse, it is kept from misconduct not by an internal moral compass but by specific laws or by the adverse business prospect of gaining so bad a reputation as to interfere with its profit-making.

Third, corporations have no loyalty to any flag or nation. Mostly this is true of modern multinational corporations, which move assets, jobs, and intellectual property around the globe at will. Exxon's former CEO is quoted as saying, "I'm not a U.S. company and I don't make decisions based on what is good for the U.S."[23] They have only a simple fiduciary loyalty to their shareholders. Some have revenues that exceed those of countries in which they operate.

Fourth, corporations do not rest, retire, or die. They are persistent and unrelenting. The legal term is "perpetual succession," meaning "artificial life extending beyond the natural lives of the incorporators, directors, and officers."[24] A corporation "does not die in the sense that a person dies."[25] Nor does it rest in the sense that a person rests.

Fifth, there is no natural limit to corporations' size; they can hold preposterous sums of money. In politics, where "money is the mother's milk,"[26] those sums can be used to acquire influence for the corporation, so as to promote policies that enrich the corporation well beyond the cost of buying that influence. Indeed, given the corporation's fiduciary obligation, it has some natural economic obligation to use its power to that end.

Finally, there is no natural limit to their appetite. No corporation says, "You know, I think I've made enough money," and pushes back from the table. No corporate lobby says, "You know, I think I've acquired enough political influence," and goes out to play with the grandchildren.

The continuity, single-mindedness, relentlessness, and efficiency that these characteristics permit are valuable qualities in economic enterprise. In the political arena, they present risks, which become acute if a corporation makes the fateful decision to pursue political influence as a moneymaking strategy. It is a voracious spiral: the more money the corporate entity can make through political influence, the more money it can justify spending to acquire that influence. The more money it spends, the greater its influence, the more it can use that influence to make more money, and so on, once acquiring political influence becomes a corporate profit-making strategy.

Rare is the human being who desires to pursue, or is capable of pursuing, this influence-purchasing enterprise with such relentless and single-minded determination. We humans ordinarily have families and churches, illnesses and distractions, hobbies and responsibilities of various kinds that get in the way. We may be passionate about our politics, but we need our sleep.

The United States Supreme Court of the twentieth century summed up the political role indicated by these corporate characteristics thus: "That invisible, intangible, and artificial being, that mere legal entity, a corporation aggregate, is certainly not a citizen."[27] As described by legal scholar Burt Neuborne, the "for-profit business corporation [is] an artificial state-created legal fiction vested with unlimited life, entity shielding, limited shareholder liability, negotiable shares, and highly favorable rules encouraging the acquisition, accumulation, and retention of other people's money."[28] Supreme Court justice John Paul Stevens reminded us that "corporations are different from human beings," because unlike us, corporations "have no consciences, no beliefs, no feelings, no thoughts, no desires."[29] Putting these observations into a political context, Justice Stevens noted that corporations are not "members of 'We the People' by whom and for whom our Constitution was established."[30] "Certainly not a citizen," "different from human beings," not "members of 'We the People'"—all these descriptors imply little or no political role for corporations.

Once let loose in the political sphere, however, the sum of these corporate characteristics is a political creature with momentous natural advantages over its human competitors. The Framers simply would not recognize the constitutional alien that is the modern corporation operating in our democracy; of course they didn't design limits on the political activities of an entity they couldn't even imagine.

Add to these characteristics the twentieth-century advertising and marketing skills corporations have developed to sell their products, which apply well to the task of manipulating human voters. Add on size sufficient to dwarf many sovereign nations, and the massive profit that political ventures can provide. Then add the twenty-first-century technologies of constant communication. Finally, add secrecy. The result is a power that could turn our popular democracy into high-tech corporate feudalism if we don't learn how to restrain it.

This book addresses how corporations have grown to a size and power and political role unimaginable to the Founders of our country; how the modern corporation has exploited the gap in the Founders' constitutional foresight; how corporations now win the "trial of strength" against our democracy that Jefferson warned about; and what political prizes are sought and seized by corporate power through its political victories in that "trial of strength." Finally, this book looks at the restraints the Founders *did* build into the system, from the civil court system to an independent press to citizens' right to vote—restraints that can and must be employed to reclaim and reinvigorate our American popular democracy and restore to its proper preeminence the office of "citizen," the one office all Americans occupy.

James Madison is said to have warned that "the day will come when our Republic will be an impossibility. It will be an impossibility because wealth will be concentrated in the hands of a few. A republic can not stand upon bayonets, and when that day comes, when the wealth of the nation will be in the hands of a few, then we must rely upon the wisdom of the best elements in the country to readjust the laws of the nation to the changed conditions."[31] I believe that the day has come, and that readjustment is needed to reclaim the power that has slipped away from the hands of regular American citizens and into the grasp of corporate concentrated wealth.

The big, politically active corporations love having us sit on the couch watching ads paid for by their front groups and deciding which of those ads appeal most to our opinions, fears, and prejudices. But that is being a consumer of their political product, not being a citizen. A citizen is more than a consumer. However much the tentacles of corporate political interference may coil around and through our democracy, at the end of the day the survival of our democratic experiment depends on the active participation of the people. Citizens need to get up off the couch and set things right.

We've gotten off the couch before.

When the Cuyahoga River in Ohio caught fire, Americans woke up to the environmental damage we were doing, started Earth Day, and passed a wealth of environmental laws that have made American life better and safer: the Clean Air Act, the Clean Water Act, hazardous waste laws, chemical safety laws, and laws protecting endangered species.[32] What had happened? The creeping reach of pollution's effects on all of us had reached a point where it sparked a reaction. Our reaction changed the country and made it a much healthier place to live.

When we realized our diets were killing us, many Americans left behind the Wonder Bread, the canned vegetables, and the TV dinners. When I was young, a health food store was a rarity, even an oddity. In 2015, Americans spent an estimated $37 billion on organic food.[33] We are living nearly ten years longer now than when I was born. What happened? The creeping effects of an all-processed-foods diet reached a point for us where it sparked a reaction. Our reaction changed our diets and made us a healthier and more vigorous people.

A similar reaction is due with respect to our democracy. Too much of our democratic debate today is the political equivalent of pollution and junk food. Other generations solved other problems; it's our turn to solve this one.

We can take example and heart from the fighting spirit of the

bipartisan Roosevelts. Democrat Franklin D. Roosevelt saw the powerful forces of "organized money" (as dangerous, he said, as an "organized mob") arrayed against him.[34] Here is how he responded to what
he had called "this resolute enemy within our gates"[35] in an address to
the nation: "Never before in all our history have these forces been so
united against one candidate as they stand today. They are unanimous
in their hate for me—and I welcome their hatred. I should like to have
it said of my first Administration that in it the forces of selfishness and
of lust for power met their match. I should like to have it said of my
second Administration that in it these forces met their master."[36]

Republican Teddy Roosevelt saw a similar enemy: "Behind the os-
tensible government sits enthroned an invisible government owing no
allegiance and acknowledging no responsibility to the people. To destroy this invisible government, to dissolve the unholy alliance between
corrupt business and corrupt politics, is the first task of the statesman-
ship of the day."[37] His call was clear: "Our government, National and
State, must be freed from the sinister influence or control of special
interests. . . . We must drive the special interests out of politics. . . .
The citizens of the United States must effectively control the mighty
commercial forces which they have called into being. There can be
no effective control of corporations while their political activity remains."[38] Ever the optimist in a fight, Teddy Roosevelt concluded: "To
put an end to it will be neither a short nor an easy task, but it can be
done."[39]

CHAPTER TWO

The Growth of Corporate Power

BEN COHEN, FOUNDER OF BEN & JERRY'S, has observed: "Unfortunately, the greatest collaboration in history has been between money and politics, which helps only the rich."[1] The corporate form has been a great facilitator of that collaboration. History shows that corporations have created immense economic value. History also shows that this value has constantly been accompanied by a political threat to popular democracy. Generation after generation has noticed; at times, this contest between corporate power and popular democracy has been the defining public issue of the day. And the key lesson of this history is that in this contest, democracy has won big victories against the tide of corporate influence. Brave Americans have stood up, fought back, and won against corporate political power.

Even at their very beginning in ancient Rome, corporations were seen as rivals to government. Sources as diverse as Blackstone's famous *Commentaries*, from the 1760s, and the 1917 *Fletcher Cyclopedia of the Law of Corporations* describe the antagonism thousands of years ago between corporations and government. According to *Fletcher*, "The development of corporations in Rome was gradual, and for a long period, in the face of more or less pronounced governmental hostility. From the time of the Twelve Tables until the days of the emperors, corporate activity was closely hedged about by restrictions, and decrees denouncing as illicit those corporations that had started upon their careers without authority, or had transgressed in any way, occurred frequently."[2] Through medieval times and guilds, the *Fletcher Cyclopedia* describes the great trading corporations of England as being "looked upon as public agencies, to which had been entrusted the duty of regulating foreign trade."³ These English corporations had the natural political limit that they "could be created only by the will of Parliament or of the Crown" and were subject to government's direct supervision.⁴

In early America, *Fletcher* reports, "there was a distrust or disfavor of private corporations," and this "cloud of disfavor" persisted through the Founding period. This distrust can be seen in the very limited number of corporations chartered in eighteenth-century America: *Fletcher* notes that "during the colonial period of American history, there were only six purely native-born business corporations." Nor was there much corporate activity between the Declaration of Independence and the drafting of the Constitution: "only 20 were added to this list during the 13-year period preceding the adoption of the federal Constitution." Though corporations were not mentioned in the text of the Constitution and their future political power was not foreseen, "misgivings respecting the power of Congress to form corporations" colored the ratification of the Constitution by the states, according to *Fletcher*. Even after ratification, in the last eleven years of the eighteenth century, "the total number of charters granted did not exceed 200"—there was growth, but not the explosion that was to follow.⁵

The United States Supreme Court's first famous and consequential case dealing with corporations concerned Dartmouth College, an early corporation, in 1819. The case was a superficially simple fight for control over the power to appoint the board of trustees.⁶ New Hampshire asserted the right of the legislature to pass a law changing the appointments, Dartmouth's trustees resisted, and Daniel Webster—a leading senator of the day, two-time secretary of state, and renowned orator—argued on behalf of the college.

Chief Justice John Marshall's decision described the corporation in the traditional way, as "an artificial being, invisible, intangible, and existing only in contemplation of law. Being the mere creature of law," he continued, "it possesses only those properties which the charter of its creation confers upon it either expressly or as incidental to its very existence."⁷ This is a recurring theme in American law. Various courts over the years have described corporations as "a mere creature of the law, invisible, intangible, and incorporeal,"⁸ "a mere conception of the legislative mind,"[9] and "a purely artificial body created by law, [which] can act only in accordance with the law of its creation."[10] A corporation, one court said, is "but a convenience, a facility, only possessing the powers conferred by the creator upon it and subject to the valid, appropriate measures of control, surveillance, and regulation governments may impose."[11] (From my perch in the Senate, I would interject, it seems that it is corporate political power that now seeks to impose its "measures of control, surveillance and regulation" upon our democracy, not vice versa.)

But Marshall decided the case for the college, espousing a new theory that legislative control over a corporate charter was not absolute. The Supreme Court determined that, once created, a corporation had certain rights against its own creator.[12] This was a fateful decision, whose dimensions have been litigated ever since.

In 1839, only twenty years after the Dartmouth College decision, Congressman Charles Jared Ingersoll of Pennsylvania gave a speech significant enough that it was published verbatim as an appendix to the January edition of the *United States Magazine and Democratic Review*, a famous anti-aristocratic periodical of the day. His speech warned that in government, "corporation power is now an overshadowing influence," and called for the "restoration of public supremacy," without which, he said, "banks are government, and the very worst government."[13]

It was the banking corporations, in particular, that concerned Ingersoll, and with good reason. As banking corporations had multiplied in number and size, so did their corrupt dealings with the legislators who had final say over which banks received charters and which did not. When the Bank of the United States's charter expired in 1812, bankers pursued a charter for what would be the country's largest bank through such corrupt means that several of their lobbyists were indicted for bribery—though none was ultimately convicted. In the 1820s, a politician from New York—future president Martin Van Buren—infamously dominated banking policy by doling out charters to friends and systematically blocking foes.[14] The corruption ran both ways: the more legislators used such power to pick and choose the winners in finance, the more incentive bankers had to lobby—and bribe— those legislators.

As Ingersoll put it, banking corporations had by then become "political engines of peculiar magnitude and moment," creating what he called "our present government by corporate supremacy." Corporations, Ingersoll said, "at this moment absolutely govern this commonwealth and this union of commonwealths with more sway than even its legitimate institutions." Ingersoll went on to describe the new banking corporations as "a novelty wholly unforeseen by the constitutions; a vast fungus grown upon government,"[15] and harked back to Jefferson's concern about what would happen in the "trial of strength" between government and "the aristocracy of our monied corporations."[16] Before long, it would be more than banking corporations that had Americans concerned.

Great and wealthy industrial corporations appeared suddenly as the nineteenth century drew to a close. Famed organizational sociologist Charles Perrow relates: "Until the 1890s there were only a few large [corporations], in textiles and railroads and the steel and locomotive industries. Then there was a spurt at the turn of the century."[17] There were thirty thousand corporations in 1860; by 1915 there were three hundred thousand.[18] Within only five years at the turn of the century, most of the two hundred biggest corporations of the time were established, many of which, according to Perrow, "still rule their industries."[19]

Bear in mind the novelty of these great beasts, too. As economists Jessica Hennessey and John Wallis observe in *Corporations and American Democracy*, "The only comparably large organizations historically were governments, armies or churches."[20] The suddenness of the emergence of these new corporate entities, coupled with their size, made them "profoundly controversial."[21] As historian H.W. Brands put it in *American Colossus*: "Capitalism threatened to eclipse democracy."[22]

Immense economic value has come to America via human effort organized through the corporate form; particularly in the industrial era, this was vital to our nation's development. As law professor Daniel Crane describes the unique benefits of the corporate structure, "[t]he mechanized processes, infrastructure investments, and enormous fixed costs that characterized the railroads, factories, mills, refineries and pipelines of the late nineteenth century required unprecedented aggregations of capital, to which the newly accessible corporate form lent a ready hand."[23] Though often producing conditions that were hellish for workers, the corporate form was an economic blessing for the country.

The mistake was to let these economic actors intrude into politics. Corporations would inevitably become brutal political players, because, as sociologist Edward A. Ross has observed, "the force devoted to wresting government from the people will correspond to the magnitude of the pecuniary interest at stake."[24] These new aggregators of capital had enormous pecuniary interests at stake, and were motivated to wrest power with a force not seen before.

This was the era of Upton Sinclair's *The Jungle*, published in 1906 to expose the horrendous conditions in the meatpacking industry, where a few mega-corporations had consolidated power. And it was the era of muckrakers including Ida Tarbell, Lincoln Steffens, and Ray Baker, who together produced a 1903 issue of the famous *McClure's Magazine* exposing the corruption that corporate power brought to the financial and political systems of the day.[25] Tarbell dove deep into the rise of John D. Rockefeller, cataloging how he aggregated power to control the means of oil production and distribution across the country, and abused it, to build Standard Oil into a monolith of unmatched proportions. A summary by historian Doris Kearns Goodwin, quoting Tarbell, captured Rockefeller's efforts to manipulate the economic system in the 1870s and 1880s to accumulate wealth and power. It stands as a warning of the dangerous ambitions corporate power can harbor, and it serves as a reminder that other businesses and enterprises are often the victims of those ambitions.

> He began his ascent by flouting the common law to secure favorable rates from the railroads, allowing him to drive his rivals out. "At the same time he worked with the railroads to prevent other people getting oil to manufacture, or if they got it he worked with the railroads to prevent the shipment of the product. If it reached a dealer, he did his utmost to bully or wheedle him to countermand his order. If he failed in that, he undersold until the dealer, losing on his purchase, was glad enough to buy thereafter of Mr. Rockefeller." In the end, "every great campaign against rival interests which the Standard Oil Company has

carried on has been inaugurated, not to save its life, but to build up and sustain a monopoly in the oil industry."[26]

Historian William Novak has noted, "though concern about public corruption was as old as the republic, what was new at the turn of the 20th century was an acute awareness of the unprecedented threat *to the polity* posed by the arrival of large scale business and corporate interests in rail, oil, meatpacking, and insurance, whose corruptions were cataloged in a seemingly endless series of reports and even fictional portrayals."[27]

State legislators across America had seen corporations gaining enormous financial and political power in the late nineteenth century, and they had tried to contain the growing threat. The general rule, according to the *Fletcher Cyclopedia*, was to restrict a corporation's powers to those "only as were expressly granted to it by its enabling act."[28] This put controlling power in the people's representatives to "enable" the corporation or not by legislative act, as the state legislatures saw fit. Corporations were denied the automatic right to do all things that a natural person could do and instead were limited to specifically granted powers. That restriction was important to allay public suspicions of this enormous new force.[29]

California offers one example. California's 1879 state constitution was designed specifically to protect against corporate power. The California Supreme Court, in a decision decades later looking back on the state's founding period, noted that the California constitution was drafted "to guard against . . . actual or potential danger existing or foreshadowed in that marvelous expansion of corporate growth in varied and widening fields of activity which mark that epoch in our state and national history." The safeguards included restrictions within the state constitution, "covering many pages thereof," including "limitations upon corporate powers, definitions of corporate liabilities and restrictions upon the otherwise unlimited right of the legislature to unduly extend the one or to remove or qualify the other."[30]

Why would Californians thus restrict even their own elected legislature? The only logical reason is that Californians sensed the danger of corporate influence over their legislature and desired to build into the state's constitution some protection from what corporate power could do if it were to control legislative power and upend the natural order.

California was not alone in seeing corporate menace: *Fletcher* reports that the development of state constitutions in the mid- to late nineteenth century was characterized by "an attitude of suspicion and fear toward the corporate mechanism."[31] The result was restrictions, lots of them. At first, as Justice Louis Brandeis later recounted, "corporations could be formed under the general laws only for a limited number of purposes. . . . Permission to incorporate for 'any lawful purpose' was not common until 1875; and until that time the duration of corporate franchises was generally limited to a period of 20, 30 or 50 years. . . . The powers which the corporation might exercise in carrying out its purposes were sparingly conferred and strictly construed."[32]

By the time the industrial boom of the late nineteenth century reached its apex, however, many of these restrictions on corporate activity were more honored in the breach than the observance; the regulatory system set up by state governments to limit corporate power had essentially collapsed. This was not because Americans felt safe, or because the restrictions had proved unwise. It was, as Justice Brandeis concluded, because of "the conviction that it was futile" for states to continue to insist upon restrictions on the size and powers of business corporations, as local restrictions in one state "would be circumvented by foreign incorporation" in another state.[33] In other words, corporations had created a race to the bottom among the states.

New Jersey was first to break from the others, with its Holding Company Act of 1891, which allowed corporations to own stocks in other firms and thus enabled the major trusts to grow and expand.[34] This move earned New Jersey the contemporary nickname the "Traitor State."[35] New Jersey benefited mightily from being the first to fold, to the tune of a nearly $3 million surplus in its treasury in incorporation-related fees. Regulation followed. As historian Daniel Crane notes, "It was little wonder that, despite grumbling about the 'traitor state,' most other states soon followed suit."[36]

Decades later, the Supreme Court would describe America during the Gilded Age as deeply suspicious of corporations. Justice John

Harlan reflected: "All who recall the condition of the country in 1890 will remember that there was everywhere, among the people generally, a deep feeling of unrest. . . . [T]he conviction was universal that the country was in real danger from another kind of slavery sought to be fastened on the American people; namely, the slavery that would result from aggregations of capital in the hands of a few individuals and corporations controlling, for their own profit and advantage exclusively, the entire business of the country, including the production and sale of the necessaries of life."[37] Justice Brandeis wrote, "There was a sense of some insidious menace inherent in large aggregations of capital, particularly when held by corporations."[38]

Another such voice was Thomas Cooley, a distinguished lawyer, chief justice of the Michigan Supreme Court, and the first chairman of the Interstate Commerce Commission. In 1874, he had warned that "the most enormous and threatening powers in our country have been created; some of the great and wealthy corporations [have] greater influence in the country at large and upon the legislation of the country than the States to which they owe their corporate existence."[39] The legendary progressive journalist William Allen White described the Senate during this period as a place where senators represented not states but "principalities and powers in business. One Senator . . . represents the Union Pacific Railway System; another the New York Central; still another the insurance interests of New York and New Jersey."[40] Charles Francis Adams Jr. looked at state legislatures and saw them "now universally becoming a species of irregular board of railroad direction."[41] Historian George Thayer, looking back at the Gilded Age, concluded, "Never has the American political process been so corrupt. No office was too high to purchase, no man too pure to bribe, no principle too sacred to destroy, no law too fundamental to break."[42]

The effect on the public of what historian Doris Kearns Goodwin refers to as a "web of corruption" between corporations and government was to shake popular confidence in American democracy.[43] Even thoughtful leaders of the establishment held that view. No one was more establishment than Elihu Root, a distinguished New York corporate lawyer before becoming secretary of war and secretary of state under Teddy Roosevelt. Root in 1894 described corporate influence as "the constantly growing evil in our political affairs, which has, in my judgment, done more to shake the confidence of the plain people of small means in our political institutions, than any other practice which has ever obtained since the foundation of our government."[44] The very non-establishment muckraker Ray Baker concurred, and wrote in 1906, "Men were questioning the fundamentals of democracy, inquiring whether we truly had self-government in America, or whether it had been corrupted by selfish interests."[45] As the nineteenth century closed, corruption-fighting President Grover Cleveland warned: "Corporations, which should be the carefully restrained creatures of the law and the servants of the people, are fast becoming the people's masters."[46]

At the end of the nineteenth century, however, while corporate power had met politicians smart enough to fear it, it had not yet met the force that could tame it, and meaningful restraint of the great railroads, monopolies, and other industrial powers was far from the order of the day. As legal historian Adam Winkler relates, it took scandals for the public to understand the true extent of corporate meddling in politics, such as a headline-grabbing insurance scandal that exposed corporate executives using policyholder funds to throw extravagant parties in New York. The investigation that followed showed life insurance companies not only abusing corporate funds but directly contributing to candidates running for office. The investigation pulled back the curtain on corporate political power for all to see.[47]

Corporations back then corrupted politics because they could, and because corrupting our politics brought them such lavish financial rewards. Indeed, it was in this era that President William McKinley's political operative Mark Hanna famously quipped, "There are two things that are important in politics. The first is money, and I can not remember what the other one is."[48] The big corporations were gushers of money. With no natural limit on the corporate effort to corrupt, American citizens had to push back, and they did. The shaken confidence of what Root called the "plain people of small means" moved the country to action.[49] And what Root memorably described as "the economic capture of representative government" brought the emergence, at the turn of the century, of the Progressive movement.[50]

The 1896 presidential race may have been the straw that broke the back of public tolerance for corporate corruption. Democrat William

Jennings Bryan had run as a reformer, "railing against railroads, big banks, the gold standard, and the concentration of economic and political power."[51] Yet he stood no real chance against his opponent, Republican William McKinley, the candidate of the wealthy whose famed political strategist, Mark Hanna, actually assessed banks at 0.25 percent of their capital to directly fund McKinley's campaign.[52] The subsequent influence of these banks in the McKinley administration was unavoidable; after all, they had paid for the campaign.

The president who carried on the fight to contain corporate political power with the greatest gusto and effect was McKinley's vice president and (after McKinley's assassination) his successor: the indomitable Teddy Roosevelt. To Roosevelt, Jefferson's concern about a "trial of strength" between corporate and government power was at hand: "the great special business interests," he said in his famous 1910 "New Nationalism" speech, "too often control and corrupt the men and methods of government for their own profit."[53] Roosevelt saw the plain difference between corporate economic activity and corporate political activity: "The Constitution guarantees protection of property, and we must make that promise good. But it does not give the right of suffrage to any corporation."[54]

To Roosevelt, the very survival of our democracy depended on whether power was held by the people or by the special interests. He wrote in a 1911 essay: "The existence of this Nation has no real significance . . . unless it means the rule of the people. . . . Unless this is in very truth a government of, by, and for the people, then both historically and in world interest our National existence loses most of its point."[55]

What he called a "matter of necessity" brought out Teddy Roosevelt's competitive spirit. Roosevelt's enemies were big, but this did not confound him; as he said in a 1912 speech, "It is imperative to exercise over big business a control and supervision which is unnecessary as regards small business. . . . a wicked big interest is necessarily more dangerous to the community than a wicked little interest."[56] As put at the time by a staffer at the muckraking *McClure's Magazine*, taking on the big corporations and titans of industry who controlled them was "a challenge such as his nature would never ignore."[57]

In this contest for power, Roosevelt made subordination of business to government a conservative cause: "The true friend of property, the true conservative, is he who insists that property shall be the servant and not the master of the commonwealth. . . . The citizens of the United States must effectively control the mighty commercial forces which they themselves have called into being." [58]

Roosevelt's solution to the corrupting influence of corporate money in elections was legislative. Focusing on "a law prohibiting all corporations from contributing to the campaign expenses of any party," Roosevelt decreed in his 1906 State of the Union address: "Let individuals contribute as they desire; but let us prohibit in effective fashion all corporations from making contributions for any political purpose, directly or indirectly." [59] With that challenge, the battle over what was to be called the Tillman Act was joined.

In a 2016 speech at the Brookings Institution, Trevor Potter, former chairman of the Federal Election Commission, called the Tillman Act "one of the first major laws geared toward reducing the corrupting influence of big money on American politics." Describing the act's impetus, Potter noted, "More and more citizens felt that government had become a tool of campaign contributors rather than responsive to average voters. State legislatures and Congress were seen as 'in the pockets' of economic interests who perverted legislation to serve private purposes rather than the public good." [60]

In opposing the Tillman Act, early twentieth-century corporate forces tried to wrap themselves in the flag of freedom and the mantle of the Constitution. Roosevelt wasn't buying it. His position foreshadowed that of his cousin FDR, who some years later referred to "the economic royalists" who "complain that we seek to overthrow the institutions of America." In his acceptance speech for renomination for the presidency in 1936, FDR wrote: "What they really complain of is that we seek to take away their power. Our allegiance to American institutions requires the overthrow of this kind of power. In vain they seek to hide behind the flag and the Constitution. In their blindness they forget what the flag and the Constitution stand for. Now, as always, they stand for democracy, not tyranny; for freedom, not subjection; and against a dictatorship by mob rule and the over-privileged alike." [61]

In the battle between big corporations and government, Teddy

Roosevelt was a government man. As he said in his Annual Message to Congress in 1907, "The fortunes amassed through corporate organiza-tion are now so large, and vest such power in those that wield them, as to make it a matter of necessity to give to the sovereign—that is, to the Government, which represents the people as a whole—some effec-tive power of supervision over their corporate use. In order to insure a healthy social and industrial life, every big corporation should be held responsible by, and be accountable to, some sovereign strong enough to control its conduct." [62]

Corporations were deeply entrenched in America's elections at the time of the Tillman Act (even Theodore Roosevelt's campaign took corporate contributions in 1904). But when Roosevelt set his sights on getting corporate money out of politics, he homed in and fought hard. And with the tools of the presidency and its bully pulpit at his disposal, he won.

The evil of corporate money in political elections was so apparent in that era that the Senate committee working on the Tillman Act deemed it unnecessary to make an expansive legislative record in sup-port of the law—it was too obvious. They had seen too much corrup-tion up close. The Senate report on the bill simply stated: "The evils of the use of [corporate] money in connection with political elections are so generally recognized that the committee deems it unnecessary to make any argument in favor of the general purpose of this measure. It is in the interest of good government and calculated to promote purity in the selection of public officials." [63]

It is a noteworthy sidebar that the final version of the Tillman Act, passed in 1907, did not require proof of corrupt intent by the corpo-ration. Corporate corruption of politics was so self-evident that the mere contribution of corporate funds to politicians sufficed to estab-lish "corruption," as the term was used in the Act.[64] When Roosevelt said, "Corporate expenditures for political purposes . . . have supplied one of the principal sources of corruption in our political affairs," the bill he championed proved that he did not mean corporate political spending was *potentially* corrupting.[65] Corporate political spending *was* corruption, plain and simple (a view that contrasts with that of the five Supreme Court justices who gave us the *Citizens United* decision a century later).

Various loopholes have come and gone since, but the principle embodied in the Tillman Act more than a hundred years ago—that inanimate business corporations are not free to spend corporate dollars to influence our campaigns for elected office—has long been an admirable and indispensable cornerstone of our political system.

CHAPTER THREE

Where We Are Now

MORE THAN A CENTURY AGO, FOLLOWING A BRUISING battle, Theodore Roosevelt and the United States Congress succeeded in taming the beast of corporate political power. With the Tillman Act in place, corporations were prohibited from contributing to federal elections and, consequently, our democracy was protected from this form of corrupting corporate influence.

The following decades saw laws enacted to target various problems in the broader campaign finance system: the 1925 Federal Corrupt Practices Act increased disclosure requirements and limits on spending; the 1939 Hatch Act regulated primary elections, protected the civil service from political demands, and established contribution and spending limits for Congressional elections; and the 1947 Taft-Hartley Act extended the Tillman Act by banning both corporations and unions from contributing to or spending on federal elections.[1] However, while the ban on corporate election spending held, the broader system was inadequate. According to the Federal Election Commission's own account, prior to the 1970s "the campaign finance provisions of all of these laws were largely ignored . . . because none provided an institutional framework to administer their provisions effectively."[2] It wasn't until the Watergate break-in and election financing scandals reached the front page that a comprehensive system was put in place.

The discovery of five burglars breaking into Democratic campaign headquarters, funded with money contributed to Nixon's reelection campaign (the Committee to Re-Elect the President, with its apt acronym CREEP), led to the Federal Elections Campaign Act of 1971 and its subsequent amendments. Together, these provisions formed the basis of our modern campaign finance system. FECA, as it is known, limited both contributions and expenditures in federal campaigns, required significant disclosure, and established the Federal Election Commission (FEC), among other things.[3]

That's not to say that corporate power ran amok during the first three-quarters of the twentieth century. The ban on corporate campaign contributions from the Tillman Act held, and corporate political power on the lobbying side was just a shadow of what we see today. In his book *The Business of America Is Lobbying*, Lee Drutman notes that before the 1970s relatively few companies even had their own Washington lobbyists, and corporate lobbying was "sparse and mostly defensive"[4]—that is, a company would come in to fight a particular bill here or there. Lobbying was not yet seen as a strategic investment, a way for corporations to increase profits by political control. Lewis Powell, later to become a Supreme Court justice, summed the situation up in 1971, the same year FECA was passed, observing, "As every business executive knows, few elements of American society today have as little influence in government as the American businessman."[5]

But just a few years later, in 1978, an FEC advisory opinion created a loophole that allowed the political parties to accept much larger contributions in what became known as "soft money," which could pay for "issue ads" around election time and, in turn, access to grateful politicians. (An issue ad is like an attack ad, except the punch line is not "Vote for Congressman Snooks's opponent" but "Call Congressman Snooks and ask him why he hates America and wants to kill American jobs.") As the legendary Washington, D.C., correspondent Elizabeth Drew describes the impact of the loophole: "In effect, the parties act[ed] as laundries for money that [wasn't] supposed to be used in federal elections."[6]

The explosion of soft money spurred the McCain-Feingold reform efforts of the late 1990s, which were doggedly opposed by incumbents in both parties and both houses of Congress. As Drew writes of Senator John McCain, "His Senate colleagues ripped into him because he had accurately called the current system corrupt."[7] After a fierce and prolonged legislative battle, the reform effort prevailed, and the Bipartisan Campaign Reform Act of 2002 (BCRA, often known as the

McCain-Feingold Act) became law, significantly limiting soft money contributions and, among other things, prohibiting corporate-funded campaign commercials within thirty days of a presidential primary. McCain said at the time that he hoped the reforms would help "change the public's widespread belief that politicians have no greater purpose than our own reelection. And to that end, [that] we will respond disproportionately to the needs of those interests that can best finance our ambition, even if those interests conflict with the public interest."[8]

With the various provisions of these two acts (1971's FECA and 2002's BCRA), Congress took many steps toward reestablishing the public's trust in our democracy as representing the interests of the people, not whichever corporation or wealthy donor could fund a winning campaign. However, many of the restrictions Congress built up in this area were torn down by a conservative, business-friendly Supreme Court, based on a premise that corporate money is speech under the First Amendment. How this came to pass, we will consider in Chapter Five. For now, it suffices to know that this was a novel theory, which today remains controversial.

Back and forth it went. Legislators in Congress approached the problem at the practical level and tried to catch up to and regulate both contributions and outside spending in support of campaigns; the Supreme Court would then strike or water down those limits. As part of this decades-old dance, in 2008 a narrow statutory provision came before the Supreme Court—the McCain-Feingold ban on corporate-funded campaign commercials within thirty days of a presidential primary. As Chapter Seven describes in detail, the Court struck down this ban in the *Citizens United* decision of 2010 and did away with the entire ban on corporate spending in place since Teddy Roosevelt's Tillman Act.

Consequently, our democracy is today once again darkened by the shadow of corporate political influence, vulnerable to its grip not only in our elections but throughout the functioning of our government as well. In the recurring "trial of strength" between corporate power and government, corporate power has been given devastating new political artillery.

The power of modern multinational corporations to wield that artillery has grown dramatically as the wealth of mega-corporations has grown. Their scale is massive. In his book *Power, Inc.*, about these massive multinational corporations, David Rothkopf reports that "the total number of people dependent on these multinationals may have been between one and two billion in 2000, a third of the world's population."[9] And the biggest corporations today are truly enormous. Rothkopf estimates that just the top three hundred companies "control over a quarter of the earth's productive capacity."[10] Walmart alone has more than two million employees.

According to Rothkopf, the financial world's largest asset manager, BlackRock, "controls assets worth almost as much as the total currency reserves of the number-one and number-two countries, China and Japan, combined. BlackRock has $3.3 trillion under management; China and Japan's combined reserves are $3.6 trillion. BlackRock controls twenty-five times the assets that the United States has in its national currency reserves."[11] The number of countries in the world that hold hard currency reserves worth over $100 billion is twenty; by Rothkopf's accounting, "the top 125 asset managers each control the same amount."[12]

Consider a comparison of the annual revenue of the largest corporations in the world to the gross domestic product (GDP) of sovereign countries—countries with armies and currencies of their own.[13]

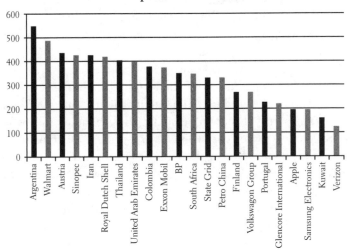

Companies vs. Countries

GDP/revenue in billions US$ for 2014

(Chart adapted from Worldbank.org and Corporationsandhealth.org)

Rothkopf's comparisons between Sweden and ExxonMobil are instructive: Sweden's 2009 GDP was $406 billion versus Exxon's 2009
sales of $442 billion, and Exxon's 2006 budgeted expenditures were
more than $400 billion versus Sweden's of less than one-third that
amount.[14] Rothkopf goes on to note that Sweden had a vote at the
Kyoto Protocol meeting on climate change, but that "ExxonMobil, as
it turned out, had a veto."[15]

As I have said, there is nothing inherently wrong with economic activity by corporations, even very large corporations. Corporate money
dominating our politics is another thing altogether. That is where the
democratic crisis lies, and that is the crisis sparked by *Citizens United*.
Specifically, corporations can now spend unlimited general treasury
funds to support or oppose a candidate (as long as the money doesn't
go to the campaign directly). Corporations can also give unlimited
amounts to super PACs (technically "independent expenditure-only
committees"), and these groups can spend unlimited sums to overtly
advocate for or against political candidates, as long as their spending
is not "coordinated" with that of the candidates they benefit. Corporations can also give unlimited amounts to 501(c)(4) nonprofits, which
(unlike super PACs) do not have to disclose their donors; the 501(c)(4)
then spends that corporate "dark money" on political activity, such
as political advertisements during election season. In sum, *Citizens
United* gave corporations a menu of avenues of influence over who is
elected in America.

The result has been staggering. In the 2012 election cycle, super
PACs and other nonprofit organizations unleashed by *Citizens United*
spent upward of $840 million.[16] The nonpartisan Center for Respon-
sive Politics estimated that 69 percent of this spending was by conservative groups, 28 percent by liberal groups, and the remainder by
other organizations.[17] In 2012, Republican presidential nominee Mitt
Romney reaped the greatest benefit of the new flow of cash: of the $450
million in outside spending dedicated to the presidential candidates,
Romney received approximately $350 million, while President Barack
Obama received an estimated $100 million.[18]

Four years later, the numbers continue to rise. As of March 7, 2016,
more than two thousand groups organized as super PACs reported total receipts of over $540 million and total independent expenditures of

over $240 million in the 2016 cycle. The Koch brothers—through their own billions, through Koch Industries, and through a network of front groups they fund—are probably the most active corporate meddlers in our politics today. Their network alone initially pledged to spend $889 million in the 2016 presidential election.[19] Super PACs supporting presidential candidates banked more than $250 million just through June 30, 2015 (about seventeen times more than at that point in the 2012 cycle).[20] And our politics is awash with "dark money" from anonymous donors (dark to us, of course; you can bet the candidates know).

The impact of super PACs has been truly seismic for our democracy. For example, Americans for Prosperity, a Koch brothers venture, disclosed election spending of $6.4 million to the Federal Election Commission for the 2014 midterm elections.[21] But that group's own officials have boasted that they in fact intended to spend as much as $125 million—an enormous and unprecedented amount to be spent in just one election by just one group.[22] Taken together, Americans for Prosperity and the Kochs' other major nonprofit, Freedom Partners, ultimately spent over $220 million in 2014.[23] Koch Industries' reported lobbying expenditure for that year was $13.7 million, a huge number but nothing like the elections expenditure of its front groups.[24] Their 2014 election spending was just an opening bid. The Koch network initially announced a plan to raise and spend $889 million (and then adjusted it to $750 million) for the 2016 elections.[25] Their 2015 spending was right on track: In January 2016, the *New York Times* reported that the Koch network had spent $400 million in 2015.[26]

The Koch brothers' sophisticated electioneering capacity now rivals or exceeds that of the Republican National Committee.[27] As one scholarly article concludes, "a network of conservative mega-donors (led by the Koch brothers) has created a shadow GOP."[28] Yes, a few very wealthy individuals in the fossil-fuel business—huge polluters— are now such big players in our politics that they rival our national political parties. Their extravagant spending has bought the Koch brothers and their corporate empire a vast political network, with platoons of employees in critical swing states, with voter databases cross-linked to your consumer data, with advertising and media buying specialists, with an intelligence-gathering operation staffed by former CIA operatives[29]—and with no limit on what they can spend. *Politico* has reported former Republican National Committee chair Michael Steele conceding that "the Koch network and other deep-pocketed outside groups have found legal ways to do most of the other things that were once the party's sole province."[30] And some new things—I'm not aware of political parties using former intelligence personnel to do their spook work against political adversaries. Unlimited money can do unlimited things.

Since *Citizens United* the large fossil-fuel polluters and their network of interests have become among the biggest spenders, relying heavily on undisclosed, untraceable dark money. According to the Center for American Progress, oil, gas, and coal companies and electric utilities alone reported *directly* spending more than $84 million on the 2014 elections—and that's just what they report.[31] Super PACs are required to disclose their donors; by contrast, the industry's undisclosed spending on so-called issue ads through groups that are not required to disclose their donors, and for "grassroots organizing," which is not subject to any reporting at all, is estimated to be in the hundreds of millions of dollars.[32] Money talks, and in politics it talks plenty loud: $100 million has a lot to say. Asked about raising hundreds of millions of dollars for conservative, corporatist causes, Charles Koch himself said, "I expect something in return."[33]

Remember that this new corporate spending on elections rides on top of all the corporate lobbying special interests do in Washington, D.C. As described by political scientist Lee Drutman in a 2015 article in *The Atlantic*, corporations spent $2.6 billion a year sending lobbyists to Washington to push their agendas in the halls of Congress; some corporations have more than a hundred lobbyists *each*. Members of Congress get plenty of attention. According to Zephyr Teachout, "private interests spent about $12.5 million on lobbying in 2012 for every member of Congress."[34] Corporate interests are by far the most powerful: "For every dollar spent on lobbying by labor unions and public interest groups together, large corporations and their associations now spend $34. Of the 100 organizations that spend the most on lobbying, 95 consistently represent business."[35] It's a blowout.

The focus of this book is not on traditional, reported lobbying so much as on the new, less well-known, and secret means of influence. Yet corporate lobbying continues to be an enormous and enormously corrosive force, as you would imagine of any force that dwarfs all opposition by a ratio of more than thirty to one. The bipartisan campaign finance group ReFormers Caucus reports that the lobbying enterprise in 1960 occupied the effort of 3,414 registered lobbyists who spent just over $30 million lobbying Congress. By 2014 the number of lobbyists had swollen to 11,781 and their lobbying expenditures for Congress had exploded more than a hundredfold, to $3.23 billion.[36]

Administrative agencies get lots of attention from lobbyists too. Long-standing corporate lobbying efforts continue to turn watchdogs into lapdogs in a practice known as "regulatory capture" that has gone on for as long as there have been regulatory agencies to capture.

And the price of political access is going up, as money floods the system. ReFormers reports that the average cost of winning a Senate seat from 1986 to 2012 grew more than threefold to $10.4 million, and a House seat more than fourfold to $1.6 million (the truly contested races, of course, cost far more).[37] Before *Citizens United*, individuals could give a maximum of $30,400 to a national party.[38] In 2016, according to the *New York Times*, "top-tier Republican donors will pay $1.34 million per couple for the privilege of being treated as party insiders, while the Democratic Party will charge about $1.6 million."[39] The higher the price of admission, the more selective the group admitted, and the more selective the group, the more likely they are to be either big corporations or very high-income people who reflect the views of the corporate structure that provided them their vast personal wealth. One percent of the 1 percent, fewer than 32,000 people, contributed $1.18 billion in political contributions during the 2014 elections.[40] By the end of 2015, the biggest one hundred political donors had spent more to influence politics in the 2016 election than the two million smallest donors combined.[41] As the *Times* concludes, "More big money can only leave less hope for voters concerned that the richest donors are buying ever more influence over politicians, with favoritism and corruption an inevitable result."[42]

Although America is home to about 120 million families, nearly half of all the money contributed through the spring of 2016 in the 2016 presidential contest came from just 150 families, most of them with corporate connections; and most contributed secretly, through super PACs and 501(c)(4)s.[43] The *Washington Post* has chronicled our politics

for 140 years; its editorial board recently warned that "campaign finance in the United States has . . . fallen into an era dominated by
'dark money,' with donors hiding in the shadows and hundreds of
millions of dollars in contributions flowing through politics without a
trace of who gave it or why."[44] While our new status quo of unlimited
dark money may work to benefit some politicians for some period of
time, in the long run it will hurt all Americans, regardless of party.
Unlimited money is not a force that anyone can hope to control, and
unlimited secret money is even more dangerous.

If money is power, then big spenders hold the keys to the kingdom.
And if that weren't bad enough, the American people often don't
even know who the new kingmakers are. The game has changed. Not
long ago, campaigns were waged by candidates and parties fighting
over ideas. If you saw an ad, at least you knew who'd put it on the air.
Campaigns are now waged by shadowy political attack groups pos-
ing as social welfare organizations, run by political operatives, and
fueled by millions of undisclosed dollars from secret special interests.
When these secret special interests ramp up their shouting in our elections this way, it inevitably drowns out the voices of regular individual
Americans.

This can matter a lot. Special interests don't much need the pillars
of a strong middle class, such as Medicare, Social Security, and Pell
Grants. Big corporations don't get sick and need a doctor's care. Big
corporations don't retire. Big corporations don't have to educate their
kids. It would be in their financial interest to see that spending moved
elsewhere—say, to offset corporate income taxes.

These government programs help a lot of families to have far better
lives and have paved the way for generations to achieve the American
dream. But they have always been the target of special interests with
different, corporate, priorities. If you like Medicare, Social Security,
and Pell Grants, and if you want to be heard in their defense, then
having your voice drowned out by an anonymous billionaire or corporate CEO at election time is a lot more than some abstract exercise
in political science. And anonymity opens up attacks on such popular
programs by forces that don't want their fingerprints on such attacks
but will go for it if masked.

Another measure of growing corporate political influence may be the declining corporate share of America's tax revenues. When I was born, America's corporations, through income and excise taxes, were contributing nearly half of the nation's revenue, with individual income tax and payroll tax making up the other half.[45] That has gradually shifted, as corporate taxes have produced steadily lower revenues. By 2013, the individual income tax and payroll tax together provided over 80 percent of the nation's revenue.[46] America's revenue is more and more being supplied by individuals, and less and less by corporations. (Of course, corporations contribute to payroll taxes, but many economists say that contribution comes out of salary the company otherwise would have paid, so ultimately it's still on the individual either way.) When Congress has the chance to fix this, it doesn't. The *New York Times* pointed out in an August 30, 2016, editorial that "Congress . . . sat idly by as American corporations have indulged in increasingly intricate forms of tax avoidance made possible by the interplay of an outmoded corporate tax code and modern globalized finance."[47] We could have done something, but that would have stopped the corporate tax-avoidance payday, and politicians bought and paid for with corporate money are not about to start reforming the corporate tax code.

This increasing corporate political power is increasingly anonymous. In 2012, at least two-thirds of election ad spending through July from groups other than candidates or parties came from secretive corporations and billionaires whose names and agendas the voters may never know.[48] The *Washington Post* has reported that at least 31 percent of all independent spending in the 2014 elections—which were the most expensive midterm elections in our history—came from groups that are not required to disclose their donors. And this does not even include so-called issue ads, whose donors are also not disclosed.[49] By the end of 2015, dark-money spending was up more than 5,000 percent just since 2004, according to ReFormers.[50]

In 2010, Karl Rove was one of the first to set up a dark-money group, obliquely called Crossroads GPS. One measure of the explosion in such dark-money spending is a study by the Wesleyan Media Project and the Center for Responsive Politics, examining the actual number

of political advertisements run with dark-money.[51] Presidential-year
dark-money ads jumped from fewer than 160,000 in 2008 to over
380,000 in 2012. Off-year dark-money advertisements jumped from
around 15,000 in 2006 to well over 100,000 ads in 2010, to over 200,000
ads in 2014. Karl Rove's Crossroads GPS aired the most dark-money
ads, exceeding even the heavyweight business lobby, the U.S. Chamber of Commerce. The Center for Responsive Politics' investigator
said, "the lack of oversight of these groups . . . has allowed nonprofit
groups to be a much more tantalizing vehicle for people who want to
hide their political spending."[52] When the top two ad-runners are Karl
Rove and the U.S. Chamber, you can guess who those "people" are.

As the *New York Times* wrote in a 2012 editorial, "Corporations love
the secrecy provided by Mr. Rove's group because it protects them
from scrutiny by nosy shareholders and consumers."[53] They want a big
influence on elections but without leaving any tracks. An unnamed
corporate lobbyist confirmed to *Politico* in 2016 that "nondisclosure is
always preferred" by corporate donors.[54]

Why is it preferred? Because it makes it so much harder for the
public, the press, and law enforcement to connect the dots—to track
down the corrupting influence of the money these corporations spend
in elections. As legal scholar Burt Neuborne has written, "Lobbyists
treat elected officials as wholly owned subsidiaries, and rivers of money
flowing from secret sources have turned our elections into silent auc-
tions."[55] We often don't even know who the winning bidder is, thanks
to secrecy.

As if all this weren't enough, the use of corporate "shields," such as
limited liability companies, to further conceal donors' identities from
the public is exploding. Super PACs must disclose their donors to the
FEC, but if the donor is a limited liability company, the actual people
behind the company may legally remain unknown. In 2015, the *Wall
Street Journal* reported, "more than 200 limited liability companies . . .
donated almost $11 million to super PACs backing six presidential
candidates."[56]

The special interests putting in their bids have big motives to
spend this kind of big money. If those motives were good for America and would be welcomed and accepted by the average American
voter, the big donors wouldn't need to keep them secret. We need to

ask ourselves: What are they hiding? Why do they demand secrecy? Whatever the answer, one thing is clear: Americans who worry that Washington is overly beholden to special interests need to be more concerned than ever.

With no identity, there is no accountability; and with no account-ability, there is no limit to what people will say. One restraint on the vitriol and the filth that is often part of American political debate is that candidates have to stand by their ads. If someone says something awful, if he engages in relentless negative attacks, voters may charge him a price for that. They may say, "Wow, he's not very nice. I'm not voting for him." That is the reason political ads are required to have that tagline at the end, "I'm Congressman Snooks and I approved this message." Now the tagline is likely to be, "This message approved by Americans for Puppies and Prosperity." Who the hell is that? No one knows. A little inquiry, and you might get a lawyer's name. Restraint, of course, disappears when the name behind the ad is just a sham entity, a phony, a shell. Joe Hagan memorably described the result in a *New York Magazine* article as a "tsunami of slime."[57]

How has this tsunami of slime worked out? Not well for an in-formed American public. An April 2012 study found that about 70 per-cent of ads up to that date in the 2012 election cycle were negative, up from 9 percent of ads in that time period in 2008.[58] If you think you're seeing more negative advertising after *Citizens United* than you used to see, it's because you are. By a lot. It's not that we are worse people; to quote renowned political analyst E.J. Dionne, "structural changes in our politics are making campaigns more mean and personal."[59] Of course it's easier to throw slime from behind a mask. As Mike Hucka-bee has said, the dark money unleashed by *Citizens United* is "killing any sense of civility in politics because of the cheap shots that can be made from the trees by snipers that you can never identify."[60]

It's also easier to lie. And lying has exploded. A study by the An-nenberg Public Policy Center looked at the four top-spending political 501(c)(4) organizations—which don't have to disclose their donors—over a six-month period in 2012. It turns out that an estimated 85 per-cent of their election spending went to ads that the Annenberg Center determined to contain deceptions.[61] So not only are 70 percent of the ads out there negative, but at least during parts of the election cycle, the big spenders were putting 85 percent of their money toward deceptive advertising.

That is what five corporate-friendly justices on the Supreme Court have wrought: campaign practice since *Citizens United* is a dark web of unknown spending by unknown groups with unknown funding sources, with who knows what conversations happening in secret.

The "transparency" the five justices foresaw was supposed to have happened when people saw the corporate-funded ads on TV and could identify the interest behind the spending: "We're ExxonMobil and we approved this message." But such clear identification of the real money behind those ads never occurs. Unfortunately, the justices built in no safety checks to ensure that there would in fact be the transparency they assumed would exist (one must ask how much they really cared), and they have taken no interest since the decision in correcting their error when the transparency they foresaw did not show up. They completely misunderstood how the regulatory regime they left standing would operate (or they did not care, having achieved their objective).

A sense of what this secrecy may do in real life comes readily to anyone who has ever investigated or prosecuted public corruption (none of the five *Citizens United* justices ever had) or who has ever run for elective office (none of the justices on the Court ever had—indeed, this is the first Supreme Court in American history that has no former elected official among the justices).[62] The special-interest lobbyist tells a fellow political operative to let the congressman's campaign manager know that if the congressman doesn't "get right" on issue X, they're in against him, big-time. The congressman will never see it coming, because the ads will be from Americans for Puppies and Prosperity or some other bogus front group, and the money will have been laundered through DonorsTrust or a similar identity-laundering organization (more on them later) or simply hidden behind shell corporations and lawyers. It will just be *POW! No fingerprints.*

What does the sudden, anonymous political attack look like in practice? On the very morning I was presenting the DISCLOSE Act—my bill to ban dark-money contributions—on the Senate floor in 2012, the *New York Times* ran an article describing an organization called the Commission on Hope, Growth and Opportunity. (In this upside-down environment, you know an organization with a smarmy name like that has to be bad.) Funded with "a single $4 million donation from an anonymous benefactor," the *Times* reported, "the group kicked off a multimillion-dollar campaign against 11 Democratic candidates, declining to report any of its political spending to the Federal Election Commission, maintaining to the IRS that it did not do any political spending at all, and failing to register as a political committee required to disclose the names of its donors. Then, faced with multiple election commission and IRS complaints, the group went out of business."[63] Done and gone. No fingerprints. The group's registered lawyer told an inquiring reporter from NPR, "You're not going to get anything out of me, so let's just end this right now."[64] Citizens for Responsibility and Ethics called this episode "the political equivalent of a hit and run."[65] Another entity, ironically named the Government Integrity Fund, popped up and spent more than $5 million in the 2012 election, mostly against my Senate colleague Sherrod Brown. Its attorney refused to name its donors, citing attorney-client privilege. They can strike out of nowhere, without limits and anonymously.[66] *Citizens United* is inherently corrupting because it empowers that threat.

And the power of the *threat* to spend money is the second major problem with this sort of secrecy. We will get more into this in Chapter Seven, where we take a close look at *Citizens United*. For now, it is enough to realize one very obvious real-life fact: what you allow big corporate or billionaire spenders to do, you also allow them to threaten or promise to do. If you're allowed to drop a $5 million campaign attack into a congressional race, you can just as easily threaten or promise to drop a $5 million campaign attack into a congressional race. And if the threat works, you save the $5 million. Anyone with an ounce of political common sense should have foreseen the problem of secret threats and promises, which remains a gaping hole in the logic of *Citizens United*. But more on that later.

In the early stages of the 2016 Republican presidential primary, the new, creepy vehicles of corporate and billionaire funding—the "affiliated" super PAC and nonprofit 501(c)(4) entities—have exploded. (Hillary Clinton had her own super PAC, so the sins are bipartisan, but in the 2016 election, the primary action was mostly on the Republican side.) In September 2015 the *New York Times* reported: "A super PAC backing Jeb Bush will spend $37 million on ads through February."[67] New Hampshire alone was slated for $22 million of that spending. Jeb Bush was not the only one; as the *Times* reported, "Rival super PACs and allied groups are also set to run TV ads primarily in early voting states for Gov. Chris Christie of New Jersey ($11.4 million), Senator Marco Rubio of Florida ($15 million) and Gov. Bobby Jindal of Louisiana ($5 million)."[68] That's nearly $70 million just for these candidates, just in that period. The total, according to the *Times*, is $106 million, of which "super PACs and other outside groups account for 82 percent."[69] And this was just the warm-up. The article continues: "TV spending in the 2016 elections is projected to reach $4.4 billion."[70]

Where does all this come from? As Eric Lichtblau reported in the *Times* in October 2015, "This rise of the 'super PAC,' which can raise unlimited donations from individuals and corporations, has put a premium on billionaire donors who can give once-unimaginable sums to support their preferred candidates."[71] Super PAC money comes not only from corporations but also from billionaires who have amassed their fortunes through the corporate form, such as Maurice "Hank" Greenberg, the former chairman and CEO of AIG, the largest life insurance corporation in the world, who gave $10 million to Jeb Bush's PAC.[72]

It's a flood of big money. An Associated Press investigation in the summer of 2015 found that "nearly 60 donations of a million dollars or more accounted for about a third of the more than $380 million brought in so far for the 2016 presidential election."[73] By August of 2015, seven donors who each gave $1 million or more made up nearly half of the funding for Hillary Clinton's Priorities USA Action super PAC.[74] Contributions of $100,000 or more made up about half of all donations to all the candidates and to their super PACs.[75] To ordinary citizens $100,000 is a huge amount; it's even a lot to candidates. But it's chump change to the big donors.

Citizens United, of course, said this would all be fine because it would all be "independent" of the candidates (whatever that meant).[76] But even if that made sense, it's just not true. As Trevor Potter, former Republican chairman of the Federal Election Commission, has said, "The theory is that super PACs are independent groups, so it's not corrupting for them to take large sums of money. Reality is that they are now joined at the hip with the candidate."[77] Indeed, they are often "affiliated" with a particular candidate.

Let's start with Jeb Bush, who began his campaign with a long, phony "pre-campaign" period. (Why do I say phony? During this time he told Mitt Romney he was "all in" on the presidential race.[78]) Not formally declaring allowed Bush to raise more than $100 million for his own super PAC without violating the rule against super PACs "coordinating" with campaigns—there was no campaign yet to coordinate with! Candidates including Jeb Bush, Carly Fiorina, and John Kasich shot film for their super PACs before they formally declared, allowing them to raise the money to film and air political ads without respect for funding limits, because they were not yet declared candidates under the election laws—a dodge if there ever was one.[79] Really? Jeb Bush wasn't sure whether he was running? Please.

Then he declared. But even after declaring, Bush could still show up for his super PAC events. The *Wall Street Journal* reports that candidates Jeb Bush, Scott Walker, Chris Christie, and Marco Rubio "all attended events organized by their affiliated super PACs after declaring their candidacy."[80] In the case of Jeb Bush, the *Journal* reports, "Mr. Bush's super PAC fundraisers are often scheduled immediately after campaign receptions at nearby homes or in different rooms in the same hotel."[81] And as is true with all of the "affiliated" super PACs, Jeb Bush's "affiliated" super PAC was specific to one candidate only: Jeb Bush. Some independence. (When did "affiliation" become "independence" anyway? That doesn't even pass the dictionary test.)

Carly Fiorina's campaign was called Carly for President; her super PAC was called CARLY for America. CARLY for America ran and paid for campaign events where Carly Fiorina showed up running for president.[82] The "biggest donor by far" to the Carly Fiorina super PAC, according to Eric Lichtblau in the *New York Times*, was a reclusive California billionaire who at one point had contributed about half of her super PAC's money.[83]

As she campaigned through South Carolina, the *New York Times* reported, Fiorina "traveled with a few campaign aides who squeezed into a white sport utility vehicle, while a team of at least seven people from the super PAC swooped in, often hours ahead, at each stop to stage her backdrops, set up sign-up tables and arrange stacks of posters and placards." Said Fiorina, "We are not coordinating."[84] One has to wonder what coordinating would look like.

Oh, and by the way, there's a Federal Election Commission regulation that prohibits using the candidate's name in the super PAC's name. No problem. "CARLY" in CARLY for America actually means "Conservative, Authentic, Responsive Leadership for You," they say.[85] (Never mind that this makes the super PAC's actual name "Conservative, Authentic, Responsive Leadership for You for America.")

How about Marco Rubio? He went beyond even that. According to reports from the Associated Press, "the Florida senator benefit[ted] in unprecedented ways from a non-profit group funded by anonymous donors."[86] As of October 2015, "every pro-Rubio television commercial so far in the early primary states of Iowa, New Hampshire and South Carolina has been paid for not by his campaign or even by a super PAC that identifies its donors, but instead by a nonprofit called Conservative Solutions Project."[87]

What Marco Rubio *said* at a town hall meeting to a voter who asked about the rise of money in politics is: "Full disclosure and sunlight into all these expenditures is critical."[88] He said it is important that "you know who's behind the money and how much they're giving."[89] What Marco Rubio *did* in his campaign for president, according to the *New York Times*, as of October 2015, was to have "all the television advertisements aired in support of the Florida senator so far this year—$5.5 million worth . . . [flow] through a political nonprofit group called the Conservative Solutions Project . . . which has raised more than $18 million [and] will never be required to disclose anything about its donors."[90] At least we know the identity of the auto dealer who gave $5 million to Rubio's super PAC. We'll never know who gave the $18 million to the Conservative Solutions Project.

Of course, the nonprofit claimed to be independent. It said it was "created . . . to help the conservative movement."[91] In fact, as the *New York Times* reported, "the group's commercials all focus on Mr. Rubio. The senator's picture is prominently displayed on its website, and a video featuring Mr. Rubio speaking is the first thing shown to the site's visitors."[92] As the *Times* went on to document, the nonprofit shared its name with the Rubio super PAC, Conservative Solutions PAC; it was run by a political operative from Rubio's Senate campaign; and the super PAC and the nonprofit used the same fundraiser. The pro-Rubio nonprofit did not even seek the approval of the Internal Revenue Service, "which means its political activities will not face the possibility of agency review"—and potential denial by the agency as a phony nonprofit—"until after the group files its next tax return, probably long after the Republican primary season is over." [93]

This combination of big money, anonymity, and connections to the candidate, taken together, powers the "tsunami of slime" Americans see in our elections. Americans know this is new, and they are disgusted. Fred Wertheimer, a respected campaign finance reform advocate, said about 2016, "We have never seen an election like this, in which the wealthiest people in America are dominating the financing of the presidential election and as a consequence are creating enormous debts and obligations from the candidates who are receiving this financial support." [94]

I see a real effect on our politics. Money isn't decisive: it can't cure the problems of a candidacy such as Jeb Bush's. But it makes a difference. It is a big advantage to have money. As Trevor Potter said in his 4th of July speech to the Chatauqua Institution in 2016: "Money and power. Power attracts money, and money maintains power. Money and power in Washington have become a closed circle." [95] Money matters.

And two things stand out. One, virtually all the candidates had a billionaire in their pocket. When one candidate told me he was going to run, he said: "Now I'm going to have to find my billionaire." Two, the money is driving the content of campaigns. No Republican will talk about climate change, because of where their money comes from. No Republican will talk about legendary Omaha investor Warren Buffett's plan for fairer taxes on Wall Street, because of where their money comes from. Indeed, as Wall Street money flowed into Marco Rubio's campaign (in the last half of 2015, about over half of his super PAC money came from financial industry donors [96]) he announced he was for Wall Street paying not just lower taxes, but no taxes at all on income they can treat as capital gains. [97] As Fred Wertheimer has said, "Who wins and loses elections is very important, but even more important is the question of what kind of policy results it buys. We have hedge fund managers who put huge amounts into our campaigns; they have the most unjustifiable tax break in our tax system."[98]

This new corporate political effort is not limited to choosing between the candidates the parties produce and driving the candidates to (or away from) a certain agenda. The Koch brothers' political enterprise has begun finding and growing its own political candidates. This is done through a variety of corporate screens, so first meet the players. One is Freedom Partners Chamber of Commerce, which has been described in *Politico* as "the central group in the increasingly powerful network of conservative public policy and political groups helmed by the billionaire brothers."[99] This outfit raised more than $160 million in the run-up to the 2014 elections.[100] We don't know from whom that money came, because this is one of the bogus nonprofits operating under a provision of the tax code known as Section 501(c)(4) that requires no donor disclosure (but also in theory requires the nonprofit to stay out of elections). Another player was called Trees of Liberty, described by the website Conservative Transparency as a "short-lived 501(c)(4) front group funded by the Koch brothers' 'secret bank,' Freedom Partners."[101] A third is called Freedom Partners Action Fund, a "candidate-affiliated" (but not "coordinated"—big difference, right?) super PAC.[102]

In 2013, Joni Ernst was an Iowa state senator with single-digit name recognition around the state. But the Kochs liked her politics as a United States Senate candidate and invited her to their secretive political gathering of wealthy conservative donors that August. A report from *Politico* describes what happened. First, the short-lived Trees of Liberty group popped up and went to work in the Iowa Republican primary.[103] With $400,000 from Freedom Partners Chamber of Commerce, Trees of Liberty began attacking Ernst's Republican primary opponent. Behind the scenes, *Politico* reported, Freedom Partners had what was needed to make Trees of Liberty's attacks effective: a $13 million payroll, nearly $2 million for focus groups, over $1 million for ad production, $1.5 million for messaging experts, and $1.4 million for a direct mail firm.[104] (This was a Koch brothers operation, so it is no surprise that the specific attack on Ernst's opponent slammed him for having supported a restriction on carbon emissions.)

The Trees of Liberty attack campaign was designed to obscure the source of the money behind it. As *Politico* reported, "Trees of Liberty carefully tailored its ad campaign to avoid triggering rules that would have required more financial disclosure during the campaign. It pulled down the television ads just before the calendar reached the one-month election countdown. Had the ad aired within that month, Trees of Liberty would have been required to report its spending—but not its donors—to the Federal Election Commission."[105] As *Politico* also disclosed, Trees of Liberty reported to the IRS, under oath, that it did not "engage in direct or indirect political campaign activities on behalf of or in opposition to candidates for public office."[106] (More on this requirement in Chapter Eight.) Ernst won the Republican primary and went on to the general election.

That's where Freedom Partners Action Fund kicked in. Even before Ernst had won her primary, the super PAC Freedom Partners Action Fund had begun what became a $1 million-plus ad barrage against her Democratic adversary, funded by $693,000 from Freedom Partners Chamber of Commerce.[107] Again, Ernst won.

As *Politico* concluded about the Koch brothers' political enterprise: "'They're building a muscular political machine capable of electing the right politicians and ensuring they implement the right policies,'" and "they're well on their way to achieving that goal."[108] From the candidate's point of view, anyone who will spend this kind of money is a force to be reckoned with. On one hand, there's the gratitude due. On the other, there's the recognition that if you don't stay in line, the stealth spending may be for your opponent next time. (As I have said, the sins are bipartisan. The *Washington Post* reported on the mysterious entity DE First Holdings, incorporated in Delaware. The day after its creation, it gave $1 million to a super PAC tied to a New Jersey Democratic officeholder. Its owner, according to the *Post*, "remains unknown."[109])

And as I describe in Chapter Eleven, the effect of the *Citizens United* decision has been particularly villainous with respect to the climate change debate in Congress. Indeed, it has been disabling—exactly as the big corporate spenders want. *Citizens United* did not add to America's policy debate; it gave big special interests a weapon to suppress debate, with political threats and bullying they did not have the power to use before. But more on that later.

Here, it's perhaps worth addressing the elephant in the room: does the surprising strength of Donald Trump's "self-funded" campaign prove that the super PACs and corporate money unleashed by *Citizens United* have no bearing on our elections? No, quite the opposite. One way to understand Trump's popularity among Republican voters is as an expression of anger at this post–*Citizens United* system—the system that is serving the powerful, not the people. Yet as we have seen, the true source of the system's dysfunction is not immigrants and foreigners, as Trump would like voters to believe. It is forces of corporate power that have infiltrated our democracy, leaving ordinary Americans out.

The irony, of course, is that the embrace of Trump was an embrace of the very same corporate power machine that is shutting Americans out of their own democracy. Trump could not have accumulated his wealth without the power of the corporation and the favorable tax and regulatory environment corporate lobbying has secured. As a real estate magnate, he may pay no taxes at all. Like a magician waving a bright scarf in one hand while he sneaks a rabbit into the hat with the other, Trump has effectively focused voters on anyone he can easily scapegoat, while himself benefiting from and perpetuating the real menace: a system that persistently serves corporations and the rich. And it's hardly throwing open the doors of democracy to say that you don't have to *have* a billionaire to win, it's enough that you can *be* a billionaire.

Even where a candidate campaigns on being outside of money in politics, the system of political money tends to seep in, sooner or later. Unsurprisingly, it didn't take Trump long after securing the nomination to turn to super PACs and their multimillion-dollar contributions for support. In fact, the day *before* Trump's acceptance speech at the Republican National Convention *Politico*'s headline read: "Trump Blesses Major Super PAC Effort."[110] *Politico* then reported on August 7, 2016 ("Trump's Economic Advisers Are Also His Biggest Donors"), that of the thirteen men Donald Trump announced as his economic advisory council, "five are major donors whose families combined to give Trump's campaign and his joint fundraising account with the Republican Party more than $2 million."[111] Trevor Potter noted of Trump that this was "the path he has said was corrupt: raising large sums of money and then giving donors special access."[112] The inevitable switcheroo pulled a fast one on Trump's primary voters, who were "an easy mark for a P.T. Barnum con man," said right-wing Iowa radio host Steve Deace.[113]

Americans of all political stripes are disgusted by the influence of unlimited, anonymous corporate cash in our elections and by campaigns that can succeed or fail depending on how many billionaires the candidate has in his pocket (or vice versa, perhaps: how many candidates the billionaire has in his pocket).[114] More and more, people feel their government responds only to wealthy and corporate interests, and they are right.[115] Indeed, there is even scientific documentation of this: a 2014 report by political scientists Martin Gilens and Benjamin Page, looking at data even before the worst effects of *Citizens United*, attempted to answer the questions, "Who governs? Who really rules? To what extent is the broad body of U.S. citizens sovereign, semi-sovereign, or largely powerless?"[116] The unhappy conclusion of the report was this: "The central point that emerges from our research is that economic elites and organized groups representing business interests have substantial independent impacts on U.S. government policy, while mass-based interest groups and average citizens have little or no independent influence."[117] The report notes the "impediments to majority rule that were deliberately built into the U.S. political system—federalism, separation of powers, bicameralism," which give the American political system a built-in "substantial status quo bias."[118] They understood that the Founders deliberately made it a somewhat uphill struggle to get things done in Washington. But this is different. "When a majority of citizens disagrees with economic elites or with organized interests, they generally lose."[119]

This is more than just a matter of ordinary people not getting what they want from government, say the authors: "we believe that if policymaking is dominated by powerful business organizations and a small number of affluent Americans, then America's claims to being a democratic society are seriously threatened."[120] And America's example as a democratic society matters a lot in a dangerous world, as I argue in Chapter Twelve.

*   *   *

While today's Congress can't make much progress on many problems facing the country, from gun control to the climate crisis, the Senate can be remarkably efficient in tackling obscure items important only to the corporate lobby. For example, on October 22, 2015, senators were summoned to the floor regarding an ambassador's nomination. I walked up to the two desks on the Senate floor in front of the parliamentarians and clerks, one for each party, where during a vote there is a piece of paper on each desk describing the subject of the vote, along with leadership's position on the vote (sometimes also the name of the lead senator in opposition, if there is one). I looked at the paper to see what appointment was important enough to call the full Senate to the floor and saw that the subject at hand was the confirmation of our ambassador to the tiny, corrupt nation of Equatorial Guinea. You've probably never heard of the place; if you have, you've probably heard nothing good.

Equatorial Guinea has been described by scholars and writers as "one of the few African countries that 'can be correctly classified as a criminal state'"[121] and as a "mafia state in which power and wealth are tightly controlled by a brutal gang family and a small number of cronies and enforcers."[122] The U.S. Department of Justice has sued to seize assets of the ruling family, alleging the assets were the product of extortion, misappropriation, theft, and embezzlement. Allegations of torture abound. I knew a bit about the country because years ago my family was posted in nearby Guinea. Of all the things to be called over for, Equatorial Guinea?

At the time of this vote in 2015, there was a de facto blockade in the Senate of the president's nominees to State Department and Defense Department civilian positions. The executive calendar had more than fifty nominations pending, including the State Department's lawyer and ambassadors to Norway and Sweden. So why did we call up for a vote on the ambassador to this nasty little country?

The one noteworthy thing about Equatorial Guinea beyond its corruption is that oil was discovered there about twenty years ago, so much that little Equatorial Guinea has been referred to as the "Kuwait of Africa."[123] Big oil and gas concessions went to American companies. A 2004 Senate report into money laundering by the ruling clan chronicled these unsavory business ties, and as Ken Silverstein's *The Secret World of Oil* reports, "U.S. oil companies remain the bulwark of Equatorial Guinea's economy."[124] Clearly, the oil and gas industry wanted a Senate-confirmed ambassador to assist their dealings with this regime.

Was it bad to confirm the ambassador? Of course not. Do I know exactly why that ambassador's nomination made it to the floor that day for a vote? I don't. But with fifty other nominees waiting on the calendar, it's a reflection of whose priorities matter in Congress when the one that gets the recorded vote is the ambassador to the "Kuwait of Africa."

CHAPTER FOUR

What the Corporate Political Machine
Wants: Four Short Case Studies

THE FORCES OF CORPORATE POWER ARE MURKY. They seek to be obscure. It can be hard to identify what they really hope to achieve. Moreover, their public relations messaging is usually designed to hide rather than clarify what they really want to achieve. There is no shopping list posted anywhere for us to examine. They often don't want us to know.

But we can drill a few core samples and extract some data to form at least a general idea. Four quick samples—the regulations corporations don't want, the taxes corporations don't want, the extreme policies the Kochs do want, and the differences in what the wealthy want—provide important clues as to the goals and possible effects of corporate power as it is deployed in the political arena.

On October 6, 2015, Senator Ted Cruz held a hearing in the Judiciary Subcommittee on Oversight, Agency Action, Federal Rights and Federal Courts.[1] The focus of the hearing was "overregulation." He called as one of his witnesses a small-business owner from Chicago, Sabina Loving, who runs a tax preparation service. The purpose of Loving's testimony was to decry the burden of a federal regulation that required her to obtain a license before preparing other people's tax returns. The thrust of the hearing was to make the case that regulations in general were burdensome on commerce, interfered with people's livelihoods, and were annoying. Loving was a nice person and an appealing witness.

But here is what was interesting: Senator Cruz had never filed a bill seeking to overturn that regulation. The Congressional Review

Act allows Congress to overturn agency regulations. It wasn't used. A review of the record shows that no senator had made any legislative effort to repeal or correct that regulation.[2] While we've seen more than a hundred legislative attacks and votes trying to repeal environmental protections per year since the Republicans took control of the House of Representatives in 2010[3] and repeated votes trying to undo the Dodd-Frank bill's restraints on Wall Street that were put in place after the Great Recession caused by Wall Street in 2008,[4] not once did anyone force a vote on Loving's little license regulation problem.

The reason I point this out is that there is a specific agenda behind a lot of the corporate mischief in Congress, and behind the generalized concern we often hear over "burdensome regulations." The Koch brothers' political groups, for instance, love to say that "burdensome and costly regulations are sucking the life out of our economy"[5] and that "Americans are suffering under the crushing burden of overregulation."[6] Oh my.

If that's so, where's the package of burdensome regulations we in Congress might well agree to repeal if they really didn't make sense? Regulations do get obsolete. The need for regulation can be affected by new technologies. Practice can show that particular regulations are ineffective. There's plenty of room for bipartisan work to clean that up. But this is never about those situations.

The corporate groups will talk generally about burdensome regulations, but what they want specifically is for Congress to help the usual suspects. Pull back the curtain marked "Burdensome Regulation" and you see some very familiar Rottweilers: Wall Street and the big polluters. The Koch brothers and Koch Industries, for instance, one of the top producers of toxic waste in the United States year after year, are the pointy tip of the corporate political spear.

A Wall Street billionaire saying he didn't want regulations on his financial schemes would not be a very appealing witness, especially after the big Wall Street meltdown and resulting bailout. Neither would a major polluter seeking relief from environmental regulations. So nice Sabina Loving is marched in to testify, although even on the Republican side there had been zero effort to do anything about the regulation she cared about. She was a prop. The real political energy is always behind Wall Street and the big polluters. That's where the big money is.

Indeed, as I was writing this section, a headline in *Politico* said: "GOP Targets Dodd-Frank, EPA for End-of-Year Fight."[7] Well, well.

Noteworthy too in this deregulation tale is the effort by big utility polluters to reregulate themselves. When it looked like state and federal regulators were restraining their profits, electric utility deregulation was their mantra.[8] Now that the cost of wind and solar power is undercutting their big coal-burning plants, various utilities are trying to reregulate themselves in order to get paid for power plants the market may not support. Some of these companies charged their ratepayers for these power plants, and then in the deregulated environment they were able to mark up prices and get consumers to pay again through that system; now, as they face "stranded costs," they are trying to get their customers, or even people using wind and solar, to pay them yet again.[9] In one happy story, the Atlanta Tea Party and Sierra Club chapters joined together to form the Green Tea Coalition. They beat back utility-sponsored legislation that would have put a tax on rooftop solar with the money going to the big polluting utilities.[10]

The lesson from this particular core sample is not to be duped by the sound of appealing generalities. Who the hell is *not* for getting rid of obsolete or useless "burdensome regulations"? But when you hear the refrain about "burdensome regulations," look out for your wallet, and for your lungs, because in practice it's almost always a cover for the deregulatory agenda of two narrow interests: Wall Street and the big corporate polluters.

Next let's drill into corporate tax priorities. More than anything, the right pursues eliminating the estate tax, which only about 0.2 percent of the very wealthiest Americans—those whose estates are worth more than $5.45 million—will ever have to pay.[11] In my time in the Senate, estate tax repeal seems to come up more frequently than any other proposed tax reduction or repeal. Over and over, when the Senate budget process opens the floor to amendments (in the process known irreverently as "vote-a-rama"), Republicans insist on votes on repealing the estate tax. In my experience, the degree of Congress's political interest in tax reform corresponds directly to the wealth of the beneficiaries of that tax reform: the wealthier the beneficiaries, the more ardent the repeal effort.

During one of these mostly symbolic budget vote exercises, there was a tie vote on an estate tax repeal amendment, and the vice president of the United States, Dick Cheney, rushed in his motorcade to the Capitol so that the vote could be retaken and won by the repeal proponents. Cheney ejected Senator Jon Tester, who was presiding, from the chair (the vice president, serving also as the president of the Senate under the Constitution, has the right at any time to claim the chair and preside in the Senate, and his vote is then added to break a tie), and the vote was retaken. Such was the distaste for Cheney in the chamber that the measure actually got *fewer* votes. But the episode shows the political energy behind estate tax repeal. As a budget amendment in the "vote-a-rama," the measure wouldn't even have changed the actual law; yet the vice president of the United States came tearing up to the Senate for that vote.

Tax cuts add to the national debt. When senators express concern about the national debt, they will often suggest that the very survival of the Republic depends upon reducing the national debt. All things considered, this is an admirable goal. But those same senators will often fight tenaciously against repealing even the worst special-interest tax breaks, even when the revenues from the repeal would reduce the deficit. Many want *still more* special-interest tax breaks. It is a contradiction.

Contributing to a national debt that "risks the survival of the country" are massive subsidies for the big multinational oil companies, who make the largest profits the world has ever seen. Corporate welfare for big oil companies should be the last place in the world to waste tax subsidies, yet even in the name of debt reduction, repealing this subsidy is a nonstarter with senators beholden to corporate interests.

Another classic is the "carried interest" tax rule, which allows hedge fund billionaires to treat great chunks of their income as if it were a less taxable long-term capital gain—a long-term capital gain that just happens to occur every year.[12] Because of this loophole, some of the most highly paid people in the world, with incomes that can run into the hundreds of millions of dollars in a single year, pay lower tax rates than a truck driver or a bricklayer.[13] There is no scheme of reason, nor any notion of justice, that could make sense of so massive a tax break. Some of these corporate highfliers make so much money they don't even notice the last million dollars they make in a year—in economic terms, that last million dollars has near-zero marginal utility to them. Yet we tax more heavily the income of people who need their earnings to pay the rent and the heat bill every month, people for whom even a hundred dollars makes a real difference.

One startling example of this special-influence tax policy at work, highlighted by economist Martin A. Sullivan, is a luxury residential building on Park Avenue in New York City so big that it has its own zip code. Since the IRS reports taxpayer information by zip code, we know, on average, what the people in this zip-code-sized luxury building make each year, and we know, on average, what they pay in taxes. The IRS reports for 2007 show that the adjusted gross income declared by the residents in this building averaged $1.2 million per household per year. The average federal tax rate paid by the residents in this building was 14.7 percent.[14]

By way of comparison, the Department of Labor reports the wage and tax rates for security guards and janitors in New York City. Security guards reportedly average a little over $27,500 in annual income, and janitors a little over $33,000. At those salaries, the statutory tax rates are 23.8 percent and 24.9 percent, respectively.[15] Thus the doorman holding the umbrella up in the rain in front of this building is likely paying a higher federal tax rate than the hedge-fund mogul climbing out of his limo under the doorman's sheltering umbrella. This disgraceful state of affairs—not reducing the national debt—is what the corporate lobby fights to protect. If they truly cared about reducing the national debt, corporate America and its high-paid denizens could pay their fair share of taxes, and fight to see that it went to reducing the debt. Fat chance.

The moral to be drawn from this core sample into the tax debate is that the political power of very highly paid corporate executives and investors, as that power gets deployed in Congress, is dedicated often to protecting the well-being of very highly paid executives and investors. In this case, it protects them from the indignity of having to pay taxes like regular working people.

Oh, did I forget to mention? That building in New York City is the Helmsley Building, as in Leona Helmsley, famously quoted as saying, "Only the little people pay taxes."[16]

*   *   *

We return to the Koch brothers for our third effort to seek out the true agendas of the corporate elite and the politicians they fund. This core sample drills back in time to the official platform of David Koch of Koch Industries, when he was the vice presidential candidate in 1980 for the Libertarian Party. Yes, that Koch, of those Koch brothers, once ran for vice president of the United States, and his political platform of thirty-five years ago reveals volumes about the Koch brothers' actual priorities. Right-wing operative Grover Norquist has said, "David Koch ran in '80 to go against the campaign finance rules. By being a candidate he could give as much as he wanted." [17] But Koch wanted to do more than give money. Time may have mellowed his views since then, or he may just have learned to keep these parts of his agenda from the public, but the platform below is just some of what David Koch actually campaigned on as vice-presidential candidate. Buckle up, because it's quite a ride.

We specifically oppose laws requiring an individual to buy or use so-called "self-protection" equipment such as safety belts, air bags, or crash helmets.

We advocate the abolition of the Federal Aviation Administration.

We advocate the abolition of the Food and Drug Administration.

We call for the repeal of the Occupational Safety and Health Act.

We oppose all so-called "consumer protection" legislation . . . and call for the abolition of the Consumer Product Safety Commission.

We propose the abolition of the governmental Postal Service. The present system, in addition to being inefficient, encourages governmental surveillance of private correspondence. Pending abolition, we call for an end to the monopoly system and for allowing free competition in all aspects of postal service.

We advocate the complete separation of education and State. Government schools lead to the indoctrination of children and interfere with the free choice of individuals. Government ownership, operation, regulation, and subsidy of schools and colleges should be ended.

[We] call for the dissolution of all government agencies concerned with transportation, including the Department of Transportation, the Civil Aeronautics Board, the Federal Maritime Commission, Conrail and Amtrak.

We demand the return of America's railroad system to private ownership. We call for the privatization of the public roads and national highway system.

We condemn compulsory education laws, which spawn prison-like schools with many of the problems associated with prisons, and we call for the immediate repeal of such laws.

We call for the privatization of the inland waterways, and of the distribution system that brings water to industry, agriculture and households.

We support repeal of all laws which impede the ability of any person to find employment, such as minimum wage laws.

We support an end to all subsidies for child-bearing built into our present laws, including all welfare plans and the provision of tax-supported services for children.

We oppose all government welfare, relief projects, and "aid to the poor" programs. All these government programs are privacy-invading, paternalistic, demeaning, and inefficient.

The proper source of help for such persons is the voluntary efforts of private groups and individuals.

We favor the abolition of Medicare and Medicaid programs.

We favor the repeal of the fraudulent, virtually bankrupt, and increasingly oppressive Social Security system. Pending that repeal, participation in Social Security should be made voluntary.

We oppose all personal and corporate income taxation, including capital gains taxes.

[We] support the eventual repeal of all taxation. . . . As an interim measure, all criminal and civil sanctions against tax evasion should be terminated immediately.

[We] support the abolition of the Environmental Protection Agency.

We support abolition of the Department of Energy.

We urge the repeal of federal campaign finance laws, and the immediate abolition of the despotic Federal Election Commission.[18]

Wow. This is obviously not the agenda of all corporate America, but it shows the antigovernment extremism of one of corporate America's most politically active voices. And, together, the Koch brothers are perhaps America's most politically active corporate voice. Indeed, with their private political operation said to exceed the capability of the Republican National Committee, their goals and intentions matter.

And don't be fooled by the Koch brothers' public statements against "corporate welfare." It's all part of a carefully orchestrated campaign to rebuild their image, following so much unwelcome disclosure by author Jane Mayer and others of their behind-the-scenes scheming in recent elections. The Kochs fight for every kind of corporate welfare that helps them: low corporate taxes, low tax rates on money earned as capital gains from corporate stock, offshoring of American jobs and profits, and of course deregulation. The Kochs' top political operative, Richard Fink, has conceded: "We want to decrease regulations. Why? It's because we can make more profit, okay? Yeah, and cut government spending so we don't have to pay so much taxes."[19]

But that's not the big one. The business that made the Koch brothers into billionaires has been called the biggest toxic waste emitter in the country. The fossil-fuel industry with which they are entwined is the biggest polluter on the planet. And they particularly want the biggest piece of corporate welfare that exists: the ability to privatize their profits but socialize their costs (yes, the Kochs are fine socialists when it comes to the costs they impose on humanity—"share the wealth" is anathema to them, but "share the pollution" is their business model).

As a quick sidebar, I recently ran across one of their efforts to clean up their reputation and found a particularly cynical trick. I was a co-author of a criminal sentencing reform moving along in the Senate Judiciary Committee. The Kochs and their political operation made a big splash when they decided to support criminal sentencing reform; the news media loved the "strange bedfellows" aspect of their alliance with liberal and minority groups, and the Kochs' usually surreptitious efforts were all at once unusually noisy.[20] I'll confess, I smelled a rat.

Sure enough, after the sentencing bill was negotiated and ready to pass out of the Senate Judiciary Committee, there came a sudden fuss from Republicans about how "mens rea reform" had to be added: an amendment to add the new mens rea provision was unexpectedly brought up in the Judiciary Committee when we voted on sentencing reform, and a committee hearing was suddenly held on mens rea reform right afterward, House members started threatening that our Senate bill would be dead without mens rea reform, right-wing groups began to insist on adding mens rea reform when the bill was taken up on the Senate floor, and the ever-obedient *Wall Street Journal* editorial page began editorializing for "mens rea reform."[21]

Well, "mens rea" is a legal term—Latin for "guilty mind"—and the "reform" was to make the government have to prove knowing, criminal intent in order to prosecute wrongdoing. While criminal intent has long been a component of trials for crimes such as murder or man-slaughter, it has not been a factor in regulatory offenses. The purpose of regulatory statutes is safety, and the method is deterrence: where safety violations would be dangerous, the idea is "to require a degree of diligence for the protection of the public which shall render violation impossible."[22] Forget about intent; just don't do it.

In such public danger cases, corporate polluters are often the defendants. Moreover, since a corporation is an artificial legal entity without a soul or mind, forcing prosecutors to prove a culpable state of mind on the part of the corporation, and not just the criminal act by the corporation, opens up a field of mischief for corporate defense attorneys and adds another snarl for prosecutors to have to untangle. So mens rea reform is a corporate payday.

If you were the biggest toxic waste emitter in the country and you could hobble the forces of government that were prosecuting you for your pollution and safety violations, wouldn't that be ideal? Such a loophole wouldn't be likely to pass on its own, though. But maybe if you snuggled up to a criminal sentencing reform effort and got in with that, you could turn it into a Trojan horse with your mens rea reform tucked inside. And in the meantime, you could get all that good publicity for looking like a nice guy as you helped build the Trojan horse.

The Koch brothers themselves of course denied this was all part of their scheme, and said they'd be happy to have criminal sentencing reform pass without adding the corporation-protecting mens rea reform. But at the same time, Koch-funded groups were the ones demanding mens rea reform as part of sentencing reform, and Koch lawyer Mark Holden has conceded they were motivated by a twenty-million-dollar settlement they paid arising out of a Department of Justice prosecution under the Clean Air Act after carcinogenic benzene releases at a Koch refinery.[23] Great combo, if you can get it: mens rea reform to help out your corporations, clean hands for the Kochs. The fronts for the Kochs in the criminal sentencing reform effort were Holden of the Koch Foundation and Edwin Meese III, the former U.S. attorney general (you may recall he was forced to resign in a swirl of ethics problems). Later, before the Judiciary Committee, Meese was actually the lead witness for mens rea reform, there representing the right-wing

Heritage Foundation, which is supported by the Koch Foundation. Subtle as a brick.

If you think there must be some reasonable boundary around this corporate agenda, think again. The extremism of David Koch's vice presidential platform shows how unrestrained and even reckless some corporate-sector voices are about uprooting programs that ordinary Americans count on for their health, their retirement, their safety, and their prosperity. This set of policies would re-create the law of the jungle in our economy. (I guess if you were born a very big cat, the jungle may not seem like such a bad place.)

America is full of responsible corporate leaders as horrified as you and I are by this vision of America. So let me be clear: there is a small but powerful segment of corporate America driven by self-interest and ideology to seek power in politics. Their priorities drive what I describe as the "corporate agenda." This agenda reflects the views of a minority of CEOs, but it is the loudest, strongest, and most persistent corporate voice in my world, in Congress. It is the voice we hear.

Other corporations come in and dabble in trade, intellectual property, or tax issues of the moment. Different sectors of the economy have their industry concerns. Their worst sin, and it is a mild one, is to crowd out other interests and other issues that don't have their lobbying clout as they jostle to get their issue resolved. The defense establishment, for instance—which is well funded and powerful—focuses intensely on defense programs and the defense budget. So every year in the Senate we do a defense bill, even if we never get to student loans.

The hard core is different from corporate America at large. The Kochs are different. This tiny group of corporations and corporate leaders has made the determination that intense engagement in politics, and particularly intense *hidden* engagement in politics, is a very rewarding business strategy. It has embraced the new political artillery that *Citizens United* provided. It manages a fleet of front groups to obscure its role. It engages in super PAC and 501(c)(4) politics on an unprecedented scale. Its impact is outsized. I feel comfortable calling what it seeks the corporate agenda, even if it's not the agenda of all or even most corporations, because it is the corporate agenda we most see and feel in Congress.

It's worth noting that, from my perspective in Congress, I've seen that the agenda of a CEO and of the corporation employing her may diverge considerably. A CEO may be honorable and fair, but the corporation itself may not prioritize her fair and honorable views when lobbying Congress. Indeed, those fair and honorable views may be left entirely on the cutting room floor by the time the corporation's government affairs folks and lobbyists communicate to Congress. The industry's trade association may then exacerbate this, representing the worst, most selfish views among the various players in the industry. The trade association's lobbying will then focus on the sketchiest industry priorities, those furthest from the public interest—such as eliminating limits on air pollution or protections from extreme risk-taking by big banks. The result is that the happy talk from an honorable and fair CEO up in the executive suite may be almost completely transformed by the time the lobbying rubber has hit the road in Congress. We in Congress will usually see the worst face of the industry.

Senator Elizabeth Warren and I did a report on the U.S. Chamber of Commerce, for instance, which has lobbying positions on tobacco and climate change that are significantly different from the public positions of the corporate directors on the Chamber's board.[24] A few corporations left the Chamber over its extreme positions, but most took no action at all.[25] The result was one set of policies in the executive suites, but a completely different push from their lobbying muscle in Congress.

And my experience is that even the very best American companies won't push back against their industry's nefarious fringe. Corporate CEOs who are sincere about climate change and effective at driving sustainability still won't lobby Congress for a serious climate bill or push back against the fossil-fuel industry. Yes, if they think something big is coming, they will rush in to make sure they get their share, as they did in the cap-and-trade bill, which would have limited overall emissions and allowed polluters to "trade" carbon allowances. But regular corporate America ordinarily won't dissociate itself from the most disgraceful lobbying, the dark political rough stuff by the hard core of corporate activists. Not when the rough bunch takes over industry associations like the U.S. Chamber of Commerce. Not even when they say things that are known to be false.

While this book is a general warning about the infiltration of corporate forces into our democracy, it is worth highlighting again that the corporate forces exerting themselves in our politics are not always representative of the larger business community. The exercise of political power by corporate forces tends to grow with the size of the corporation. The big boys dominate. Moreover, the desire to exercise political power tends mostly to animate a few highly regulated sectors, particularly finance and fossil fuels, but also insurance, pharmaceuticals, chemical manufacturing, and, to a lesser degree, defense. These industries monopolize the deployment of corporate power in our government, and do so to such an extent that small businesses, and even big businesses in other sectors, may be as much the victims of hidden corporate power as regular human citizens are. Many—perhaps even most—corporations should actually have common cause with regular citizens in resisting these hidden forces as they exert themselves in our politics.

My last core sample of "what the corporate political machine wants" explores the policy preferences of the wealthy compared to the general public to reveal just how much the priorities of individuals with great wealth diverge from those of regular citizens. Big CEOs now earn on average three hundred times the average wage of a worker in their company, so those CEOs, in addition to representing their corporate interests, also reflect personal views that are associated with great wealth and increasingly are out of step with the realities and wishes of modern Americans.[26]

A 2011 study by Benjamin Page, Larry Bartels, and Jason Seawright showed stark differences between the opinions of the very wealthy and those of other Americans on America's economic needs.[27] Polls consistently show that Americans care much more about job creation and economic growth than they do about reducing the deficit.[28] In contrast, the study found that high-wealth interviewees' top concern was "budget deficits or excessive government spending"; this was mentioned far more than any other issue.[29] Unemployment and education "ranked a distant second and third to budget deficits among the concerns of wealthy Americans."[30]

The 2011 study showed this pattern repeated again and again. Should "the government in Washington . . . see to it that everyone who wants to work can find a job"? Sixty-eight percent of the general public thinks so, but only 19 percent of wealthy respondents agreed. Should "the federal government . . . provide jobs for everyone able and willing to work who cannot find a job in private employment"? A majority (53 percent) of the general public says yes, compared to only 8 percent of wealthy respondents. What about a minimum wage "high enough that no family with a full-time worker falls below the official poverty line"? Seventy-eight percent of the public are in support, whereas only 40 percent of the wealthy agree. As for spending on Social Security, food stamps, and health care, the wealthy favor cutting such spending, whereas most Americans would like to see it expanded.[31]

The study extracted these policy views from a highly affluent group of Americans corresponding roughly to the top 1 percent.[32] It provides some key lessons. One is that the rich are indeed different, as F. Scott Fitzgerald observed. Because they are different, they don't make good proxies for the public. Because these very wealthy Americans have very different views than the public at large, there is actually a disenfranchisement that occurs when their views carry outsized political weight in our democracy. In other words, we can't delegate running the country to them and trust them to deliver results we will want.

One specific difference is that the very rich will not fight for middle-class employment and for social programs that support and sustain the middle class. When the interests of the rich control the political process, the central pillars of American middle-class security are in peril. To use a phrase from my childhood, they're the "pull up the ladder, Jack, I'm on board" crowd. As the talented writer Peggy Noonan has said, "The donor class . . . [i]nevitably . . . see to their own enthusiasms and policy priorities."[33]

There are undoubtedly other core samples that could be drilled into the complex geology of corporate political influence, but I would wager that almost all of them would confirm the following principles: (1) when you pull back the curtain, the interests of Wall Street and the big polluters will always be at the forefront of the deregulatory agenda (other business interests, look out—you may be being suckered!); (2) the very well-off will usually fight for the economic interests of the very well-off even if the result is plainly unfair to those who are less well-off; (3) for some of the most powerful corporate voices, there is no end to the law-of-the-jungle extremes they have championed publicly as their goals; and (4) the very rich are indeed different, and see things so differently that consolidating power in their hands will disenfranchise ordinary Americans.

As Americans career into levels of income inequality not seen since the Gilded Age, when robber barons ruled the roost, these core samples suggest a link between all this hidden corporate political power and worsening income inequality. The corporate chokehold on Congress certainly contributes to our inability to do anything about our widening income inequality. And the forces of corporate power have been on the winning economic side of the income inequality divide. At a minimum, they don't feel its injury. At worst, they are lapping it up.

CHAPTER FIVE

The Powell Memo and the Corporate Strategy

IN 1906, THE UNITED STATES SENATE proclaimed that the evils of corporate money in politics were "so generally recognized" that the threat was deemed too obvious to need to discuss.[1] In 2010, five corporate-minded Supreme Court justices ruled that corporations had a constitutional right to spend unlimited amounts of money to influence elections, and that this would pose no possible threat of corruption. Such a dramatic change could not, and did not, happen by accident. Rather, a coordinated, deliberate strategy by corporate and conservative interests built a system that, over time, allowed big business to have its way.

The sea change is often said to have begun with a corporate lawyer named Lewis Powell and a 1971 memo that he wrote, now known as the "Powell Memo."[2] Shortly after writing the memo, Lewis Powell would be appointed to the Supreme Court by President Richard Nixon. Once on the Court, Justice Powell laid the legal groundwork for corporate political rights.

Powell was a Virginian, educated and trained for the law at Washington and Lee University. He became a prominent partner in Virginia's biggest corporate law firm. He was active in the American Bar Association, ultimately becoming its president. He was both a lawyer for and board member of Virginia tobacco companies. He was courtly and polite, the ultimate "establishment lawyer." Indeed, Powell was so established that when in 1969 Nixon first offered him a seat on the United States Supreme Court, Powell turned the president down.[3]

Beneath Powell's establishment gloss lay a sharper edge: Powell was a member of right-wing billionaire Richard Mellon Scaife's League to Save Carthage, described by Jane Mayer in her book *Dark Money* as "an informal network of influential, die-hard American conservatives."[4]

Lewis Powell wrote his 1971 memorandum at the request of the United States Chamber of Commerce.[5] The Chamber of Commerce was then a less partisan organization than it is now. Today the U.S. Chamber of Commerce supports virtually only Republican candidates. It is usually more representative of multinational than American corporate interests; in a 2010 letter to the Senate opposing a bill that sought to prevent offshoring of American jobs, the Chamber actually wrote to us, "Replacing a job that is based in another country with a domestic job does not stimulate economic growth or enhance the competitiveness of American worldwide companies."[6] And among American corporate interests, it is dominated by fossil-fuel interests and Wall Street.[7] Indeed, one might say that the U.S. Chamber of Commerce has been captured by these particular narrow interests.

The 1960s were an anxious time for the business establishment. Long-haired sons and bell-bottom-wearing daughters openly scorned a CEO dad's straitlaced corporate world. The wildly popular movie *The Graduate* famously mocked "plastics." Napalm symbolized American productive capacity gone morally adrift. Tectonic forces in the antiwar and civil rights movements were shaking our social consensus.

In this turbulence, the late 1960s and early 1970s saw a surge of new regulation, including the establishment of major new agencies, including the Department of Transportation (1967), the Environmental Protection Agency (1970), and the Consumer Product Safety Commission (1972). As political scientist Lee Drutman puts it, American businesses were "reeling from a remarkable expansion of government regulation and a general rise in anti-business sentiment."[8] In the wake of this new regulatory activity, the Chamber sought advice from Powell on how to increase the influence and power of its big business clients. Powell laid out "possible avenues of action" to aid American big business.[9] His recommendations ranged from enhancing corporate public relations departments to promoting pro-corporate faculty at universities and textbooks in schools. The strategy's centerpiece, however, was a new focus on government. "Business must learn the lesson . . . that political power is necessary," Powell instructed.[10]

The quest for political power in the Powell Memo did not just focus on business interests' traditional regulatory and lobbying influence in the administrative agencies and the executive and legislative branches. Powell included in his recommendations a section entitled "Neglected Opportunity in the Courts." It was not enough to have your lobbyists prowling the legislature and executive agencies. "Under our constitutional system," Powell argued, "especially with an activist-minded Supreme Court, the judiciary may be the most important instrument for social, economic and political change."[11] Powell called on the Chamber of Commerce to assemble "a highly competent staff of lawyers" and hire "lawyers of national standing and reputation" to file amicus briefs in the Supreme Court.[12]

Powell had in mind a sophisticated strategy of what we now call "impact litigation," litigation where the purpose is not so much to represent the client as to change the law. In keeping with this direction, in 1998 the Chamber launched its Institute for Legal Reform, which has described itself as a "national legal reform advocate . . . working to change the laws, [and] also changing the legal climate."[13] Impact litigation had a distinguished history in the civil rights and environmental movements. *Brown v. Board of Education*, the decision desegregating America's schools, could be said to be public-interest impact litigation. But Powell was going to turn those public-interest strategies in a new direction having little to do with the public good.

Powell sent his memo to the Chamber on August 23, 1971. President Nixon announced Powell's appointment to the Supreme Court on October 21 of that same year.[14] It is unclear whether Powell knew when he turned in the memo that he would be the president's next appointee to the Court. (There must have been considerable discussion prior to the October announcement, particularly within the Powell family, because Powell biographer John Calvin Jeffries reports that at Powell's swearing-in, Powell's wife, Josephine, said, "This is the worst day of my life. I am about to cry."[15])

The business community responded quickly to the recommendations of the Powell Memo. As I've mentioned, Lee Drutman, author of *The Business of America Is Lobbying*, has pointed out that scarcely any Washington lobbyists were deployed by corporations prior to the 1970s. That changed fast. Political scientists Jacob Hacker and Paul Pierson

have reported, "The organizational counterattack of business in the
1970s was swift and sweeping—a domestic version of Shock and Awe.
The number of corporations with public affairs offices in Washington
grew from 100 in 1968 to over 500 in 1978. In 1971, only 175 firms had
registered lobbyists in Washington, but by 1982, nearly 2,500 did. The
number of corporate PACs increased from under 300 in 1976 to over
1,200 by the middle of 1980. On every dimension of corporate political
activity, the numbers reveal a dramatic, rapid mobilization of business
resources in the mid-1970s."[16]

In the 1970s, the Chamber doubled its membership and tripled its
budget; its fellow lobby group, the National Federation of Independent Businesses, doubled its membership; and the CEO lobby group
the Business Roundtable was formed.[17] Corporate political spending
ramped up, as well. According to Hacker and Pierson, "From the late
1970s to the late 1980s, corporate PACs increased their expenditures in
congressional races nearly fivefold."[18] These were expansions of existing activities, so it is not surprising they would happen quickly.

But some of Powell's ideas were novel. In particular, his call for
mobilizing in the courts was inconsistent with the common view that
courts were neutral places where decisions were handed down dispas-
sionately and corporate influence would have little role.

In 1978, now a Supreme Court justice, Powell delivered a decision
that kicked wide open a whole new realm of opportunity for corporate
America. Contrary to prior Court precedent, Powell wrote in the case
of *First National Bank of Boston v. Bellotti* that the First Amendment
protects corporate speech in political discourse.[19] With that decision,
two things happened. First, a new front was opened for corporate political engagement under the umbrella of protected speech, a front
that corporate power would explore and expand for decades to come,
leading the Court ultimately to the profoundly misguided *Citizens
United* decision. And second, Justice Powell presented to the corporate
community a living example of what can be accomplished through
aggressive efforts to build an "activist Court" with like-minded judges.
If the Chamber hadn't fully believed his memo about the prospects
of judicial activism on behalf of corporations, they certainly did after
they saw his decision. He had delivered a prize, proven the potential of
an activist Court, and illuminated the pathway.

The business community and the conservative movement got the message from Powell and the Chamber and began to build a sophisticated legal infrastructure. In 1982, for instance, the Federalist Society, a conservative, pro-corporate legal organization, opened its doors at prestigious law schools. Legal historian Steven Teles has described the role of the Federalist Society in the Reagan administration:

[Federalist] Society membership was a valuable signal for an administration eager to hire true-believers for bureaucratic hand-to-hand combat. In addition, by hiring the Society's entire founding cadre the Reagan administration and its judicial appointees sent a very powerful message that the terms of advancement associated with political ambition were being set on their head: clear ideological positioning, not cautiousness, was now an affirmative qualification for appointed office.[20]

The Federalist Society provided a means of signaling the ideological bona fides of ambitious conservative and pro-corporate lawyers, but it was only one of many such legal organizations. Some were created with the explicit goal of grooming and vetting the ideological purity of foot soldiers in the conservative movement. Others were created to look for opportunities to systematically and strategically advance conservative and pro-corporate legal theories. I ran across one of these advocacy institutions as attorney general of my state.

When I became Rhode Island's attorney general in 1999, I inherited a long-standing regulatory quarrel over a small parcel of land on the shores of Winnapaug Pond, along our southern coast. The parcel was owned by a gentleman named Anthony Palazzolo, who was something of a local character. Mr. Palazzolo's parcel of land was mostly tidal wetlands, which made the parcel not buildable under Rhode Island's centuries-old "public trust" doctrine. After several of his proposals to develop the property were denied, he filed a lawsuit against the state asserting that the Rhode Island Coastal Resources Management Council's effort to protect coastal wetlands rendered his property worthless and was thus an unconstitutional "taking" without just compensation. Palazzolo's case came up through the state's coastal regulatory body, and from there into the state courts, as a small and unassuming part of the great flood of business of the Department of Attorney General. But this small case would soon take me to the litigant's podium of the United States Supreme Court.

To understand how that came to pass, it's helpful to have some background on the takings clause of the United States Constitution. The takings clause, reasonably, requires the government to pay you if it condemns your land for a highway, for instance. Corporate interests, however, have long argued that it also requires the government to pay you if a government regulation reduces the value of your property from its "highest and best use"—for instance, if you can no longer build a shopping mall or nuclear power plant on it. In part this is a property rights movement ("Who are you to tell me what I can and cannot do with property I own?"), and in part this is a corporate effort to make it harder for regulators to regulate. Corporations have a powerful tool when they can threaten litigation and ultimately perhaps even demand a money judgment against a little state regulatory agency by claiming that a regulatory restriction violates their constitutionally protected property rights under the takings clause. On the front lines of this battle lie corporate-funded legal organizations, exactly as suggested in the Powell Memo, which troll through court records and news reports for cases that they think can be useful in this cause.

Anthony Palazzolo's case was noticed from across the country by an entity in Sacramento, California, called the Pacific Legal Foundation. This is a corporate-funded entity whose employees read case reports from lower courts around the country all day long, looking for platforms to advance their pro-corporate, pro-property-rights argument.

Someone in Sacramento read legal reports about Mr. Palazzolo's little lot on Winnapaug Pond and thought it would make a good case for impact litigation. So they swooped in, became Palazzolo's attorney of record, and took over the case. Unlike the usual situation of a client choosing a lawyer, this law group chose its client from across the country, and next thing you know we're in the U.S. Supreme Court.

As it turned out, the property rights movement gained no ground in that particular effort in the Supreme Court. We held them off. There was a technical error in the state court's decision, so the case was sent back to the state court.[21] From the Pacific Legal Foundation's perspective, the Supreme Court case ended with a whimper, not a bang.

With no prospect remaining of any national impact, the Pacific Legal Foundation declined to represent Palazzolo in the subsequent state proceedings. Nothing has been built on the lot to date, and Mr. Palazzolo has since passed away.

Corporate America has these kinds of front groups on duty every day, actively looking for litigation that will advance their causes. The front groups don't represent real clients in the ordinary course; they swoop into existing litigation and offer to litigate for free to make their point, then vanish once they have. And the Pacific Legal Foundation is not alone—these front groups have become endemic. The docket of the United States Supreme Court is riddled with parties, intervenors, and "friends of the court" that are corporate-backed "advocacy advocates," rather than regular lawyers advocating for regular clients in the ordinary course of litigation.

These entities are the new buckled-and-feathered corporate courtiers of the Supreme Court, seeking "impact" exactly as the Powell memo prescribed. They have made the Supreme Court an arena for political combat. It is not uncommon to find five or six of these groups filing amicus briefs on matters before the court, parroting each other's arguments and providing the conservative justices an instructive and reassuring right-wing echo chamber. (Indeed, there were five such briefs in the Palazzolo case.)[22]

Let's be clear: these are not public interest organizations taking key civil liberties cases through the courts to vindicate the rights of ordinary American citizens. These are well-funded corporate front groups that have co-opted a strategy pioneered by the great advocates of the civil rights movement, and put it to the service of special interests. The goal is not to give voice in court to citizens whose voices are all too often not heard; it is to manipulate courts in the service of corporate power and wealth. These corporate-funded groups masquerade as independent organizations, but they are tools of a self-serving corporate network.

Again, I will take the liberty of calling these groups corporate-funded, whether the funding comes directly from big corporations, has been contributed by individuals who have amassed huge wealth through corporate activity, or derives from trusts or front groups set up by such individuals and corporations. All these roads lead to Rome, and Rome is the pro-corporate agenda.

As if this "impact" machinery were not bad enough on its own, a not-so-subtle signaling system has emerged between the conservative judges and these entities, sending the groups hints as to which cases and arguments the conservative justices would like to have come before them. One recent example of this signaling was described by the *New York Times*. It involves a pet peeve of the union-busting right wing and the corporate sector: a decision from 1977 called *Abood v. Detroit Board of Education* that allows unions to collect dues from nonmembers whom they represent in collective bargaining. If *Abood* were reversed, unions would lose the revenues they now get from the fees of nonmember employees, employees would be encouraged to become "free riders" and get the benefit of union membership without paying, and the balance of power between corporations and unions would shift further toward corporations. As Supreme Court reporter Adam Liptak tells the story in the *Times*:

> In making a minor adjustment to how public unions must issue notifications about their political spending, Justice Alito digressed to raise questions about the constitutionality of requiring workers who are not members of public unions to pay fees for the unions' work on their behalf. . . .
>
> Justice Sonia Sotomayor saw what was going on. "To cast serious doubt on longstanding precedent," she wrote in a concurrence, "is a step we historically take only with the greatest caution and reticence. To do so, as the majority does, on our own invitation and without adversarial presentation is both unfair and unwise."
>
> Michael A. Carvin, a leading conservative lawyer, also saw what was going on. He and the Center for Individual Rights, a libertarian group, promptly filed the challenge Justice Alito had sketched out. Indeed, Mr. Carvin asked the lower courts to rule against his clients, a Christian education group and 10 California teachers, so they could high-tail it to the Supreme Court.

(A brief interruption here to underscore that the conservative impact litigation outfit wanted to *lose* the case, to get more quickly to the

forum they really wanted: the U.S. Supreme Court, where they anticipated a welcoming audience. Now back to the *Times* story.)

> Last year, Justice Alito wrote a second majority opinion at-
> tacking the central precedent in the area, a 1975 decision called
> Abood v. Detroit Board of Education. But the majority in the
> new case, Harris v. Quinn, stopped short of overruling Abood.
>
> By now everyone saw what was going on. "Readers of today's
> decision will know that Abood does not rank on the majority's
> top-ten list of favorite precedents—and that the majority could
> not restrain itself from saying (and saying and saying) so," Justice
> Elena Kagan wrote in dissent.
>
> Last week, the court agreed to hear Mr. Carvin's case, Fried-
> richs v. California Education Association, No. 14-915, and it may
> soon complete the project Justice Alito began in 2012, that of
> overruling Abood.[23]

The Supreme Court heard oral argument in *Friedrichs* in January
2016, and it certainly looked like another 5–4 decision in favor of corporate interests was coming down the pike. It was only the unexpected
death of Justice Antonin Scalia in February that took history on a different course. A tie vote on March 29 effectively left the Ninth Circuit Court of Appeals decision in place, upholding the long-standing
precedent.[24]

The extent of the planning and expectations between the conservative justices and the corporate world is displayed in the reactions in
major newspapers—the *Wall Street Journal*, the *Washington Post*, and
the *New York Times*—to Justice Scalia's death. "Corporate America
had high hopes," the *Journal* said, because "the Supreme Court appeared poised to deliver long-sought conservative victories," in the
form of "body blow[s] that business had sought against consumer and
worker plaintiffs."[25] The cases "had been carefully developed by activists to capitalize on the court's rightward tilt," including "'test cases
tailor-made for a court including Justice Scalia.'"[26]

The *Post* noted that each of the "cases and causes that had the right
so excited at the beginning of the term" was "'an attempt to push the

law sharply to the right.'"[27] "Conservatives . . . welcomed a new docket in October studded with cases that seemed poised to move the law to the right," said the *Times,* a new docket that included "a half-dozen potential blockbusters."[28] "Conservative advocacy groups hoped," the *Times* continued, that these cases "would help business interests and Republican politicians, while dealing setbacks to public unions, colleges with racial admissions preferences and abortion providers."[29]

But "things soon changed," noted the *Times.*[30] "Conservative hopes for a transformational term at the Supreme Court ended with Justice Antonin Scalia's death," said the *Post,* quoting law professor Pamela Karlan, who noted that an "era of aggressive conservative legislation and litigation at the Supreme Court may largely be over."[31] Concluded the *Journal* after Scalia's death: "The court frustrated conservative expectations."[32]

In the corporate effort to influence the judiciary, a cottage industry has even cropped up of conservative, pro-corporate organizations hosting "continuing legal education" sessions for judges at luxurious resorts where, between the golf and fishing outings, they can hear from "experts" in pro-corporate legal theories. An investigative report by the Community Rights Counsel, now the Constitutional Accountability Center, examined this practice and concluded that the groups hosting these events are "run by ideologues and funded by special interests."[33] One such group actually bragged of its intention in these sessions "to serve the interests of its contributors effectively."[34]

The retreats are free to the judges, since they are bankrolled by oil, timber, and other corporate interests, and they are so luxurious that the judges often bring their spouses along to enjoy the occasion.[35] The locales have included Amelia Island and Sea Pines plantations, Florida beach resorts, Arizona golfing destinations, and private ranches out west.[36] Another investigation found that "the seminars take place at truly plush resorts (many of them the same used by ALEC [the American Legislative Exchange Council] for their annual meetings involving legislators) during all expense [paid] trips provided to the judges by a number of conservative funded organizations."[37] (Focused on state legislators, ALEC is also in the business of saturating decision-makers with pro-corporate, conservative ideology.)

This is no small effort. One group gloated that "more than one-third of the sitting federal judiciary" had attended its retreats.[38] At one time, about 10 percent of the federal judiciary was attending one of the various retreats each year, reaching by one count an overall total of 40 percent of the federal judiciary.[39] The nonpartisan Center for Public Integrity has estimated the attendance count at around 185 federal judges from 2008 to 2012.[40] The partisan nature of this effort is apparent, too; for one group, Republican-appointed judges accounted for 97 percent of the guests[41]—at which point it becomes sort of a right-wing judicial jamboree and team-building exercise. The judges who were listed as having attended the most retreats were all appointed by Presidents Reagan or George H.W. Bush.[42]

The sponsors get value for their money, as the investigative report described: "Imagine one wealthy foundation, interested in shaping the law in a conservative, anti-regulatory fashion. That foundation decides on a strategy, which has two parts. First, fund groups that are going to litigate. Second, fund seminars that will try to persuade judges."[43] And sure enough, the report showed, sponsors funding these retreats "are simultaneously bankrolling litigation in federal courts to limit environmental regulation, often before the same judges."[44]

Not surprisingly, the report found "no balance whatsoever" in the presentations.[45] Presenters include former oil company CEOs and "Free Marketeers," people who "weave together . . . doctrines from economics and political science to attack federal environmental laws."[46] A more recent report by the Voters Legislative Transparency Project summarized: "These junkets are designed to provide attending judges with an ultra-conservative, pro-corporate outlook on key issues. During these free trips judges attend daily seminars provided by purported scientists, corporate executives and others advancing a one-sided, pro-corporate, free-market conservative ideology."[47]

The materials provided to the judges are pretty extreme. A "Desk Reference for Federal Judges" prepared by one group for conference attendees says this about air pollution: "The first step is to realize that an external cost is not simply a cost produced by the polluter and borne by the victim. In almost all cases, the cost is a result of decisions by both parties. I would not be coughing if your steel mill were not pouring out sulfur dioxide. But your steel mill would do no damage if

I (and other people) did not happen to live downstream of it."[48] Darn me for living downwind and having these pesky lungs.

Activism is a desired result. One instructor at these seminars is an advocate for "unabashed activism."[49] He has complained that "the Reagan revolution will come to nothing as these judges sit on their hands in the name of a simplistic theory of judicial restraint."[50] He applauds judges who depart from Supreme Court precedent in the service of a "libertarian Constitution."[51]

And the strategy has worked. The report found a "remarkable correlation between seminar attendance and judicial activism."[52] "In case after case, the judges writing the opinions that strike down environmental statutes have attended [these groups'] seminars."[53] This should come as no surprise, given who's funding them and what they want: "The seminars offer something that is more helpful to a conservative judge and more dangerous to the independence of our judicial system: the tools to reach the results conservatives favor as a matter of politics or ideology."[54] And no wonder: as a recent Voters Legislative Transparency Project report disclosed, "six of the seven [groups] providing such judicial trips are funded with money from one or more of the Koch-controlled family foundations. In addition many known conservative foundations also fund these trips and seminars for judges, including: John M. Olin Foundation, Inc., M.J. Murdock Charitable Trust, Castle Rock Foundation, Claude Lambe Foundation (Koch controlled) and the Lynde and Harry Bradley Foundation."[55]

Many of the judges did not even disclose on their mandatory ethics reports that they attend these corporate-funded retreats. I don't know what would be worse if you are a party litigating an environmental claim—knowing your judge was being indoctrinated at partisan seminars paid for by your adversary, or having the judge keep it a secret from you. Either way, litigants may well see justice perverted by both the indoctrination and the secrecy.

Does this have a bad odor to you? You are not alone. One newspaper editorialized that it "creates an egregious ethical conflict of interest, bordering on wholly improper out-of-court communication with special-interest lobbyists or representatives of people who have filed lawsuits."[56] Another said it looks like "an interest group has put part of the federal judiciary in its saddle."[57] A third said, "The conflict is clear, and the judges' participation is mind-boggling."[58] And lest you think I've gone to liberal, elitist, Yankee publications for these quotes, every one comes from a newspaper below the Mason-Dixon Line. Northerners were tough, too: one writer described these junkets as "popular free vacations for judges, a cross between Maoist cultural reeducation camps and Club Med."[59]

Another task of the conservative legal groups has been to create an aura of academic legitimacy around the pro-corporate cause. Seminars, publications, and societies have sprouted, and traditional law reviews have been barraged with submissions. Some of these submissions are highly strategic, even targeting specific cases.

I ran into this too as attorney general, in a civil action I brought against the lead paint industry seeking a remedy for lead paint having poisoned so many children in Rhode Island. It was a big case. Our state's assistant medical director for the Department of Health had said lead poisoning was "Rhode Island's number 1 children's environmental health problem."[60] The lead paint defendants lawyered up massively: dozens of lawyers appeared for them at court proceedings, and more than a hundred lawyers were involved in various stages of the proceedings. I remember looking across the courtroom at one point and guesstimating that the companies were burning more than $10,000 per hour in legal fees just from the lawyers present that day.

The companies really began to panic when we won the case at trial, before a Rhode Island jury. Cleaning up the trail of poison from their product in buildings across Rhode Island was not going to be cheap, and the case could point the way for other, bigger decisions in other, bigger states. So they pulled out the stops in their appeal of our trial victory to the state supreme court.

One tactic they used was to have their own paid consultants write "articles" purporting to be regular scholarly work, but which were in fact written during the pendency of the case to be cited as legal authority by the lawyers for the big corporations in the case. It worked. The Rhode Island supreme court's decision overturning our jury verdict relied in part on a law review article in the *University of Cincinnati Law Review* written by a professor of law at the University of Maryland School of Law who was also a paid consultant to the lead paint companies.[61] It appears that the Rhode Island supreme court was unaware while citing the "article" that it was a piece planted mid-litigation by a paid advisor to the lead paint companies.

My consolation was having put the Lead Industries Association, the industry's front group, out of business. They closed up shop rather than answer questions under oath.

The corporate effort runs broad as well as deep. Do the phrases "runaway jury" or "frivolous litigation" ring a bell? Planting those phrases in your consciousness is the work of this enterprise. If the phrase "burdensome regulation" resonates with you, that's the work of this enterprise, too.

Of course, all the argument and indoctrination in the world might be unavailing without, as Lewis Powell observed before stepping onto the Court himself, "an activist-minded Supreme Court"—one that is willing to make the judiciary "the most important instrument for social, economic and political change." [62] That task appears to have been accomplished as well, judging from the direction in which five conservative, pro-corporate justices took the Court in recent years.

The steady march of the activist right-wing bloc on the Supreme Court to establish its political priorities as the law of the land should come as no surprise. It represents the fruits of a long-standing and often very public effort to turn the law and the Constitution to the advantage of special interest groups and conservative activists. It is the realization of the "activist-minded Supreme Court" that Lewis Powell originally dreamed about in his memo.

The results of this meld of political ambition, ideological positioning, and activist judicial appointments have been terrible. What were once fringe conservative ideas—hostility to our nation's civil rights, environmental protection, and consumer protection laws—have been steadily dripped into the legal mainstream by endless repetition. The mainstream of American law has been shifted steadily to the right by the force of this effort, backed by seemingly endless corporate funds. This new "rights movement"—for the rights of corporations, the rich, the powerful, and the fortunate—has been aggressive and explicit.

CHAPTER SIX

Capture of the Court

FOLLOWING A DECADES-LONG CAMPAIGN FOR INFLUENCE over the Supreme Court, the corporate effort, under Chief Justice John Roberts, reached a pinnacle.[1] During his confirmation hearings, Chief Justice Roberts had cast himself as an "umpire," promising that he would just call "balls and strikes."[2] Yet a study by law professors Lee Epstein and William Landes and Judge Richard Posner analyzed more than two thousand cases argued before the Supreme Court between 1946 and 2011 and found that the Roberts Court's decisions have been, as reported by the *New York Times*, "far friendlier to business than those of any Court since at least World War II."[3] As described by renowned law professor Arthur Miller to the *Times*: "The upshot . . . is that businesses are free to run their operations without fear of liability for the harm they cause to consumers, employees and people injured by their products."[4] And, as Jeffrey Toobin noted in the *New Yorker*, this pattern of decisions "has served the interests, and reflected the values, of the contemporary Republican Party."[5] The strike zone has been moved.

Activism is not the Supreme Court's proper role. Justice Felix Frankfurter once noted that "it is not the business of this Court to pronounce policy. It must observe a fastidious regard for limitations on its own power, and this precludes the Court's giving effect to its own notions of what is wise or politic."[6] The conservative bloc on today's Supreme Court has done nothing of the kind; instead it has blatantly used its power, while it had a five-vote majority, to promote an agenda.

Corporate and conservative interests provided powerful support for the conservative justices' nominations; and it appears, to paraphrase the old song, that those judges were determined to "dance with the guys that brung them." The dance even included, for Justices Antonin Scalia and Clarence Thomas, attending the Koch brothers' secretive annual political conference.

This may sound like a harsh indictment. However, taking a fair look at the patterns of the Court's decisions during the power period of the five conservatives, and considering the strategies employed to achieve their results, it is difficult not to see the hand of activism at work. Over and over, the conservative justices ignored traditional, conservative judicial principles when those principles obstructed a political result favorable to corporations. Over and over, the conservative justices laid groundwork in one decision to shape pro-business policy in later decisions. Over and over, given the choice between achieving consensus and attaining the most ideological result, even if they had to get there by a narrow 5–4 decision, Chief Justice Roberts and the conservative bloc repeatedly chose to max out their agenda in 5–4 decisions. In those 5–4 decisions, the chief justice was amazingly reliable, taking the conservative side of the case 85 percent of the time.[7] A recent study co-authored by conservative Seventh Circuit judge Richard Posner found not only that the Roberts Court was more favorable to business interests than its predecessors but also that all five members of the recent corporatist bloc were among the top ten most business-friendly justices in the past sixty-five years—with Chief Justice Roberts number one and Justice Samuel Alito number two.[8]

There remains an unmistakable pattern suggesting intentionality and purposefulness here. The clear beneficiaries of the conservative justices' agenda were corporate and conservative interests, winning in the Supreme Court at an unprecedented rate. The role the five justices played in implementing a robust corporate agenda was far from conservative in the judicial sense; they were aggressive activists with a purpose. They were, clearly, the corporate, big-business bloc.

Concern over the Roberts Court's activism is not limited to lawyers, advocacy groups, and those in the partisan fray in Washington. Recent polling shows that less than one-third of Americans have confidence in the Supreme Court.[9] By two to one, Americans think the justices often let political considerations and personal views influence their decisions.[10] Americans massively oppose the *Citizens United* decision

(80 percent against, with 71 percent "strongly" opposed).[11] And, most tellingly, by a ratio of nine to one, Americans now believe the Court treats corporations more favorably than individuals. This sentiment is true even of Americans who identify themselves as "conservative Republicans." They agree by a four-to-one margin.[12]

While Americans across the political spectrum are disillusioned with the Court's apparent lack of neutrality, a nexus clearly exists on the Court's right wing between politically conservative ideology, the corporate agenda, and the Republican Party's interests. The five corporatist justices seemed also to rule in favor of the ideology and the party whenever they could. Even renowned *New York Times* reporter Linda Greenhouse, who had long resisted labeling those justices partisan ideologues, ultimately wrote that she found it "impossible to avoid the conclusion that the Republican-appointed majority is committed to harnessing the Supreme Court to an ideological agenda."[13] Other noted Court watchers such as Norm Ornstein at the conservative American Enterprise Institute and the *New Yorker's* Jeffrey Toobin had long before reached a similar conclusion.[14] *Washington Post* columnist Dana Milbank observed wryly of a recent decision: "The Roberts Court has found yet another way to stack the deck in favor of the rich."[15]

The obvious retort to these arguments is the "Obamacare" decision.[16] It may seem that the Court's decision upholding the Affordable Care Act disproves any accusation that the Court has been politicized by the conservative movement. But the Obamacare decision was predictable—and anticipated by many of us—under a "politicized Court" theory. It was actually the smart play for the chief justice and his fellow conservatives.

First, being against Obamacare was a big conservative rallying effort; why should the Court deprive the party of such a unifying cause? Second, if the Court had actually ruled the Affordable Care Act unconstitutional, then what? The Republican Party would own the resulting mess, and the party had no plan whatsoever to offer as an alternative. Like the dog chasing the car, there was the problem of what they'd do if they caught it. Third, the health insurance industry needed Obamacare. However things turned out, one thing was clear: there was no going back to letting the insurance industry deny insurance coverage for preexisting conditions. To do that would have been political Kryptonite. If there were no Obamacare (which stabilized the insurance industry with the "tax" on uninsured individuals) and also no way to avoid covering preexisting conditions, the health insurance industry would be imperiled by what it calls "adverse selection." Undoing Obamacare would have been a nightmare for the insurance industry, and the corporatists on the Court would not want that.

Finally, under cover of the decision allowing Obamacare, the Court could provide some big conservative deliverables—and it did. Rhetorically, the Court could call the program a "tax" (providing a very successful conservative talking point to the right).[17] Further, the conservative justices could and did narrow the scope of the commerce clause (thereby narrowing federal legislative power).[18] And on top of that, the chief justice invented a new "dragooning" theory limiting Congress's ability to attach conditions to federal spending programs.[19] Those latter two constitutional novelties would have been the subject of much notice ordinarily, but they were drowned out in the "Supreme Court Upholds Obamacare" headlines.

A governor I once worked for, Bruce Sundlun, liked to say, "If you have a disadvantage, make use of it." The five conservatives made great use of the Obamacare decision.

Usually, political efforts to "capture" great public institutions come, as it were, in sheep's clothing. But the conservative takeover of the Supreme Court came as a wolf. Consider the official Republican Party platform of 2000, which "applaud[ed] Governor Bush's pledge to name only judges who have demonstrated that they share his conservative beliefs and respect the Constitution."[20] They didn't just have to share those beliefs; they had to be willing to impose them too.

The political deal that leads to this result is not complicated. America's big corporate interests fund Republican candidates for office. Those corporate interests want those Republicans to help them. That is as old as politics. So Republicans make it a priority to appoint judges who also want to help—judges who may in their confirmation proceedings pay obligatory lip service to opposing "judicial activism" but who, once on the bench, will actually deliver on core Republican political interests. When Republican appointees to the Court have not adequately delivered on the corporate agenda, the *Wall Street Journal* editorial page has accused them of "political betrayal."[21]

A series of landmark Supreme Court decisions in the second half of the twentieth century provided fertile soil from which the rage of the Republican voter base has grown. *Brown v. Board of Education* ended the segregation of schools across the South, infuriating southern conservatives, who came out for "massive resistance" to it.[22] *Roe v. Wade* recognized a woman's right to decide to have an abortion in the first trimester of a pregnancy, infuriating conservatives and fundamentalists.[23] The Court created rights including Miranda warnings ("you have the right to remain silent . . .") for arrested suspects, infuriating the law-and-order crowd.[24] And the Court said that burning the American flag as a form of protest was protected by the First Amendment.[25] The Republican "base" was mad as hell about these decisions and others.

Elements of the modern Republican Party base thus saw judicial appointments as a vital means of political action to unwind those decisions. A Republican can raise far more money than a Democrat can from a fundraising email railing about "activist judges." The baseline Republican voter cares a lot more about judicial appointments than the baseline Democratic voter does.[26] With the "base" ginned up about appointing conservative judges, adding a pro-corporate payload to help the big donors out was as natural as cake with ice cream. And if election laws too can be made favorable to Republican political strategies, that's a cherry on top.

Despite the Court's professed political neutrality, election decisions of the Court's recent Republican-appointed majority always seemed to come down on the side that helped the election prospects of the Republican Party. The sockdolager of political decisions, of course, is *Bush v. Gore*, in which five conservative justices determined who the next President of the United States would be. Constitutional law scholar and Yale Law School professor Akhil Amar has described the ironies of that decision this way:

> Justices who claim to respect states savage state judges. Jurists who condemn new rules make up rules of breathtaking novelty in application. A court that purports to frown on ad hoc,

after-the-fact decision making gives us a case limited to its facts.
A court that claims it is defending the prerogatives of the Florida
Legislature in fact unravels its statutory scheme vesting power in
state judges and permitting geographic variations. . . . The case
that bears the name of a professed strict constructionist is as activist a decision as I know.[27]

Principles galore were trampled to achieve that decision's result.

More recently the Court intervened in voting rights in a way virtually guaranteed to help the Republican Party at the polls. Access to
the polls for minority voters is facilitated by the aptly named Voting
Rights Act, a federal law that was a key victory in America's civil rights
struggle. Section IV of the Voting Rights Act is the act's preventative
mechanism to protect minority access to the ballot from local laws
designed to restrict that access; this section operates only in those
states that had long histories of discriminating against minority voters.
The conservative majority's 5–4 *Shelby County* decision in 2013 fired
a torpedo into that section. Minority voters tend to vote Democratic,
so sinking the section that proactively safeguarded their ballot access
tipped the balance at the polls to Republicans.[28]

With the safeguard gutted, there came swift enactment in many of
those states of a raft of voter-identification laws, cuts to early voting,
bans on same-day registration, and voter-roll purges.[29] Voter suppres-
sion laws such as these, freed up by *Shelby County*, work exclusively in
favor of Republicans. In January 2016, the *Washington Post* described
the "surgical precision with which North Carolina Republicans approved certain forms of photo IDs for voting and excluded others"—
"passports, motor vehicle department IDs, expired IDs for those over
age 70, and veteran and military IDs" were in, while "student IDs, government employee IDs, and . . . public assistance IDs" were out.[30] Ultimately, a federal appeals court saw through the ruse in North Carolina,
declaring in July 2016 that the restrictions "target African Americans
with almost surgical precision" (in an echo of the *Post*) and striking
down the law.[31] Of course, the law had been in place since 2013; Republicans still enjoyed the benefit of fewer Democrats in the electorate
during the time it took to litigate this blatant voter-suppression strategy.

Notably, the conservative justices ignored a voluminous bipartisan congressional record that supported the preclearance requirement. The Court's disrespect for Congress in this matter is odd, because the Fifteenth Amendment to the Constitution gives Congress a vital role in enforcing the voting rights of racial minorities (it explicitly gives "Congress . . . power to enforce this article by appropriate legislation"),[32] yet the conservative justices trampled over this express power. The late Justice Scalia even suggested during oral argument that the overwhelming bipartisan support within Congress for reauthorization of the Voting Rights Act in 2006 actually made the statute more suspect.[33]

A closer look at *Shelby County* suggests that the conservative justices were determined to disable Section IV, and planned, years in advance, to achieve that outcome. Four years before *Shelby County*, in 2009, Chief Justice Roberts, writing for the conservative majority in a decision called *Northwest Austin Municipal Utility District No. 1 v. Holder*, criticized Section IV of the Voting Rights Act and announced a doctrine of the "equal sovereignty" of all states.[34] Later, in *Shelby County*, he relied on his *Northwest Austin* "equal sovereignty" concept to disable Section IV, gutting the "preclearance" safeguard provisions of the Act.[35] Far from just "calling balls and strikes,"[36] it looks like the chief justice (to switch sports metaphors) actually "teed himself up" in *Northwest Austin* for the later decision he rendered in *Shelby County*.

Federal appeals court judge Richard Posner, in an essay about *Shelby County* tellingly titled "The Voting Rights Act Ruling Is About the Conservative Imagination," noted: "There is no doctrine of equal sovereignty. The opinion rests on air."[37]

The conservative justices' decisions on gerrymandering gave a second election boon to Republicans. Gerrymandering is the political technique of designing the shape of a legislative district to make sure a legislator has a friendly electorate. In the early nineteenth century, a salamander-shaped district, designed at the behest of Massachusetts governor Elbridge Gerry to shape a state senate district he needed to protect, was described by Massachusetts newspapers as a "Gerrymander," which gave us this word.[38]

Gerrymandering has been seized on by Republicans as a way to enhance their legislative power in the U.S. Congress. One notable example of how this has succeeded comes from Pennsylvania. In the 2012 elections, Pennsylvania voted statewide to reelect President Obama. Pennsylvania also voted statewide to reelect my Senate colleague Bob Casey, a Democrat. You'd think that would have made Pennsylvania a Democratic state in its House delegation, too. But Pennsylvania in that same election sent thirteen Republicans and five Democrats to Congress from its eighteen congressional districts.[39]

How is that possible? A new and clever form of gerrymandering has emerged. Old-school gerrymandering helps a friendly congressman by shaping his district to make sure he wins. Nasty gerrymandering takes on an undesirable incumbent by reshaping his district to make sure he loses. Modern "bulk" gerrymandering is more strategic and looks at a state's whole congressional delegation. Such bulk gerrymandering isolates Democrats into heavily (80 percent or more) Democratic political districts, "wasting" Democratic votes, and constructs 60/40-majority Republican districts out of the remainder of the state. It thus delivers congressional delegations that don't reflect the state's popular vote.

These diagrams give a good illustration of how this "bulk" gerrymandering works:

Gerrymandering, Explained
Three different ways to divide 50 people into five districts

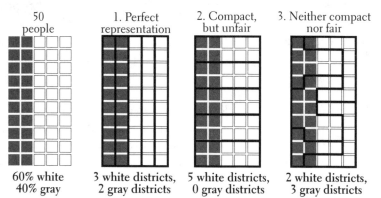

50 people	1. Perfect representation	2. Compact, but unfair	3. Neither compact nor fair
60% white 40% gray	3 white districts, 2 gray districts	5 white districts, 0 gray districts	2 white districts, 3 gray districts

(*Chart adapted from Stephen Nass*)

To lay the groundwork for acquiring this power in Congress, Republicans launched the Redistricting Majority Project (REDMAP). They spent more than $30 million—much of it dark money—to help elect majorities in state legislatures in battleground states including Ohio, Michigan, North Carolina, Pennsylvania, and Wisconsin.[40] Winning those state legislatures was the key that opened the door to redistricting the federal congressional delegations, since it's state legislatures that usually draw those maps. In Pennsylvania, REDMAP spent nearly $1 million to win three state representative races, helping Republicans take over the Pennsylvania House of Representatives.[41] It seems like a lot of money for three state representative races, unless you see the bigger prize.

Sure enough, when voters in Pennsylvania came to the polls in 2012, a total of 2.79 million voters statewide voted for Democratic candidates for Congress.[42] Only 2.71 million voters statewide voted for Republican candidates for Congress.[43] It was close, but Democrats won—83,000 more people in Pennsylvania voted for Democratic candidates for Congress than voted for Republican candidates for Congress.[44] Yet although Democrats won more votes overall, Pennsylvania sent a delegation to Congress that year of five Democrats and thirteen Republicans, as we have seen.[45] Because of the supersaturated Democratic voting districts that had been created, Democratic members of Congress averaged over 76 percent of the vote in their districts, with one district over 89 percent! Republicans averaged 59 percent, winning more districts by smaller margins.[46]

This was not just a Pennsylvania fluke. Ohio in 2012 voted for Barack Obama for president and returned my Democratic colleague Sherrod Brown to the Senate in the statewide vote, but on the same day Ohio elected twelve Republican congressmen and only four Democrats. Wisconsin voted for Obama in 2012 and elected Tammy Baldwin, a progressive, to the Senate; yet Wisconsin sent a delegation of five Republicans and three Democrats to Congress.[47]

Across the country in that 2012 election, 1.59 million more Americans voted for Democratic candidates for Congress than voted for Republican candidates for Congress.[48] Yet the ensuing Congress fell into Republican hands by a majority of thirty-three seats.[49] It was gerrymandering that won the Republicans control of Congress, not winning more votes. And the strategy was plainly admitted.[50] Indeed, the Republican organization behind REDMAP sent out a memo bragging of its achievements:

Farther down-ballot, aggregated numbers show voters pulled the lever for Republicans only 49 percent of the time in congressional races, suggesting that 2012 could have been a repeat of 2008, when voters gave control of the White House and both chambers of Congress to Democrats. But, as we see today, that was not the case. Instead, Republicans enjoy a 33-seat margin in the U.S. House seated yesterday in the 113th Congress, having endured Democratic successes atop the ticket and over one million more votes cast for Democratic House candidates than Republicans.[51]

In 2004, in a gerrymandering case called *Vieth v. Jubelirer*, a group of Pennsylvania Democrats objected to gerrymandering by the Republican-controlled Pennsylvania legislature.[52] The case went all the way to the U.S. Supreme Court. The Republican-appointed judges on the U.S. Supreme Court held, in simplified terms (and again with a 5–4 vote), that the question of gerrymandering was just too hard to agree how to decide, so they wouldn't try to decide it. Four Republican justices announced in their decision that they would no longer even try to determine if gerrymandering interfered with any constitutional voting rights; one, Justice Anthony Kennedy, left a glimmer of light. But the effect was open season for gerrymandering, no matter how crass or obvious the political motive, and no matter how strong the evidence of partisan strategy in the redistricting. The American Bar Association's publication on redistricting law now states: "The Court's recent decisions appear to give legislators leeway to preserve partisan advantage as zealously as they like when drawing district lines."[53] As we have seen, Republicans took full advantage, and by 2012 had seized Pennsylvania's, Ohio's, and Wisconsin's congressional delegations with a minority of voters.

For a Court that regularly addresses vague and challenging constitutional doctrines such as "due process of law" and "equal protection of the laws," to say that this was too hard seemed like a very convenient admission of defeat. It was also dishonest: because of the protected status of race under the Constitution, when districts are gerrymandered for race rather than for politics, the Court must grapple with the hard questions of gerrymandering, so evidently gerrymandering presents problems that, while difficult, are not impossible to resolve.

*   *   *

A series of campaign finance decisions has also helped tip the political balance toward big donors (who tend to be corporate entities, front groups, and super-wealthy individuals), with the predictable result— proven out since in practice—that this would tend to help the Republican Party. The most notable of these is *Citizens United*. That decision (again 5–4) is so extraordinary that it merits its own chapter (which follows this one). But a constellation of decisions surrounds *Citizens United*, beginning with United States Supreme Court justice (you guessed it) Lewis Powell's original decision opening up political rights for corporations.

The notion that the First Amendment protects political activity by corporations as if it were free speech by humans traces back to Powell's 1978 opinion in *First National Bank of Boston v. Bellotti*.[54] In a (guess what) 5–4 vote, the Court gave First Amendment protection to corporations' political expenditures and recognized a corporate constitutional right to influence the political process. A direct line can be drawn from Powell's reasoning in *Bellotti*, through cases like *Buckley v. Valeo*, to the outcome in the Court's 2010 ruling in *Citizens United*. Indeed, Justice Kennedy's majority opinion in *Citizens United* referenced *Bellotti* twenty-four times. In the wake of his own memo urging more corporate political activity, Powell gave corporations the tools for that activity once he was on the Court.

Thus Attorney Powell's memo providing a strategy to enhance the political power of corporations begat Justice Powell's opinion recognizing a corporate constitutional right to political influence, and that in turn begat *Citizens United*, which forbids any limitations on corporate use of campaign spending to acquire political influence.

What merits noting before we move on is that even speech is not always protected "speech" under the First Amendment. Courts over the years have affirmed that the First Amendment doesn't protect the yelling of "Fire!" in a crowded theater and that it doesn't protect fraudulent statements. Some language we utter is libelous and can be punished in civil proceedings. Treasonous statements, criminal threats, and certain other acts of speaking are prosecutable crimes. Offering a bribe is not protected speech. Conspiring to fix an election is done using speech, but it's not protected. Commercial speech by corporations may be regulated to protect the integrity of markets and the expectations of consumers.

So if all actual speech isn't even protected "speech," it makes little sense to think that all corporate spending in politics is necessarily protected "speech." Corporate money is a selfish and driven force with few natural limits in the hydraulic pressures and counterpressures of our politics. It selectively amplifies the voices of a corporate CEO class, giving that class precedence over everyone else. Corporate money in politics can be used for bullying; it can be used for propagandizing falsehoods; it can be used to drown out other voices and deafen the electorate; it can be used for buying political loyalty or punishing political disobedience; it can be the bait on a hook; it can be artillery; it can be blandishment; it can be a "tsunami of slime."[55]

In a country that has made such effort to create a meaningful and open democracy, it is both wrong and simple-minded to refuse to grapple with all the mischievous effects of massive money let loose in politics, to just say it's "speech," and to walk away wiping your hands. It is both wrong and simple-minded to equate corporations, as political actors, with human citizens; they are very different creatures. This ignorance is the price we pay for having the first Supreme Court in America's history with not one justice with any political experience. This ignorance and an associated rashness rushing in to unleash the forces of money have done enormous damage to our democracy— damage that we see all around us.

The Court also has a proclivity in favor of the conservative agenda on social issues, from prayer to abortion to gun control. Curiously, to get to the politically conservative result, the judges will often violate judicially conservative doctrines.

A politically conservative result is something political conservatives want, as an end result, like laws that are pro-gun or anti-gay-marriage, pro-prayer or anti-choice, pro-fossil-fuel or anti-undocumented-immigrant. A judicially conservative doctrine is a theory of jurisprudence, usually a principle that will discourage change in the law and more closely tie the law to the past. It is a conservative *means*, not a conservative end. It is conservative in that it is steadying, prizes continuity, and resists change. (William F. Buckley is said to have observed: "A conservative is someone who stands athwart history, yelling 'Stop.'")[56]

For example, the principle of originalism, or faithfulness to the original meaning of the Constitution, is a conservative judicial doctrine. Some scholars and lawyers believe that the drafters of the Constitution launched in that document very general principles, which they articulated as best they could, but which they left to future generations to define anew as society developed, in what has been described as a "living Constitution." Originalism is the conservative counter to that argument, tying constitutional theory much more closely to the manners and the mores of the Founding era. A "living Constitution" could find the death penalty unconstitutional as "cruel or unusual" or inconsistent with "due process of law"; originalism would scoff at the notion that the states, which all executed criminals during the Founding era, could possibly have sent to the Continental Congress men who wrote a document that could be read to ban the practice. More generally, filtering constitutional theory through the eyes of well-off, eighteenth-century white men is not very likely to lead to dramatic change.

But originalism became inconvenient to the conservatives in the *District of Columbia v. Heller* case about gun control.[57] The Second Amendment had always in prior precedent been tied up with the idea of local militias. In a radical decision, the Court entirely recast the Second Amendment, implying for the first time in our history that the Second Amendment protects an individual right to keep and bear arms for self-defense. The individual right had no Court precedent. As recently as 1991 this doctrine was such a fringe theory that it was described by retired chief justice Warren Burger as "one of the greatest pieces of fraud, I repeat the word 'fraud,' on the American public by special interest groups that I have ever seen in my lifetime."[58] U.S. Appeals Court judge Richard Posner has noted wryly that "the true springs of the *Heller* decision must be sought elsewhere than in the majority's declared commitment to originalism."[59]

The result of the *Heller* decision was the long-sought dream of the National Rifle Association (NRA), the gun industry, and the right wing: recognition of an individual right to bear arms. As Amanda Hollis-Brusky noted in *Ideas with Consequences*, the role of the right-wing legal infrastructure was profound: "With the properly framed

case brought by Federalist Society–affiliated litigators and with intellectual capital nurtured and supported through the Federalist Society
network, five Justices on the Supreme Court were able to reinterpret,
by some standards radically, the Second Amendment's right to keep
and bear arms as a personal, not a collective right in *Heller*."[60] Standing right behind the Federalist Society was the NRA, and standing
right behind the NRA were the gun manufacturers.

In order to give the gun industry its win, the conservative judges
also cast aside the conservative judicial principle of respect for precedent. The Latin name of this doctrine is *stare decisis*, or "it stands
decided." If you do not favor change in the law, you want to respect existing precedents from past decisions. Those precedents are an anchor
against modernity and change, and a stabilizing influence protecting
settled expectations against new ideas. Again, that all became inconvenient in *Heller*. No Supreme Court in history had ever found an
individual right to gun ownership in the Second Amendment; hence
the former chief justice's comment that the idea was a "fraud." But the
NRA wanted it, the right wing wanted it, and the gun manufacturers
wanted it—and that was that. Right-wing Justice Alito has since said
of *stare decisis*, "It is a Latin phrase. It means 'to leave things decided
when it suits our purposes.'"[61]

Alito's dismissal of *stare decisis* may have been tongue-in-cheek, but
Chief Justice Roberts has gone further, announcing that he evaluates
precedent in light of whether his bloc of justices objects to it. He is surprisingly up front about this: "*Stare decisis* effect is . . . diminished . . .
when the precedent's validity is so hotly contested that it cannot reliably
function as a basis for decision in future cases."[62] He continues, "The
simple fact that one of our decisions remains controversial . . . does undermine the precedent's ability to contribute to the stable and orderly
development of the law."[63] As anybody looking at this can see, this is
a completely self-fulfilling theory. It allows the right-wing bloc on the
Court, like sappers, to gradually undermine a settled precedent simply
by "hotly contesting" it—until the day comes when they can blow it up.

A Court with five conservative justices who would tip America's politics toward one party in voting rights, gerrymandering, and campaign
finance cases (toward the party that appointed them, if it need be said),

and who would deliver conservative social policy victories to the party that appointed them (even though these decisions run against traditional conservative legal doctrine), should also have no trouble delivering the substantive goods on legal issues important to the corporate hierarchy backing that party. And the conservative five had no trouble at all with that.

According to the Constitutional Accountability Center, between 2006 and 2015 the Roberts Court supported the legal position of the United States Chamber of Commerce (by then the Chamber had become a de facto organ of the national Republican Party—or vice versa) 69 percent of the time.[64] The Chamber's side had won 56 percent of the time during the Rehnquist Court and 43 percent of the time during the Burger Court.[65] If it was Lewis Powell's dream to have the Chamber actively litigating before an "activist" Court, it has been Justice Roberts's achievement to provide them that Court.

The Chamber's impressive "win" rate in the Roberts Court is itself an understatement of the pro-corporate direction of the Court. An aggressive, confident Chamber, knowing it had an active conservative majority on the Court, could file cases where it expected a win would have "impact" and move the law in its direction. A "loss" in a case like that meant no more than that the status quo remained intact. An opportunity may be lost, but if the status quo remains, no actual harm is done to corporate interests.

Many Chamber victories have been significant. In the *Ledbetter* case, the Court overturned a verdict of employment discrimination, concluding that an employer could not be held liable if it successfully hid the discriminatory treatment from the victim long enough—that is, after decades of unequal pay, the plaintiff could recover damages for only the single paycheck received within the 180-day window allowed for filing a complaint.[66] In the *Leegin* case, the Court reversed precedent that had long prohibited manufacturers and distributors from setting minimum prices for the sale of retail goods to consumers.[67] In the *Janus* case, the Court limited the ability of mutual fund investors to recover for securities fraud, holding that fund advisors cannot be found liable for knowingly including misstatements of others in the documents they prepare.[68] And in the *Gross* case, the Court overturned a jury decision in favor of a victim of age discrimination in the workplace.[69] Each of these cases was decided by a 5–4 margin, with the five Republican appointees voting as a bloc in support of the corporate position.

Corporations have also won a series of cases that make it harder for people, and groups of people, to bring them to court for wrongdoing. As we'll discuss in detail later, big corporations hate being hauled into court and having to face juries, and the Supreme Court has protected them from this equalizing mechanism of justice in several ways. Through the *Iqbal* and *Twombly* decisions, corporations benefit from heightened pleading standards—meaning that the bar is now higher for plaintiffs who want to take a defendant such as a big corporation to court.[70] They have won rulings pushing disputes into corporation-favoring arbitration, as in *Rent-A-Center, West, Inc. v. Jackson.*[71] They have won rulings making it harder for injured Americans to band together to press cases of large-scale corporate wrongdoing, such as in *Wal-Mart v. Dukes* and *AT&T v. Concepcion.*[72] They recently won a two-fer ruling that pushed disputes into corporation-favoring arbitration *and* made it harder for injured Americans to band together.[73] They won *Vance v. Ball State University*, in which the Court made it more difficult for workers to hold their employers accountable for harassment in the workplace under the 1964 Civil Rights Act; *Mutual Pharmaceutical Co. v. Bartlett*, in which the Court made it harder for consumers who experience serious side effects from medications to sue drug companies; and *Comcast v. Behrend*, where the Court made it even harder for consumers to bring class actions.[74] They won *Hobby Lobby*, where the Court put the religious rights of corporate entities over the rights of those entities' employees (corporations, being people, can have religion, I guess), and *Harris*, already discussed, in which the Court not only dealt a significant blow to the political and economic clout of unions but issued an invitation to come and take another slug at them.[75]

It is highly improbable that corporate interests have prevailed so often and so reliably by mere happenstance, by neutral calling of "balls and strikes."[76] When you add in the rate at which Republican election interests have prevailed and the rate at which conservative social positions have prevailed, the case for happenstance becomes even more remote.

CHAPTER SEVEN

Capture of Elections

Citizens United

IN DECISION AFTER DECISION, the five-man conservative bloc that dominated the Roberts Court found a way to hold in favor of corporate and conservative interests with alarming predictability. Given the Court's corporate bent—in areas from civil procedure to workers' rights—perhaps it should not have been surprising when, in 2010, the Court unleashed unlimited corporate spending in our elections. Nevertheless, to court-watchers and Congress alike, *Citizens United* came as a shock. It was once the opinion of the United States Supreme Court that "to subject the state governments to the combined capital of wealthy corporations [would] produce universal corruption."[1] No more.

Citizens United, another 5–4 decision, marked the crowning victory for corporate interests. It opened the floodgates for unlimited, anonymous corporate cash in our elections, causing the "tsunami of slime" that we have seen in recent election cycles. *Citizens United* granted inanimate corporations and their special-interest fronts new power in our elections, not just through the corrupting ability to buy elections for favored candidates but also through the corrupting but less visible ability to threaten officeholders with a barrage of negative attack ads if they fail to cast a pro-corporate vote.

Such a dominant role for corporations in our government would shock our Founding Fathers, who foresaw no important role in our republic for the corporations of the time. They certainly did not foresee today's massive agglomerations of corporate wealth, nor the corporations' now-unlimited power to deploy that wealth in our elections. I believe they would be disgusted.

The *Citizens United* decision was wrongly handled jurispruden-tially, wrongly managed procedurally, wrongly founded factually, and wrongly decided substantively. Even for the Roberts Court, with its near-explicit support for the corporate agenda, the decision was extreme, a rare kind of error-plagued and mischief-riddled legal monstrosity.

To unleash that corporate power in our elections, the conservative justices had to go through remarkable contortions.[2] I will discuss those contortions shortly. For now, let's just say it was a dirty business. And it has produced lamentable results.

The Founders worked hard setting up the Constitution to protect against the emergence of a new aristocracy. It is therefore saddening to see the five conservative justices create a new political aristocracy with the stroke of a pen. But they did.

We each bring to our American democracy our own voice, and we each bring to it our own pocketbook. Some of us may have a more compelling or thoughtful voice than others, and some may have a big-ger or more free-spending pocketbook, but fundamentally we Ameri-cans have all historically been equal with one another in the respect that it was our own voices and pocketbooks we brought to politics. First the Founders, and then the leaders of our great civil rights movements, fought hard to make it so.

After *Citizens United*, that is no longer true. After *Citizens United*, if you are in America's corporate elite, you have been given a super-empowered voice and pocketbook to put to work in politics, on top of your own. In addition to their own voices, corporate leaders now have the megaphone voices of the corporations they command. In addition to their own pocketbooks, corporate leaders now have the vast treasur-ies of the corporations they control.

Unleashing corporate power into elections thus super-empowered the men and women who command those corporations. They already had the advantage of greater-than-average voices through the net-work of influence their corporate position provided to them (and their corporate lobbyists and PACs). They also already had the advantage of greater-than-average pocketbooks, through the generous incomes their corporate positions provided them. So they would do just fine in our democracy on their own. Corporate CEOs were not a hurting, beleaguered class.

But on top of that, they have now been given the voices and pocketbooks of the corporations they command. They are "double-decker" citizens now: once through themselves, and once through the enormous constitutional aliens the corporatist justices have brought to such robust political life. And this state of affairs has produced a massive deformation of American politics.

Elections are the lifeblood of democracy. The U.S. Constitution is established by and for "We the People of the United States." Humans are clearly different from artificial legal fictions called corporations. And nothing in the Constitution gives CEOs the right to amplify their voices over all of ours through the corporations they control. The activist bloc that drove the Supreme Court to *Citizens United* did not seem to appreciate this foundational, commonsense principle of our republic.

Our government is intended to be "of the people, by the people, and for the people." By refusing to distinguish between people and corporations, the Court allowed CEOs special privileged status and unleashed a foreign force into our politics against which the Constitution provided no adequate protections. We can remind ourselves that the Founders never imagined that such a power would emerge, and that they would never have wanted such a power to intrude into our political life.

We are not alone in that thought. The decision's nightmarish consequences have been recognized by leaders of all stripes. Senator John McCain, Republican of Arizona, has called *Citizens United* "one of the worst decisions in history." Due to the Court's "absolute ignorance of what happens in politics," he said, they created a "flood of money into campaigns, not transparent, unaccounted for."[3] Richard Posner, the conservative legal scholar and federal judge, put it even more bluntly: "Our political system is pervasively corrupt due to our Supreme Court taking away campaign-contribution restrictions on the basis of the First Amendment."[4] And as Senator Chuck Schumer, a Democrat of New York, said in 2010 about *Citizens United*: "The Supreme Court has just predetermined the winners of next November's elections. It won't be the Republicans or the Democrats and it won't be the American people; it will be corporate America."[5]

Republican former officeholders are just as dismayed. Former senator Alan Simpson of Wyoming has written: "Ending the tyranny of big money corruption isn't partisan—it's patriotic. It's essential to preserving the most deeply held values and beliefs we share."[6] Former congresswoman Connie Morella of Maryland has written: "Democracy requires constant vigilance. When the interests of major campaign donors and their allies are favored over the needs of ordinary citizens, we all pay the price."[7] President George W. Bush's political advisor Mark McKinnon has said, "Money in politics is . . . discordant with a free market philosophy because currently our public policy markets are not free—they are hostage to crony interests that pay for what they get."[8] We now live in a country where the conversation intended to be between American citizens and their candidates for public office has instead been overwhelmed by unlimited spending by corporate power: spending by corporations themselves, by the front groups they have established, and by the billionaires they have heaved up.

Corporations, as Justice Stevens has reminded us, are "invisible," "intangible," "artificial," "mere creature[s] of the law,"[9] with "no consciences, no beliefs, no feelings, no thoughts, no desires."[10] Unsurprisingly, the corporate power unleashed by *Citizens United* has turned things into a mess. As legal scholar Burt Neuborne summarized:

> Billionaire oligarchs have a First Amendment stranglehold on the electoral process. Wealthy ideologues on the left and right dominate the electoral agenda. Huge for-profit corporations are guaranteed the power to pour unlimited sums into buying political influence. Public officials and candidates spend most of their time trolling for support from wealthy donors, who often view campaign contributions as economic investments. Political investors can now choose whether to buy influence directly, with checks to specific leaders, or indirectly, as independent spenders. Election winners repay their wealthy supporters with excessive political influence; election losers mortgage their souls trying to persuade investors to bankroll their comebacks. Giant loopholes in the disclosure rules let wealthy individuals and corporations

spend huge sums in secret to manipulate unwitting voters, and well-meaning legislators are forbidden to break the economic stranglehold of the rich by using the most efficient form of campaign subsidy—matching public funds tailored to the sums raised by privately funded opponents.[11]

This unbalances our politics. As legendary investor and CEO Warren Buffett has said, "They say it's free speech, but someone can speak 20 or 30 million times and my cleaning lady can't speak at all."[12]

The Supreme Court's 2010 decision in *Citizens United* was a shocking assault on the electoral system in our democracy. The *New York Times* called it "a sharp doctrinal shift."[13] One defeated congressman described *Citizens United* as "the polluters['] triumph." He told the *New Yorker*'s Jane Mayer: "There was a huge change after *Citizens United*. When anyone could spend any amount of money without revealing who they were, by hiding behind amorphous-named organizations, the floodgates opened. The Supreme Court made a huge mistake. There is no accountability. Zero."[14] By unleashing corporate money and the money of corporate billionaires and front groups, much of it now anonymous or laundered through intermediary organizations, the Court let loose into our political discourse waves of out-of-control spending, anonymous corporate influence, negative and false advertising, and unpunished lying. The American public is understandably disgusted and disillusioned. It seems like madness.

My point here is that there was method in the madness. *Citizens United* was cast by the conservative justices as being about the rights of individuals—in this case, the all-important right to hear more corporate speech.[15] Seriously, that's the way they framed it: our individual right to hear unlimited corporate speech. Burt Neuborne's *Madison's Music* describes it thus: "The Court allows the corporate speaker to borrow the hearer's First Amendment rights to receive the information."[16] Notwithstanding that "right" supposedly of ours, the decision's practical effect was to benefit corporations—Big Oil, pharmaceutical companies, debt collection agencies, health insurance companies, credit card companies, banks, coal barons, tobacco companies.

Unfortunately, the public doesn't know the half of it. The true

impact of *Citizens United* on our elections and our policy making can
be understood only by taking a closer look at the ins and outs of politics. I see that impact every day in the Senate. Let's have a look at some
of its practical effects.

Months prior to the *Citizens United* decision, the U.S. Chamber
of Commerce already had announced in the fall of 2009 "a massive
effort to support pro-business candidates."[17] *Citizens United* enabled
the Chamber's spending on this effort to be both limitless and face-
less. By 2014, the Chamber was the single largest dark-money spender
in the midterm elections and the single largest dark-money spender
in twenty-eight of the thirty-five individual races in which it was involved.[18] The corporate lobby was now free to attack political candidates
from behind a cloak of anonymity. The response from Republicans to
Citizens United, as reported by the *Washington Post*, should come as
no surprise: "Republican leaders . . . cheered the ruling as a victory for
free speech and predicted a surge in corporate support for GOP candidates in November's midterm elections."[19] A team of economists has
since "found that *Citizens United* shifted the odds of electoral success
detectably and in a clear direction: from Democratic to Republican
candidates."[20]

Since the Court took the fateful step of forbidding any limits on
corporate spending, nothing now prevents corporate polluters under
investigation by the Department of Justice from arranging unlimited
ads supporting a more sympathetic presidential candidate who'll tell
his attorney general to go easy. Nothing prevents financial services
companies from spending their vast wealth to defeat members of Congress who are tired of the way business is done on Wall Street and dare
to become a thorn in Wall Street's side. Nothing prevents big defense
contractors from overwhelming candidates who might dare question a
multibillion-dollar weapons program that they build.

But the problem runs far deeper than corporate interests spending their money. More insidious, corporations (and their front groups
and billionaires) can now *threaten* to spend their money. Put simply,
what big money can do, big money can threaten to do, or promise
to do. And those threats and promises are very likely to be private.
There's nothing "independent" or "transparent" about private threats
and promises in a back room. The public will never know of the secret

threats and promises, and corruption will inevitably follow. It doesn't take a constitutional scholar to figure that out.

The *Citizens United* decision opened this avenue to corruption, while pretending corruption was impossible.[21] Pretending that political corruption through corporate campaign spending is impossible is a notion that is laughable on its face, but even that laughable conclusion overlooks the problem that limitless untraceable political money doesn't actually have to be spent to corrupt our democracy. It can corrupt through the threat of spending it, or through the promise of spending it. And although the public won't see those back-room corporate threats and promises, or be aware of the deals that result, the candidate will know, and the special-interest dealmaker will know. Just the public will be left in the dark.

A well-funded super PAC can now make a single giant expenditure—or just threaten to make one—and have a major impact on a race. The overwhelming influence of outside money and dark money is particularly significant in congressional races with smaller media markets and campaign budgets than a presidential race or most Senate and gubernatorial races. In my state, members of Congress can run a $2 million race for reelection and feel they spent a lot of money. Spending $5 million would be a huge election effort. But $5 million is play money to big corporate interests when big money—perhaps tens of billions of dollars—is at stake in Congress.

Voltaire made a famous wry remark about the Royal Navy hanging Admiral Byng, saying that every once in a while the English have to hang an admiral "to encourage the others."[22] A similar effect can be had by picking off a particularly vexing member of Congress, or one whom colleagues in Congress look to for leadership on an issue. Take Bob Inglis, for example: a conservative Republican South Carolina congressman whose respect for science and love of his children caused him to take up the issue of global warming. He traveled to Antarctica to hear from the scientists directly. His children told him, "Dad, you're going to have to clean up your act on the environment." So he took the plunge and tried to make a conservative, faith-based case for taking on climate change. The response was immediate. Bombarded by outside money in his next primary, he was crushed by a margin of two to one, the kind of beating it usually takes an indictment to produce. Republicans in Congress got the message: Inglis says that for a time after that, his name "became a verb" in political circles—to be "Inglissed."

Corporate power doesn't have to hang all the admirals: hang one, and all the others will get the message. The smart strategy for a corporate-funded political attack would not be to fund massive attacks against everyone; it would be to make an example of someone. The efficiency of that strategy makes the threat all the more real, because it makes so much sense to attack for the sake of example. It's such a bargain.

That reality gives politicians an incentive not to be the example— not to be the admiral the corporate powers want to hang "to encourage all the others." So the overall message this threat conveys to members of Congress is to pull in your horns, be docile, don't be an annoyance, and perhaps you won't become a target. What a bargain for big special interests, if just having the *capability* to attack is enough to "encourage" everyone! You don't actually have to spend the money at all.

And that's the gift five pro-corporate justices gave the big special interests.

The threat of an attack doesn't even have to be specific to one particular candidate to be politically effective. Threats that are general, that are more in the nature of an announcement and that would never qualify in court as criminal bribery or extortion, can nevertheless ping loudly on the political radar of candidates and campaigns and influence political behavior in corrupting ways.

A sense of what that might look like comes from the actual warnings some special interests have issued. The climate-change-denying, Koch-backed campaign group Americans for Prosperity (a helpful name at letting the public know who is really behind it, for sure) within months made two big announcements: one, that the group was going to raise and spend $889 million in the 2016 election (since adjusted downward to merely $750 million); and two, as Carol Davenport reported in the *New York Times*, that the group would put anyone who crossed them on climate change at a "severe disadvantage."[23] Later, as reported by Davenport, the group warned that supporting a price on carbon pollution would be a "political loser."[24] According to an article in *Politico*, they bragged of the "political peril" that would result for those who crossed them.[25] You can practically imagine a big brute walking into some campaign office in a black trench coat, slapping a bat into his palm. "Nice little campaign you got going here, bub, be a shame to see it 'severely disadvantaged' . . . oh, and by the way, what're you doing on climate change?" Smack, smack.

If you want another example of how special interest politics works in Washington, read *Politico*'s story, "Drug Lobby Plans Counterattack on Prices," from August 4, 2016: the plot of the story is that PhRMA, "a sleeping giant, which routinely spends more on lobbying than any other health care group and took in more than $200 million in member dues in 2014," is "gearing up to spend hundreds of millions of dollars on a post-election ad war," seeking "to reassert its dominance in Washington after several years in which it has taken a public shellacking over prices." The punch line of the story: "Targeting politicians is not part of the initial plan, but lobbyists say the organization is prepared to do so if members of Congress or the executive branch push agendas that are seen as detrimental to the industry."[26] *Citizens United* has made all the difference in targeting politicians, and it's not for nothing that the opening bid is lobbyists telegraphing the threat before the money has to be spent.

There is an equation in political threats: size times intensity equals danger. If someone is furious at you and is going to go all in for your opponent and give them $200, the intensity may be high but the size of the threat is low, and the threat is not particularly acute. An anxious congressman can still go about his job of representing the many. If there's a billionaire in your state, one not particularly interested in politics, a prudent congresswoman may want to steer around him, since the size of his fortune is a political threat. But if he's not intensely engaged, his threat is not particularly acute. However, mark the size of the threat at $889 million (or $750 million) to be spent all in one election, and mark the intensity at "you'll be 'severely disadvantaged' if you cross us," and a very big warning beacon pings very loudly on the radar of every campaign and candidate.

Before the flood, a corporate CEO could threaten to host a fundraiser for your opponent, he could put his support for your opponent in the employee newsletter, or he could send your opponent a $10,000

PAC check, and that was about it. And he'd have to do it all publicly. It was a crime, for instance, for the CEO to launder a donation through an employee, friend, or family member to boost his giving clout or hide his role. Now the corporate CEO (or more likely his political operatives, as he probably doesn't want to get his hands too dirty with the new "wet work" of politics) simply has to approve a dollar number and unleash the new apparatus. Since corporations regularly seek benefits in Washington worth many billions of dollars for their industry, the natural limit on the dollar number it makes economic sense for the CEO to unleash is very, very high.

One example is when hedge fund CEO Robert Mercer took umbrage at a proposed federal transaction tax by Oregon's Representative Peter DeFazio that would have taxed hyper-fast "flash trades" of the type done by the hedge fund. As *Time* reported, Mercer retaliated in force: the "hedge-fund boss has financed challenges to the Oregon Democrat for four election cycles running. 'DeFazio pissed him off,' says a Republican consultant who has worked with Mercer." Showing bipartisan spirit, the hedge-fund magnate also went after John McCain for participating in a Senate hearing investigating an accounting maneuver used by the hedge fund to avoid nearly $7 billion in taxes. Again from *Time*: "with McCain locked in a primary fight, the financier cut a $200,000 check to a group supporting McCain's right-wing challenger. 'We issued a scathing report about this guy evading taxes— his firm. I'm sure there's no connection,' McCain quipped."[27] While McCain and DeFazio did not quail, lesser members of Congress certainly could have; and for a $7 billion dollar tax dodge, the political attacks and related threats could easily get into enormous numbers.

In areas where the Supreme Court actually has some experience and some idea of what it's talking about—say, with respect to the buying of judges—it has been somewhat less generous to the big special interests. In the case of *Caperton v. A.T. Massey Coal Co.*, an elected West Virginia Supreme Court of Appeals justice had been the beneficiary of more than $3 million in election support through a nonprofit started and funded by the owner of Massey Coal and through that owner's independent expenditures.[28] The money was raised and spent for the state supreme court judge's election while a case involving Massey

Coal—in which the coal company lost a $50 million trial verdict—
was coming up through the West Virginia courts. The coal company
owner's nonprofit political group ended up spending three times more
money on the judge's election than the judge's own campaign spent.
(Rather like today's candidate-specific super PACs that spend more
than the campaigns.)

Obviously, the coal company owner wanted a friendly court for the
appeal of a $50 million loss, whether Riviera vacations or campaign
contributions were the inducement. (Another judge on the court
had been photographed vacationing on the French Riviera with the
same coal company owner, but that judge prudently recused himself from the case.) The judge whose election was funded by Massey
Coal's owner turned out to be the swing vote in favor of the coal company when the appeal was decided, and the $50 million verdict was
overturned.

When the case went up to the United States Supreme Court in
2009, this was all too smelly for Justice Kennedy, who wrote the majority opinion for the Court, stating, "We conclude that there is a serious
risk of actual bias—based on objective and reasonable perceptions—
when a person with a personal stake in a particular case had a significant and disproportionate influence in placing the judge on the case
by raising funds or directing the judge's election campaign when the
case was pending or imminent."[29] So from now on, if a litigant before
a judge has such massive influence over the judge hearing his case,
the remedy must be recusal of the judge—at least if the case is pending or imminent when the influence is acquired. (Otherwise, maybe
the influence is okay; who knows?) No similar remedy is available
for members of Congress, no matter how "significant and disproportionate" the influence acquired by a big interest through campaign
spending.

(Stunningly, the other four hard-core members of the Supreme
Court's pro-corporate bloc all dissented from the majority decision in
the *Massey Coal* case. Even this level of corporate influence-buying
through campaign spending, even in the election of a judge actually
hearing the coal company's case, even when that judge was the swing
vote in the company's favor, was not too much for them. Corporate
money can do no wrong.)

*   *   *

As noted, this is the first Supreme Court in American history to have
no justice with experience running for or holding elective office. With
that experience gap on the Court, many people believe the decision
in *Citizens United* by the five conservative justices was the product of
ignorance and error. Trevor Potter is a well-respected and thoughtful
campaign lawyer who has represented both John McCain's presidential campaign and Stephen Colbert's tongue-in-cheek super PAC, and
has also served as chairman of the Federal Election Commission. He
says, "The conservatives on the court seem to fail to understand what
leads to corruption or the appearance of corruption." He considers
them "out of their depth" in campaign finance law, yet "forging ahead
without understanding the consequences." He notes that the conservatives completely blew their forecast of what would happen in the wake
of their decision, in the way of transparency of donors and independence from campaigns. Contrary to their expectations, he says, "what
we got was a tsunami of money in the 2012 elections from tax-exempt
groups that did not disclose their donors and from supposedly independent super PACs run by candidates' former top aides, close friends
and family members. This was easy to predict. But the five justices
who signed the majority opinion didn't see it."[30] Similarly, former Federal Election Commission chairman (and current commissioner) Ann
Ravel says that the justices "did not understand what the implications
were going to be of what they did."[31] Maybe.

There is another theory: that the conservatives specifically wanted
to open the floodgates of corporate spending, and went through elaborate machinations and contortions to accomplish their purpose. They
may have been ignorant of how badly it would work out, but they had
a plan.

To explore that possibility, we now move from what's bad *about*
the *Citizens United* decision, to what's bad *within* the *Citizens United*
decision.

Unleashing the corporate power *Citizens United* set loose in our
elections required the conservative justices to go through some pretty
remarkable contortions: reversing previous decisions by the Court
that had said the opposite, making up facts that are demonstrably
flat-out wrong, creating a make-believe world of "independence" and

"transparency" in election spending, and maneuvering their own judicial procedures to prevent a factual record that would belie those facts they were making up. Each of the contortions was unusual, objectionable, wrong, or all of the above.

The sins of *Citizens United* are many, but the most venal is the strategy that links them. Let's look at the individual sins of *Citizens United*, and then at the strategy. Together, these make abundantly clear that the conservative corporatists on the Court got exactly the results they were shooting for from the get-go.

Let's start with their "facts." Despite more than a century of warnings by the elected branches of government about the real dangers of corporate political corruption, despite harsh experience of corporate-funded corruption that had led to those warnings, despite recent precedents from the Court itself protecting against corporate corruption in elections, despite extensive records on corporate corruption developed in those prior precedents, and despite 100 years of settled law from Congress, the conservative justices used their bare 5–4 majority to make the fateful (many would say fanciful) finding of fact that "independent expenditures, including those made by corporations, do not give rise to corruption or the appearance of corruption."[32] They didn't stop there. They went on to find that "the appearance of influence or access, furthermore, will not cause the electorate to lose faith in our democracy."[33] These assertions in *Citizens United* stood on nothing. They were bald assertions, in air.

As you wonder about these puzzling assertions, remember something else: there is a well-established judicial principle that courts of appeal, and especially the Supreme Court, *do not make findings of fact.* That is the job of trial courts and juries. In our judicial system, the fact-finding is done by those who take the testimony and hear the witnesses. Appellate courts seek errors of law and simply take the facts as found for them by the trial courts. From its earliest days, the Supreme Court has defined its job as deciding "what the law is."[34] So it is not just weird that the *Citizens United* justices made up *bad* facts; it's weird that they made up facts *at all.*

This was no small thing. The rule against higher courts' fact-finding is one way the American system of separated powers restrains courts from gallivanting off into policy making. Courts don't get to pick the topics they want to rule on; they have to wait for cases to come to them in the ordinary course of litigation. And they can't meddle with the facts of the case as it comes to them. The appellate courts are thus tethered to the facts as the lower courts have found them. In a government based on separated powers, this limitation on the free-range wanderings of higher courts is not an idle principle; it's a key one. A judge "is not a knight-errant, roaming at will in pursuit of his own ideal," to borrow Justice Benjamin Cardozo's words, and tethering appellate courts to the facts in the case is an important judicial constraint against such roaming.[35] Here, that principle simply went out the window. Why? Read on.

The Supreme Court usually has a factual record presented to it and then must interpret the law based on that factual record. Here, the case *had no factual record* on the fundamental question of corrupt corporate political influence. As Justice Stevens objected in dissent: "In this case, the record is not simply incomplete or unsatisfactory; it is nonexistent."[36] In this respect *Citizens United* differed from the cases it overruled, which had voluminous records on the danger of corporate corruption—including the hundred-year-old Senate finding that the dangers of corporate corruption of elections were too obvious to need elaboration. Having no record, in a case of this magnitude, was unusual.

It was unusual that there was no factual record on this question, but it was no accident. There was no factual record because of a procedural maneuver pulled by the Court itself. Every case that goes to argument in the United States Supreme Court has a "question presented" that confirms what the case is about. The briefs that parties file in the Court are required to have a section stating the "question presented"—it is one of the Court's formalities. It makes sure everyone knows what the issues before the Court are. In a very unusual procedural maneuver, in the *Citizens United* case the chief justice late in the proceedings *changed* its "question presented."[37]

Citizens United was initially an extremely narrow case challenging whether the McCain-Feingold campaign finance law prohibited, in the thirty days before primary elections, airing an on-demand cable video critical of a candidate—Hillary Clinton, in this case.[38] Late in the proceedings, after the legal briefs were in and oral arguments by all the parties were done, the Court issued a *new* "question presented," which reframed the case as a broad challenge to the government's power to regulate corporate spending on elections. In dissent, Justice Stevens aptly explained, "five Justices were unhappy with the limited nature of the case before us, so they changed the case to give themselves an opportunity to change the law."[39] Balls and strikes, indeed.

By changing the question presented so late in the proceedings, they also gave themselves an opportunity to change the law *without a record*. An extensive legislative record or trial court record concerning corruption from corporate political activity would ordinarily have been developed in the preceding stages of a case of such magnitude. Past experience from similar cases shows what such a record would have revealed: a massive, reeking, obvious, and persistent threat of political corruption by corporate forces. Without any record, however, the conservatives conveniently avoided that obstacle to the ruling they were pursuing.

In sum, changing the "question presented" late in the case was an unusual procedural maneuver. That maneuver created the unusual circumstance of the Court not having a full record on the new question it had presented itself, but it was necessary to have no record in order to open the way for that equally unusual assertion of fact about corruption.

Without a record to the contrary, the justices were free to break the "no fact-finding" rule, take that one little fact-finding liberty, and pretend that corporate money, even spent in unlimited amounts, can't corrupt politics or even create the appearance of corruption. To use their exact phrase, it would "not give rise to corruption or the appearance of corruption." This finding, made in that exact language, was more than just an observation; it was a key.

The last piece of the *Citizens United* puzzle to understand is a basic principle of First Amendment law that limits free speech rights under the First Amendment. Free speech rights must be weighed against the government's efforts to police corruption, or even the appearance of corruption, in elections—and if the efforts to control corruption are reasonable ones, the right to speech must yield.[40] For instance, conspiring to fix an election likely involves talking, but it's not protected free speech. The test is whether the government is reasonably protecting against "corruption or the appearance of corruption."[41] The Court's puzzling finding of fact that "independent expenditures, including those made by corporations, do not give rise to corruption or the appearance of corruption," suddenly comes into focus.[42] It synchronizes exactly to this core principle of First Amendment law, even matching its language. It was the key to turn this lock.

If it was their goal from the outset to open up unlimited corporate spending in elections, the five justices knew they *had* to find that corporate political spending was not corrupting. Otherwise their First Amendment rationale for allowing unlimited corporate political spending would flop. The factual assertion by the justices may have been ludicrous, but it was *necessary*. Without it, the corporate "First Amendment right" they wished to create would lose to the government's legitimate interest in protecting the integrity of elections. That governmental interest in fair and honest elections, and in protecting against "corruption, or the appearance of corruption," would be an insurmountable barrier without that precisely matching finding that corporate money in elections *can't cause corruption*. That door had to be opened to get to the desired result, and this key turned the lock.

And then on you go through the rest of the scheme. To make the findings of fact you need in order to knock aside the political corruption concern, you have to break the rules about appellate courts making findings of fact. To make the specific findings of fact that turn the lock, you also have to keep out of the case any factual record, since the records established in previous cases show that a factual record on this question would blow your imaginary facts out of the water. To avoid having a factual record on the question, you have to fiddle with the question presented late in the proceedings, when the time for creating a troublesome record is long past. And, of course, you have to make the laughable findings of fact.

Each of these is an error, but they are not separate errors. They link together in a chain of necessity to form the only avenue to the decision's result. And that result was a massive explosion of corporate political power and influence.

When all the effort and craft it took to link these steps is deconstructed, only one rational conclusion can be drawn: that the five pro-corporate justices were bound and determined from the very start to unleash corporate power into our elections—to deliver that political boost to those big corporate interests willing and able to spend big political money.

And that line about how "the appearance of influence or access, furthermore, will not cause the electorate to lose faith in our democracy"? Like other "factual" findings in *Citizens United*, this just ain't factual. An independent poll conducted in 2012 by the Brennan Center for Justice found that approximately 70 percent of Americans believe super PAC spending leads to corruption.[43] In the same survey, 75 percent of Republicans and 78 percent of Democrats agreed that there would be less corruption if there were limits on how much could be given to super PACs.[44] A June 2015 *New York Times*/CBS News poll found that more than four out of five Americans believe money plays too great a role in political campaigns, while two-thirds say that the wealthy have a greater chance of influencing the electoral process than other Americans.[45] In a November 2015 *Washington Post* column titled "Americans See a Government of, by and for the Rich," Harold Meyerson described within the American public "one area of remarkable agreement: Across party lines, Americans believe that our economic system is rigged to favor the wealthy and big corporations, and that our political system is, too." Indeed, he notes that "by nearly a 2-to-1 margin (64 percent to 36 percent), Americans believe their 'vote does not matter because of the influence that wealthy individuals and big corporations have on the electoral process.'"[46]

That is new since *Citizens United*. People are mad: 69 percent of poll respondents recently confirmed that they "feel angry because our political system seems to only be working for the insiders with money and power, like those on Wall Street or in Washington, rather than working to help everyday people get ahead."[47] And eight out of ten Americans disapprove of *Citizens United*.[48]

Aside from the peculiar method the Court needed to get to its result in *Citizens United*, the path to that result ran right over several judicial principles usually thought of as conservative principles. One collateral casualty on the road to the *Citizens United* decision was the conservative judicial doctrine called "originalism," discussed in Chapter Six. Originalism is seen as a conservative principle because conservative

judges favor it and because its approach to constitutional interpretation focuses on the original intent of the Founders. If your touchstone
is the mores and prejudices of property-holding white men of the
late eighteenth century, you have a pretty good conservative weapon
against modern readings of the Constitution.

In *Citizens United* the five justices made the leap that corporations
are people and that money is speech. Thus they were able to give corporate money First Amendment protection as speech. They went a more
roundabout route than that, but that's effectively where they ended up.
And that's quite a leap when you think how suspicious the Founding
Fathers were of corporations, and when you consider that there is no
mention whatever of corporations in the Constitution. The conservative justices' fidelity to "originalism" is inconstant, and *Citizens United*
is another case in which the conservatives ignored this principle in
getting to their desired result.

In *Citizens United*, the only thorough discussion of the Founders'
"original intent" appears in Justice Stevens's dissent, not in the majority opinion or in Justice Scalia's concurrence. Justice Stevens correctly explains the Founding Fathers' dim view of corporations. They
were suspicious of corporations. They considered corporations prone
to abuse and scandal. And, as discussed, the corporations that did exist
at the time of the Founding were largely creatures of the States. They
bore little resemblance to enormous contemporary corporations, and
had no lawful role in electioneering.[49]

Justice Stevens rightly describes it as "implausible that the Framers
believed 'the freedom of speech' would extend equally to all corporate speakers, much less that it would preclude legislatures from taking
limited measures to guard against corporate capture of elections."[50]
Avoiding any discussion of originalism, the *Citizens United* majority
reached a result that would have astounded the Founding Fathers: unlimited corporate spending in American elections, with big corporations in a more robust political position than human persons.

Another core judicial doctrine abandoned in the *Citizens United*
decision is respect for precedent, for previous decisions of the Court.
As noted, respect for precedent gives the law stability, and is usually
seen as a conservative judicial doctrine. To treat corporations as people and money as speech, the conservative justices had to throw over

previous Supreme Court decisions that had said the exact opposite, upending a century of law, including *McConnell v. Federal Election Commission*, decided in 2003, and *Austin v. Michigan Chamber of Commerce*, decided in 1990.[51] Justice Stevens recognized in his dissent that the principle of *stare decisis*—"it stands decided"—ensures that our Nation's "bedrock principles are founded in the law rather than in the proclivities of individuals."[52] The conservative bloc undid these judicial precedents with almost no hesitation. Justice Stevens reviewed those recent prior precedents of the Court that had gone the opposite way, and noted that since those precedents "the only relevant thing that has changed . . . is the composition of this Court."[53]

The big winners of *Citizens United* were the forces of corporate power; the justices' ruling tipped the balance of power in their favor. The Republican Party was a direct beneficiary of *Citizens United*. For example, the largest corporate lobbying group in America is the U.S. Chamber Committee. The Chamber virtually exclusively supports Republican candidates and spends big money for them, to the point where the boundary between the Chamber and the Republican Party has become nearly indistinguishable. Beyond the Chamber, super PACs and other nonprofit organizations unleashed by *Citizens United* spent upward of $450 million in the 2012 election cycle to support Republicans or attack President Obama.[54] At one stage in the 2016 election cycle, PACs and super PACs supporting Republicans had raised 93 percent of all outside political donations.[55]

Citizens United fits the pattern of the conservative justices favoring Republican interests in election cases, and it also fits the pattern of the Roberts Court favoring corporate interests. Americans have noticed these patterns. Now by a ratio of nine to one, Americans doubt the Supreme Court will give an individual a fair shake against a corporation.[56]

Less than a decade after the *Citizens United* decision, the two premises on which it rests—that all this corporate election spending would be "transparent" to the public, and that it would be "independent" of the candidates[57]—have both proven to be false. The notion was that if big corporations were just out there on their own saying their piece ("We like free trade so we support Congressman Snooks"), and if it were clear to everyone who they were ("We're Mammoth Corporation and we approved this message"), then they wouldn't collude with candidates for favors, and they would be accountable for what they were saying and doing. It is brutally evident in the decision's aftermath that neither premise is even close to true. The current system is rotten with collusion and bereft of accountability. Yet, despite repeated opportunities, the conservatives have taken no action to correct for those errors or to police the slime they have created.

They had the chance in a case that came to them out of Montana, *American Tradition Partnership v. Bullock*.[58] Since 1912, Montana state law had prohibited corporate political spending, be it for or against a candidate. When the law was challenged based on *Citizens United*, the Montana Supreme Court upheld the ban as constitutional.[59]

A few things were different in the *Bullock* case than in *Citizens United*. First, there was an extensive factual record in Montana, based on Montana's long history of political corruption by mining interests.[60] The political corruption by corporate interests in Montana's history was almost theatrical. For one instance, in the early 1900s, Montana copper baron William Andrews Clark famously bought himself a U.S. Senate seat, bribing state legislators at a time when U.S. senators were still picked by state legislatures.[61] He was unrepentant, saying, "I never bought a man who wasn't for sale." [62]

A second difference was that the law in question was a state law, not a federal law. The Court had the chance to reconsider whether as a matter of "states rights" state legislatures in states with an abundant local history of corrupt corporate political influence could act locally, though Congress couldn't act nationally.[63]

Third, by the time the Montana case came to the Supreme Court in 2011, it was already evident that neither the "transparency" nor the "independence" premise of *Citizens United* was true in the real world. The world the five justices had dreamed was not the world as it was. This new decision gave them the chance to correct for those errors.

In a bipartisan brief to the Court, Senator John McCain and I argued all these points, and also argued that *Citizens United* had failed to consider the problem of private threats and promises in its evaluation of how noncorrupting this corporate campaign spending was all going to be.[64]

The Supreme Court didn't even give the case a hearing. The

Montana legislature had passed this law a century earlier. The Montana Supreme Court had carefully distinguished Montana's circumstances from those present in *Citizens United*. Montana had a rich historic record of local corporate political corruption. Montana's attorney general defended the Montana law before the Supreme Court.[65] None of that mattered. The five pro-corporate justices summarily dismissed the case in a terse order, again 5–4.[66]

Later on, another campaign finance case called *McCutcheon* reached the Court, challenging a campaign finance law that had survived *Citizens United*: the aggregate limits on the amount of money individuals could contribute in total to candidates, parties, and committees in one election cycle.[67] Once again, the five conservatives relied on their own "facts" about corruption, transparency, and independence, even after these had been so thoroughly disproven in practice.[68] Again they turned down the opportunity to correct their plain errors, instead throwing out another protection put in place by Congress to safeguard the integrity of our elections. It seems they were happy with the way *Citizens United* had worked out. Mission accomplished. Money unleashed.

But the horror of *Citizens United*'s effects is so great that some glimmers of regret are appearing. Justice Kennedy has said that it's "not working the way it should."[69] Justice Scalia before he passed away was more defensive, saying, "If the system seems crazy to you, don't blame it on the Court."[70] Actually, I blame it squarely on the Court.

In the end, our faith in the Supreme Court is founded on its constitutional role as a neutral arbiter of our laws. I submit that *Citizens United* does not merit that faith. Corporate power helped get that conservative majority onto the Supreme Court. In return, the conservative majority on the Supreme Court very deliberately opened American democracy to massive, unprecedented levels of corporate political power and influence.

It's a disgrace for the Court.

CHAPTER EIGHT

Capture of Regulatory Agencies

I GREW UP IN FARAWAY PLACES, AMONG AMERICAN families who had left behind the safety and comforts of home to serve their country. These families were willing to face risks and discomforts to represent the United States in grim and dangerous places overseas. They inspired me.

As a United States attorney and as my state's attorney general, I worked with lawyers and prosecutors who could have doubled their salary in private practice, but they loved the work and service, and they stayed. I've worked with first responders who go out at all hours and in all weather, and who are required in the course of their duties to see things that we would never want to see, things that would dwell on in our nightmares. I have watched talented men and women throw themselves energetically into solving the big problems that only government can solve, working appalling hours week after week without complaint. I've seen our armed forces and intelligence agencies doing their duty bravely in areas of conflict far away. I've admired the work of government scientists who are defining the cutting edge of knowledge in areas such as cyber technology and disease research. These government employees are admirable, principled, talented, hardworking people. I know there are petty bureaucrats out there, and government workers who are "retired in place." But that, in my experience at both the state and federal levels, is the exception, not the rule.

So there is my bias. I confess it. I admire hardworking government people. I'm also a fan of the mechanisms government uses—rules and regulations—to help us live together in a civilized way. I've seen overseas how desperate life can be in countries where government regulation has failed. We are very lucky to live in America.

I accept that some rules and regulations are hard to understand. Arrival to Washington, D.C., for instance, is through Union Station, where you walk from your train through the soaring great hall of the station out to a long sidewalk where fifty taxis may be waiting, with fifty people waiting for taxis. Someone decided that it would be a good idea to make a rule that only one person could be loaded into a taxi at a time, creating a completely artificial wait. You could load all the people into all the taxis in about three minutes if the linekeeper just went away, or better yet helped those travelers who need assistance. But that sort of time-wasting regulation for regulation's sake is, in my experience, the exception in America and not the rule. (In less developed and more corrupt societies these artificial gateways can be created just to provide an opportunity for someone to collect a little fee to get you through the gateway, but that's a whole different issue.)

In the private sector, I've also seen plenty of time-wasting, incompetence, and worse. I've seen big banks ruin people's lives making decisions so dumb the decisions hurt the bank itself as well as the beleaguered homeowner. I've spent frustrating hours trying to get through corporate phone trees that seem designed to exhaust rather than help you. Pick the company that has annoyed you most. You cannot convince me that government has a monopoly on incompetence and the private sector a monopoly on efficiency. At the extremes of private sector misconduct, I've over and over had to clean up in the courtroom after instances of corporate fraud, corporate crime, and corporate pollution.

I'm not arguing that government should run everything, or even most things. Corporate competition on a fair playing field is often not only the right course but a fantastic blessing for humanity. All I ask is that you remember, when you hear about the evils of "bureaucrats" and "big government," the "trial of strength" Jefferson warned us of. Big corporations are in a contest against government as their only real rival for power. If they can convince you that all corporate activity is good and efficient and helpful and that all government activity is bad and wasteful and interfering, they win an advantage in their "trial of strength." Whipping up scorn for government is very convenient in the corporate contest for political power. So take whatever side you wish in that contest, but at least be aware that there's a contest under way.

Clearly, some government regulations are ill-advised, some are stale, and some are overly broad. But look at the safety that regulation provides. Medicines are not snake-oil mysteries any longer. People are rarely burned or killed nowadays in boiler explosions. Automobiles have airbags. Smokestacks mostly have pollution controls. Stock jobbers have a harder time suckering innocent investors. Most insurance policies actually pay when the insured risk occurs. Quacks can't be doctors and barbers can't be surgeons. We take for granted the safety and reliability that a regulated world has built.

We also take for granted how regulation helps advance our economic progress. Regulation helps channel America's competitive enterprise into good and helpful innovations instead of into new tricks and traps for consumers, or new ways of cutting safety corners, or new ways of conning gullible buyers. Confidence in our industries grows when consumers know they can count on the safety and reliability of the product. Ask yourself: would the American pharmaccutical industry be a world powerhouse if patent medicine hucksters were still allowed to operate? Regulation sets a positive frame for our economic progress. Just as the solution to medical malpractice is not to get rid of medicine, so the solution to bad regulations is not to get rid of regulation.

In his book *The War on Science*, Shawn Otto makes an interesting point about regulation and freedom. Our initial reaction might be to think that regulations constrain freedom, which is certainly the narrative that big, regulated industries want to sell about regulation. But that is not necessarily true. "[W]e accept limitations on our individual freedoms to gain greater freedom," Otto argues. This greater freedom comes through "regulations that reduce smog, acid rain, ozone destruction, the use of DDT, backyard burning of garbage, driving while intoxicated, noise pollution, lead in paint and gasoline, certain carcinogens, water pollution—and more recently, exposure to secondhand smoke, injuries caused by not wearing seat belts, and texting while driving." As he describes it, the freedom we gain from these regulations is "the freedom they provide from the tyranny of others' stupid decisions," freedom from "a tyranny of trash—of ignorance."[1] Of course, to the creators of the trash and the purveyors of the ignorance, regulation is indeed a constraint; but it's one that delivers freedoms the rest of us enjoy.

Over the past fifty years, Congress has tasked an alphabet soup of regulatory agencies—the EPA, NHTSA, FDA, SEC, and countless others—with protecting the public interest. These agencies have been given the job of enforcing laws that ensure the safety of the water we drink, the air we breathe, the cars we drive, the medications we take, and the markets we invest in for our retirement and our children's future. These regulatory agencies have vast and vital responsibilities to Congress and the American people.

The incentive of regulated industries to work mischief with these regulatory agencies is equally vast and vital. Big corporate interests do not overlook the administrative agencies. Lobbying legislatures, securing agreeable appointments to the Supreme Court, pouring money into politics, and trying to elect a friendly president are all important priorities of the corporate political effort. But over the long haul, influence over regulatory agencies can be an equally valuable proposition.

As we've seen too often, wealthy and powerful industries can acquire excessive influence over regulatory agencies. When they do, the consequences can be grave. The basic tactic to control a regulatory agency has been in place for as long as there have been regulatory agencies, and the phenomenon of a regulated industry seizing control over its regulator is widely known as "regulatory capture."[2] When a regulatory agency is captured, it becomes the industry's tool, overlooking errors and misdeeds, setting rules that favor the industry, and keeping out competition that might challenge the big incumbents. That's when regulatory agencies stop working for us and become pawns of the industry they were supposed to regulate.

Two recent catastrophes—BP's *Deepwater Horizon* oil spill in the Gulf of Mexico and the giant 2008 Wall Street financial meltdown— I see as direct results of regulatory capture. They offer powerful examples of what happens when regulatory agencies come under the influence of corporations and industry.

*   *   *

Responsibility for regulating oil and gas drilling in the Gulf at the
time of the *Deepwater Horizon* disaster fell to the U.S. Department of
Interior's Minerals Management Service (MMS). But the relationship
between MMS and the oil and gas industry had become completely
toxic. Agency staff failed to collect millions of dollars in royalties
owed to the American people.[3] MMS district managers were docu-
mented telling their investigators, "Obviously we are all oil industry."[4]
Agency employees accepted gifts from regulated companies: trips to
the Peach Bowl on a private airplane, skeet shooting contests, hunt-
ing and fishing trips, and golf tournaments.[5] Social events hosted by
industry for MMS representatives involved illegal drug use and sex.[6]
An MMS inspector inspected the oil drilling platforms of a company
with which he had a job application pending[7]—yes, while they were
considering whether to hire him, he was inspecting their oil drilling
rigs. It should come as no surprise that he found no violations.[8]

The *Wall Street Journal* published an opinion piece about the Gulf
oil spill, saying: "By all accounts, MMS operated as a rubber stamp
for BP. It is a striking example of regulatory capture: Agencies tasked
with protecting the public interest come to identify with the regulated
industry and protect its interests against that of the public. The result: Government fails to protect the public."[9] Even my hometown
paper, the *Providence Journal*, editorialized trenchantly about the role
of MMS in the Gulf disaster: "The Deepwater Horizon accident has
made it painfully clear that, in its current form, MMS is a pathetic
public guardian. Neither it nor BP was prepared for a disaster of this
magnitude, and MMS's cozy relationship with industry is a big reason
why."[10]

The regulatory failures at the Securities and Exchange Commission (SEC) in the run-up to the Wall Street meltdown were less pun-
gent, but still extraordinarily painful and damaging for America. Led
on by Wall Street, the SEC, which should have been regulating the
financial industry stringently and limiting the amount of debt any one
institution took on, instead allowed "leverage ratios" of up to thirty to
one, meaning that for every dollar a bank had in equity, it could hold
$30 in debt.[11] If you're an ambitious Wall Street speculator, leverage is a

beautiful thing. If you're in a deal at thirty-to-one leverage and the deal doubles the investment made, you earn thirty times your investment, less whatever you paid the lenders you brought into the deal. If you're a bank using depositors' money on which you pay 4 percent annual interest, they share your risk but you keep the big payday.

Do the math. You put your $1 and your depositors' $29 into the kitty, and you get $60 when the deal pays back double the investment. You return the $29 you borrowed plus 4 percent (if the deal took a year, that would be $1.16 in interest), and you win a $28.84 payday on your $1 investment. What's not to love?

Until one of the deals blows up. If it's a total loss, on your own $1 gamble you've got nothing, and you still owe your depositors their $29 and their $1.16 in interest. That's where leverage can hurt. And it will particularly hurt if it happens widely, if a whole market turns sour and lots of bets fail at once. Maybe paying back the $29 to the depositors wipes out the capital of the bank entirely. If the whole bank can't stay solvent, then the government has to step in to provide any money still owed to the depositors (the government guarantees those deposits up to $250,000 per account). The government may even have to bail out the banks themselves if it looks like their collapse will take down the whole economy, which is more or less the story of the Great Wall Street Meltdown at the end of George W. Bush's presidency.

Regulatory capture has been around for a long time, with discussions of it all over economic treatises and administrative law textbooks. In a column in the *Wall Street Journal*, Thomas Frank told a fascinating early tale of regulatory capture involving the Interstate Commerce Commission (ICC) at the very inception of federal regulatory agencies in the 1880s. The ICC was designed to regulate railroad freight rates. Grover Cleveland's attorney general, Richard Olney, had been a prominent railroad lawyer. When Olney's former boss at the railroad corporation asked Olney to get rid of the regulatory agency completely, Olney replied, "The Commission . . . is, or can be made, of great use to the railroads. It satisfies the popular clamor for a government supervision of the railroads, at the same time that that supervision is almost entirely nominal. Further, the older such a commission gets to be, the more inclined it will be found to take the business and railroad view of things. . . . The part of wisdom is not to destroy the Commission, but to utilize it."[12]

That remains the recurring goal of regulated industries: to tame and "utilize" the regulator. And regulatory agencies are often not very good at pushing back against that corporate pressure.

In 1913, the year he was inaugurated as president, Woodrow Wilson wrote: "If the government is to tell big business men how to run their business, then don't you see that big business men have to get closer to the government even than they are now? Don't you see that they must capture the government, in order not to be restrained too much by it?"[13]

The first dean of Princeton's Woodrow Wilson School of Public and International Affairs, Marver Bernstein, wrote more than half a century ago of the pattern that regulators tend over time to "[become] more concerned with the general health of the industry," even to try "to prevent changes which adversely affect" the industry; and ultimately to "surrender," when the regulatory agency "finally becomes a captive of the regulated groups."[14] He noted that this problem of regulators captured by industry "is a problem of ethics and morality as well as administrative method."[15] He properly pointed out that this ethical failure is also "a blow to democratic government."[16] After all, it is democratic government that is cheated when an agency of the government is secretly working for the industry and not the people.

A regulatory agency is constantly engaged with the regulated industry. The industry is pushing on it all the time. The industry has lawyers and lobbyists working the agency. The industry threatens lawsuits if it gets regulations it does not like, and is accommodating and friendly when it gets regulations it does like. The industry often twirls a revolving door: nice jobs for regulators who have been good to the industry, or industry operatives cycled into regulatory positions and then taken care of when they return to the private sector.

Regulated entities have a strong incentive to gain influence over the drafting and enforcement of regulations. The Food and Drug Administration, for instance, regulates industries that represent a trillion-dollar market.[17] The bank robber Willie Sutton is said to have once explained that he robbed banks "because that's where the money is."[18]

When it comes to why regulated entities seek influence with regulators, the answer is the same: that's where the money is. In the high-stakes derivatives market—derivatives are financial contracts that "derive" from real assets, such as a "futures contract" to buy or sell an asset at a given price at a future date—the notional value of derivative products alone is more than thirty times greater than the gross domestic product of the United States.[19] That's a lot of incentive.

It's the same reason powerful interests spend millions of dollars to lobby Congress. In the Eisenhower era, Senator Everett Dirksen was rumored to have commented about a congressional appropriation, "A billion here, a billion there, and pretty soon you're talking real money."[20] With regard to drugs, derivatives, and other massive industries, the billions are approaching trillions. So while the big bucks spent to influence decision making may seem amazing, the money spent is actually trivial compared with the stakes. These are well-placed political "investments."

With such large rewards, industry ends up at a major organizational and resource advantage compared with the more diffuse public interest. In a volume of articles dedicated to examining regulatory capture, law professor and economics blogger James Kwak notes that while industry resources can focus with great precision and persistence, public interest groups are "likely to lack the organizational infrastructure and staying power to knock on regulators' doors month in, month out on issue after issue."[21] Intensity of interest matters in the regulatory as well as the political world. And the intensity of industry interest in regulatory decision making is difficult to match.

On the side of the public interest, nonprofit groups are ordinarily spending down scarce resources with no reasonable expectation of financial profit from their regulatory exertions. Corporate influence machinery can be self-perpetuating and pay for itself, where the public interest machinery requires constant replenishment. Up against corporate influence, the public interest is the eroding seawall holding back the ocean.

This mess is made worse because so much regulatory decision making and oversight occurs outside of public attention. Figuring out where capture has occurred is not easy. Regulatory capture is notoriously difficult to detect. Little-known agencies are often the target. Rarely does a corporate entity plant its flag victoriously over a regulatory agency, to announce that the agency has been successfully captured. By its nature, regulatory capture is a stealth operation.

Corporate interests have the patience and resources to play the long game. The revolving door between industry and government is an example. University of Chicago economist Luigi Zingales explains that "this form of regulatory capture does not require an explicit quid pro quo between regulators and regulated, where a job is offered in exchange for a favorable decision."[22] It's not necessary or smart to be that obvious. The implicit prospect of a high-paying industry job may sufficiently induce a regulator to favor industry as he thinks about moving on. He may notice how well the industry's friends do when they leave the agency, compared to how coldly consumer-oriented members are treated. Zingales describes this subtle pressure as "much more legitimate" and thus "quite pervasive."[23]

Regulatory capture can cause terrible damage. We often hear how high the cost of burdensome regulation is, but the cost of inadequate regulation can be catastrophic. I will never forget the families of the men killed on the *Deepwater Horizon* rig, who came to Congress asking for help and answers after lax enforcement of regulations led to conditions on the rig that a judge later characterized as "reckless" and "grossly negligent."[24] I will never forget the hardworking Rhode Islanders who lost their jobs when the Wall Street meltdown shattered our economy and who then lost their homes to foreclosure—after having worked honestly all their lives in good jobs and done nothing wrong. They were the collateral damage of the government agencies failing to regulate Wall Street. And I'm sure the families let down by the Mine Safety and Health Administration who lost loved ones in the Sago Mine and other mining disasters bear from that loss an incalculable agony. News stories describing the agency as a "meek watchdog" with a revolving door of industry appointees must have come as bitter solace.[25]

There's another, more general harm, too: agency capture assaults democratic government. "We the People" pass laws through a democratic and open legislative process. We then pay public representatives with public funds to take on public responsibilities in our administrative agencies and enforce those laws. Those administrative agencies craft regulations to enforce the laws and to protect the public interest. All is well until industries co-opt and control those regulatory agencies. When they do, the agencies are pried out of the matrix of our government of laws to become silent corporate servants. The public's voice is lost. The "trial of strength" in that arena is won by industry.

In the Senate, I held a hearing on regulatory capture that revealed bipartisan agreement across all the witnesses on all these points:[26]

First, agency capture is a real problem, and a threat to the integrity of government.

Second, the enormous stakes for regulated entities give them an incentive to gain influence over regulators.

Third, regulated entities usually have organizational and resource advantages in the regulatory process compared to public interest groups.

Fourth, regulatory procedures can be gamed by regulated entities in their quest for influence over regulation.

Fifth, regulatory capture by its nature happens in the dark, as invisibly as possible.

Sixth, the potential damage to the public from agency capture is enormous.

The takeaway from that hearing was best summarized by one of the witnesses, administrative law professor Nicholas Bagley, who said, "The core point that I would want to take away from our testimony today is that when you talk about agency capture, you are talking about a complex of problems whereby well-organized, well-heeled interest groups are likely to be able to bring a lot of pressure to bear on agencies under the cover of darkness."[27]

Madison and Jefferson left us warnings about corporate power. They also left us advice useful in considering regulatory capture. Thinking of the revolving doors from the regulator to industry reminds me of

Jefferson: "Whenever a man has cast a longing eye on offices, a rotten-ness begins in his conduct."[28] Madison saw conflicting interests, such as those between the industry and the public, as questions of "faction." Though he felt "the causes of faction cannot be removed," he still found hope "in the means of controlling its effects."[29]

On June 10, 1999, two ten-year-old boys, Wade King and Stephen Tsiorvas, went out to play in a field near Whatcom Creek in Belling-ham, Washington. They were fourth graders at Roosevelt Elementary School. An eighteen-year-old boy, Liam Wood, who had just gradu-ated from high school a few days before, was fishing in the creek not far away.[30] They did not know that Olympic Pipe Line Company had a poorly maintained, leaking gasoline pipe nearby that was gushing over 200,000 gallons of gasoline into the creek.[31] Excavations years earlier had damaged the pipe, the damage was never corrected, and that af-ternoon a pressure surge over 1,400 pounds per square inch ruptured the pipe at the site of one of the gouges.[32]

Liam was overcome by gasoline fumes and collapsed. Incapaci-tated, he drowned, and his body was later found partly submerged in the creek.[33] His autopsy report later stated that he had been "over-come by volatile hydrocarbon fumes, lost consciousness and died from hypoxia by freshwater drowning."[34] A spark of some kind ignited the gasoline spill, sending a smoke and fire column miles into the air. "It looked," said one witness, "like the explosion of Mt. St. Helens."[35] Rescue personnel responding to the explosion found Wade and Ste-phen. They had suffered what the official accident report described as "extensive second and third degree thermal burn injuries of the head, trunk and extremities (80 to 90 percent body surface area)."[36] The boys were rushed to St. Joseph's Hospital in Bellingham, and then by air ambulance to a burn unit at Harborview Medical Center in Seattle.[37] Both boys died the next day.[38] The gasoline fire raged for over an hour, and it took days to finish putting out brush fires. Twenty-five acres were burned. The county fire chief said, "I've been here 30 years, and I've never seen anything like this before."[39]

In the investigations that followed, blame settled on a regulatory agency, the Office of Pipeline Safety. The head of the National Trans-portation Safety Board (NTSB) faulted every aspect of the agency: "its regulations, its inspections, its assets, its staffing and its spirit."[40] The Pipeline Accident Report from the NTSB listed as one of the "major safety issues identified during this investigation" the "adequacy of Federal regulations regarding the testing of relief valves used in the protection of pipeline systems."[41]

Criticism of the agency went way beyond the Bellingham disaster. A state pipeline safety official, disappointed by his federal counterparts, said, "From the get-go, the regulations get watered down. There's not a lot of teeth behind them."[42] A *Politico* investigation found "gaping holes in pipeline safety regulations" and an agency "that grants the industry it regulates significant power to influence the rule-making process, and that has stubbornly failed to take a more aggressive regulatory role, even when ordered by Congress to do so."[43] One frustrated congressman, Peter DeFazio, ranking member on the House Transportation and Infrastructure Committee, complained to *Politico*, "They only seem to act when confronted by and forced by Congress to act. And even then, they don't act."[44] Even those laws from Congress, the Bellingham disaster victims' families thought, had been "watered down by those who pay homage to the powerful oil and gas lobbyists."[45]

In the wake of the Bellingham disaster, the agency's name was changed to the Pipeline and Hazardous Materials Safety Administration, or PHMSA. Not much else changed. As one practitioner reported to *Politico*, "With PHMSA, there's only one wind, and it blows from the industry."[46]

These obscure agencies are ripe for regulatory capture. The public takes little interest, until something goes horribly wrong; the industry attends to the agency day in and day out. Revolving doors spin—the last head of PHMSA was a former pipeline industry lawyer who had to recuse herself in a major spill inquiry because of conflict of interest.[47] Safety and environment groups struggle to hold their own against industry, particularly an industry that consists of behemoths such as ExxonMobil. A judge described the efforts of one public interest group to go up against the oil pipeline industry as "Bambi taking on Godzilla."[48] And no part of the federal government anywhere has as its task to systematically seek out and flag instances of regulatory capture, nor even to identify warning signs. There is no "regulatory capture cop" on the beat.[49]

As Representative DeFazio told *Politico*, this isn't just cost/benefit, dollars and cents: "This is life or death. Pipelines blow up and people die."[50] When Wade King died, the local paper reported, his parents "shut the door to his room and left it closed." There was simply too much pain. His mother said afterward, "The first three years were a fog. I look back and I don't know how we got through those days. It was hell. It was like waking up every day in hell."[51] As the tenth anniversary of Wade's death approached, she was asked about Olympic Pipe Line Company and all the mistakes that were made. "If I go down that road," she said, "it's with a lot of hostility. I don't forgive any of it."[52]

Regulatory capture plays a role in the massive corporate intrusion into America's elections. Here the stories of regulatory capture and corporate election mischief converge, in the now virtually lawless area of campaign finance regulation.

The Federal Election Commission is supposed to regulate federal elections. It is supposed to enforce the Federal Election Campaign Act.[53] In that law, Congress defined an "independent expenditure" as one "not made in concert or cooperation with or at the request or suggestion of such candidate, the candidate's authorized political committee, or their agents, or a political party committee or its agents."[54] This is the law meant to ensure that super PACs are independent of candidates and never coordinated with their campaigns.

In one actual case a supposedly "independent" super PAC, which supported one candidate, and one candidate only (again, how plausible is it that a super PAC set up to support one candidate only is an "independent" organization?), was founded by the candidate's former campaign lawyer, and employed the same consulting company the candidate's campaign uses. Not enough? The consulting company's founder was a former strategist for the candidate's campaign, and married to a current campaign advisor to the candidate.[55] In another actual case, a super PAC was run by the candidate's mother.[56] Are we really to believe that these super PACs are "independent"?

Larry Noble, a witness at a Senate hearing I held on this mess, is now general counsel of the Campaign Legal Center and was formerly general counsel at the FEC. He blames the FEC for not enforcing the law against coordination between super PACs and political campaigns:

"The FEC narrowed the coordination rules over time to the point where they were seen as totally ineffective."[57] The rules against coordination between super PACs and campaigns are now "narrowed" to the point where candidates now customarily post campaign ad footage online so that super PACs supporting them can incorporate the candidate's own campaign footage directly into the super PAC's ads.[58] Hard to get more "totally ineffective" than that.

At the "totally ineffective" FEC, regulations pertaining to disclosure fare no better. Disclosure of who's behind political spending is also supposedly the law of the land, believe it or not. Even that grotesque Supreme Court decision, *Citizens United*, recognized the importance of political spending disclosure to proper democratic citizenship.[59] The Federal Election Campaign Act states that groups making independent expenditures must disclose "each person who made a contribution in excess of $200 . . . made for the purpose of furthering an independent expenditure."[60] That seems pretty straightforward, no? The FEC is supposed to enforce it.

Yet the three Republican commissioners at the FEC, using their power to deadlock the six-member commission's votes 3–3, have narrowed their interpretation of the law to say that it applies only to funds the donor explicitly gives to fund a specific advertisement.[61] If the contribution is intended to fund the general effort to elect or defeat a candidate and the donor's check can't be tied to a specific advertisement, the law does not apply, says the regulator.[62]

Giving money to a campaign to fund a specific advertisement? Who does that? Money usually comes in to a campaign before ads are scripted and produced. How would an early donor ever know what ad he would like to have his money fund? The ad wasn't yet produced when he cut the check. It's ridiculous. The law is defanged, and lawlessness is the result.

Another clear federal statute prohibits giving a contribution "in the name of another."[63] Yet in the 2012 elections, we saw blatant use of shell corporations to conceal multimillion-dollar contributions to super PACs.[64] The FEC has been unwilling even to investigate.[65] One shell company appeared, contributed $5 million to a super PAC supporting a presidential candidate, and then dissolved shortly thereafter. A complaint was filed, but no official inquiry appears to have emerged from the FEC deadlock.[66] No one knows who gave the money—except, of course, the donor, and very likely the candidate.

One type of organization need not disclose its donors: an entity registered with the Internal Revenue Service under Section 501(c)(4) of the federal tax code as a "social welfare" group.[67] Groups that want to hide the identities of their donors so the donors can support candidates anonymously love this status. It's a political operator's dream.

But there's a rub. Section 501(c)(4) of the Internal Revenue Code is only for "civic leagues or organizations not organized for profit but operated exclusively for the promotion of social welfare,"[68] and IRS regulations had long made it clear that spending money in political campaigns does not constitute "promotion of social welfare."[69]

See the word "exclusively" in the law? Rather than enforce the law on those terms, the IRS began to allow organizations to spend money in campaigns as long as that was not their "primary" activity. "Exclusively" came to mean "primarily."[70] The dark-money groups seized on this and began using 49 percent of their spending on political expenditures.[71] If big money is at stake but the donor wants anonymity, the donor would in effect pay a 51 percent fee to put up anonymous political ads, with the other 49 percent funding the ads.

But folks got even cleverer. Dark-money groups began using the other 51 percent to run "issue ads."[72] These are just thinly veiled political attack ads, but they exploit yet another loophole by not "expressly" advocating election or defeat of the candidate. Instead they just urge that the viewer call the candidate and ask him why he hates America, or prosperity, or puppies (I exaggerate, but not very much).

Then the dark-money groups tried sending the 51 percent to *other* organizations that spend money on political ads. They got away with that, too. So now "exclusively," the standard set in law by Congress, comes to mean in IRS regulatory practice "virtually not at all." Where the FEC was blockaded by three commissioners who refuse to act, the IRS has been terrorized by relentless Congressional hearings, budget attacks, and threats to impeach the IRS commissioner. It is an agency curled up in a fetal crouch.

There's one more wrinkle. Even in the midst of this no-regulatory Dodge City of lawlessness, there are federal forms that need to be filed. Drill down into those federal forms, and you find groups filing IRS forms to acquire that much-treasured 501(c)(4) status. Remember, even a super PAC can't hide its donors; becoming a 501(c)(4) is what allows secrecy. Those IRS forms, filed under penalty of perjury, require the organizations to affirm that they are spending no money to influence elections, or explain what they are spending. Whatever percentage of their money they may be spending, many do not bother to explain; they just affirm that they are spending no money to influence elections. Back at the Federal Election Commission, those very same groups then report, again under penalty of perjury, that they spent millions of dollars on elections. Yes, the same groups file conflicting forms at different agencies, both under penalty of perjury.

Let me be specific. The IRS initial application form for 501(c)(4) status includes question 15: "Has the organization spent or does it plan to spend any money attempting to influence the selection, nomination, election, or appointment of any person to any Federal, state, or local public office or to an office in a political organization?" The filer is instructed to state "no" or explain.

Clear enough? I sure don't see much wiggle room there.

In addition to the initial application, a 501(c)(4) entity has to file every year the IRS Form 990 tax return for tax-exempt organizations, which asks: "Did the organization engage in direct or indirect political campaign activities on behalf of or in opposition to candidates for public office?"[73] Answer "no" or explain. Again, seems clear enough.

But organizations answer "no" to these questions and then go out and spend millions of dollars in election advertising. One organization answered "no" to these questions while sending more than $33 million to other affiliated groups explicitly for the purpose of spending in elections.[74] In one investigation, ProPublica, a Pulitzer Prize–winning nonprofit news organization, found thirty-two organizations that answered "no" to question 15 and then went out and spent money in political races. And that was out of seventy-two IRS filings ProPublica reviewed.[75] By that measure, nearly half were false, one could reasonably conclude. Some organizations had political ads running on the day they mailed their filings in with the answer "no"; some had run their ads beforehand.[76] Some spent millions on political ads.[77]

Starting from another angle, the ProPublica investigation found

104 organizations that had told state or federal elections officials in 2010 that they'd spent money on candidate-specific political ads, what the FEC calls "electioneering" communications. When ProPublica cross-referenced these with the forms these same groups had filed with the IRS, thirty-two of them had said they spent no money to influence elections.[78] That's about a one-in-three rate of discrepancy.

Even when some information is provided on these forms, the information often looks false. One organization said it would spend 50 percent of its effort on a website and 30 percent on conferences. Investigation showed its website consisted of one photograph and one paragraph, with no sign of any conferences. The same group declared it would take contributions "from individuals only" and then took $2 million from PhRMA, the big pharmaceutical lobby.[79] Another declared to the IRS it had spent $5 million on political activities, but told the FEC it had spent $19 million on political ads.[80] A third pledged that its political spending would be "limited in amount and will not constitute the organization's primary purpose," and then went out and spent $70 million on ads and robocalls in one election season.[81]

Some entities never even apply. They just start spending and file a tax return after the fact, potentially as their last act before they disband. That way they're gone before the mail brings their filing to the IRS, and before anyone can come around to ask nosy questions. One never filed the IRS tax form at all, not even after the fact.[82]

No federal enforcement action has been taken against anyone, as far as anyone knows. As Melanie Sloan, former executive director of Citizens for Responsibility and Ethics in Washington, has said, "You can go into business and violate the law and then go out of business. And what's ever going to happen about that? There's no consequence."[83]

One news article described the reaction of a state election official, Ann Ravel (who later went on to become an FEC commissioner), when she was asked about a particular 501(c)(4) group that had been active in electioneering in her state and had been the subject of her agency's scrutiny: "When ProPublica read the group's description of its activities on its IRS application to Ann Ravel, [then-]chairwoman of the California Fair Political Practices Commission, she laughed. 'Wow,' she said, upon hearing that the group said it would not try to influence elections. 'That's simply false.'"[84]

Despite her best efforts, Ravel has had little luck reviving the Federal Election Commission. Indeed, as its chairwoman, she declared it dead: "The likelihood of the laws being enforced is slim," she has said. "It's worse than dysfunctional."[85] Well-regarded Republican campaign finance lawyer Jan Baran agrees: "The agency is just not providing any legal guidance on what the rules are in the aftermath of all these momentous court decisions. That's the job of the FEC, and it hasn't done its job."[86] The *Los Angeles Times* recently headlined an editorial "The Federal Election Commission Is Worse Than Useless."[87]

At the regulatory agencies, lawlessness is the rule.

That brings us to the Department of Justice. It is a federal crime under 18 U.S.C. § 1001 to make any material false statement on federal filings like these. It is also a specific federal crime under 26 U.S.C. § 7206 to make a material false statement on an IRS form. Yet exactly zero groups have been referred by the FEC or by the IRS to the Department of Justice for investigation into whether any of these conflicting answers were false.[88]

False statement cases are bread-and-butter cases for DOJ. I did them as U.S. Attorney. Yet there has evidently not been any FBI or grand jury investigation into the apparently false statements on these forms. Perhaps there is a legitimate explanation. But when an entity declares millions of dollars in election spending under oath on one form, and then answers "no" under oath on another form to the question "Has the organization spent or does it plan to spend any money attempting to influence the selection, nomination, election, or appointment of any person to any Federal, state, or local public office?," isn't it worth investigating? Shouldn't such an apparent falsehood merit a question or two to see if there is a legitimate explanation? Is it not the DOJ's duty to examine the records to see if there has been unlawful conduct?

If there's a good explanation, great. Everybody can go home. If not, well, lying like that is a federal crime.

The "hot potato" phenomenon likely explains this multiagency failure by the IRS, the FEC, and DOJ. The forces behind the dark-money flood are powerful, intimidating, and vindictive. With responsibility shared among three agencies, each was likely happy to leave to the others the responsibility for acting, and happy to keep itself out of harm's way. When all three said, "Not me," the ball fell plop between the fielders, and we now have this disgraceful spectacle.

This has been regulatory capture of a peculiar sort. Regulatory capture can come through revolving doors with industry, through favors and perquisites from industry, or through actual encroachment of the regulated industry into the regulatory agency. But it can also come from plain old fear of the regulated industry—in this case the corporate political front groups—hectoring and bullying and pillorying the regulator. And it can come from political appointees on a commission whose very purpose in serving is to disable the commission's operations.

Whatever the method of its capture, a captured regulator fails the public it was sworn to serve. And we have been failed. These examples from the campaign finance context illustrate the importance of getting regulations right and the importance of creating responsive enforcement regimes. They also illustrate the importance of independent prosecutors willing to step in when timorous regulators, buffaloed by forces they are supposed to regulate, fear to do their jobs. We've been failed there too.

CHAPTER NINE

Capture of the Civil Jury

UNSHACKLED FROM THE CHAINS of campaign finance limits, corporate power marauds across our politics. That power has set its sights on bending a wide range of policies to its advantage, everything from corporate taxes to safety regulation. It has also set its sights on a target that is one of the fundamental constitutional pillars of our government: the civil jury.[1]

The civil jury has a unique role in our uniquely American constitutional system. In the United States, a civil jury determines the facts and decides fault in non-criminal trials, ranging from property disputes between neighbors to multimillion-dollar class-action lawsuits against corporate behemoths. The Founders deliberately built this institution into the system of government established by our Constitution and Bill of Rights. Alexis de Tocqueville, in his *Democracy in America*, observed that the jury should be understood as a "political institution" and "one form of the sovereignty of the people."[2] It gives ordinary citizens direct exercise of an American constitutional power.[3] It is the element in our constitutional system most dedicated to protecting ordinary citizens from the wealthy and powerful. Corporate political machinery, by seeking to undermine the civil jury and change the very structure of our system of government, shows the extent of its ambitions.

You may think of the civil jury as an annoyance. You may think of jury duty, and what a bother a jury summons can be. But consider why the Founders prized the institution of the civil jury so highly and defended it so fiercely.

The earliest tendrils of the jury system appeared in England way back in the twelfth century.[4] By the fifteenth century, civil juries had blossomed into their modern form: independent persons who gathered together and heard witness testimony presented by opposing counsel, and then had the power of decision.[5] It was an original form of "power to the people" and local decision making. When the earliest colonial settlers came from England to this land, they transplanted juries here: by 1624, juries were established in Virginia; by 1628, in Massachusetts; by 1677, in New Jersey; and by 1682, in Pennsylvania.[6]

Civil juries provided a treasured means of self-governance to colonial Americans as they chafed under British rule.[7] Efforts by the British government to interfere with American juries helped foment the American Revolution.[8] We know those early American forefathers cared about this, because they said so. In the Declaration of Independence itself, when the Founders protested Britain's "history of repeated injuries and usurpations, all having in direct object the establishment of an absolute Tyranny over these States," they singled out that Britain had been "depriving us in many cases, of the benefits of Trial by Jury."[9]

When our original Constitution was silent on the civil jury, Americans sounded the alarm and the Seventh Amendment, putting the civil jury right into the Constitution, was promptly sent to the states in the Bill of Rights.[10] Alexander Hamilton described the importance of juries in Federalist No. 83: "The friends and adversaries of the plan of the convention, if they agree in nothing else, concur at least in the value they set upon the trial by jury; or if there is any difference between them it consists in this: the former regard it as a valuable safeguard to liberty; the latter represent it as the very palladium of free government."[11] "Representative government and trial by jury are the heart and lungs of liberty," wrote John Adams.[12] The jury was a big deal to the Founding generation.

Sir William Blackstone was the best-known jurist in England and America at the time of the Revolution and the author of *Commentaries on the Laws of England*, probably the most widely available legal text in the colonies (still often cited today by American courts). Blackstone gave the two major arguments for trial by jury in one sentence: trial by jury, he said, "preserves in the hands of the people that share which they ought to have in the administration of public justice, and prevents the encroachments of the more powerful and wealthy citizens."[13]

Let's start with the first argument. Colonial Americans understood the civil jury to be a means of directing power to the people and recognized Sir William Blackstone's 1768 warning that "every new tribunal erected, for the decision of facts, without the intervention of a jury . . . is a step towards establishing aristocracy, the most oppressive of absolute governments."[14] The Founders intended the civil jury to serve as an institutional check by giving ordinary American people direct control over one vital element of government—giving them, in Blackstone's words, "that share which they ought to have" in the administration of justice.[15] The civil jury serves the constitutional purpose of dividing and disaggregating governmental power. And it does so in an immediate way, putting the people themselves as the decision makers.

On the second argument, in a Constitution largely devoted to protecting the individual against the power of the state, the civil jury is unique in that it is also designed to protect the individual against the power of other individuals. Wealth, power, and connections can give unfair advantage. Wealth, power, and connections can also influence officials in the performance of their duty. The remedy for this was to let an independent group of randomly selected members of the community decide whether someone was being treated unfairly, or in violation of law.

Because each jury is new—"a rotating cast of laypeople," as law professor Nathan Chapman puts it[16]—it is hard to put in an institutional fix. To amplify this protection, we have made it a crime even to try: it's a criminal act to "tamper" with a jury.[17] Contact by an interested party with a juror, unless approved by the judge in charge of the case, is forbidden. Thus does the jury prevent the "encroachments of the more powerful and wealthy citizens" who can wield influence so effectively in other arenas.[18] In the jury, our Founders set ordinary people as our Constitution's watchman against encroachments by the powerful and wealthy.

Corporations now have become the most powerful and wealthy entities in our society, and it is often corporations whose encroachments a jury will thwart. Thus, the civil jury has become the target of sustained corporate attack. The immediate corporate wish is to reduce liability exposure. But that's only part of it. As law professor David Marcus notes, "When juries decide cases, elites lose their stranglehold on legal power"[19]—and big corporations don't much care for institutions where an ordinary American citizen can have an equal voice and equal standing.

Big, wealthy, powerful corporations are accustomed to the benefit of enormous special influence, whether acquired through campaign contributions, traditional lobbying, regulatory capture, or the big political spending unleashed by *Citizens United*. They bring this influence to bear on executive officials. They bring this influence to bear on administrative agencies. They bring it to bear on elected legislatures. They even bring it to bear on judges.

But big corporations lose the advantage of all that special influence in front of a jury. Tampering with executive, legislative, and administrative agencies is a licensed activity of special interests under our lobbying and campaign finance laws. Tampering with a jury is a crime.

The civil jury can be a potent political institution. It fosters civic engagement. It educates citizens about the workings of their government. It knits together people from all walks of life. It devolves power down to the people. It offers a final check on abuse when other institutions of government are compromised by influence. But the jury trial is now close to vanishing.

When the federal Civil Rules of Procedure were adopted in 1938, about 20 percent of federal cases were resolved by either a jury or a bench trial.[20] Now, less than 2 percent of federal civil cases reach a jury or a bench trial.[21] Most litigants do not have a reasonable prospect of presenting their claims to a jury of their peers. The chief judge of my home state's federal court recently told me he had not seen a civil jury trial in his courtroom for three years.

Some reasons for this trend are practical. The economics of modern legal practice press litigants into early settlement. Judges add to this pressure their desire to manage and expedite their dockets. Jury trials are work; signing off on a settlement is easy. The growing practice of judges tolerating "paper blizzard" defense strategies rewards defendants who can bankroll aggressive and imaginative defense pretrial strategies until the plaintiff simply collapses from lack of resources before getting near a jury.

One example of this blizzard defense practice occurred in a case I brought as attorney general, where the industry defendants gave us a witness list of a hundred names. That required us to go all around the country to take these witnesses' pretrial depositions. Knowing what the other side's witnesses will say is an essential part of trial preparation, so we had no choice. At trial, the defendants called exactly zero of these witnesses. The witness list was a sham, a wild-goose chase thrown into the works of that case to waste our time and money. They got away with it.

Other changes diminishing the jury's role came via the Federal Rules of Civil Procedure. It starts with getting through the courthouse door. Corporations want this to be more difficult, and the Supreme Court as it has defined these rules has helped their cause. The Supreme Court has made it far easier for corporate defendants to dismiss cases and has helped them limit plaintiffs from gathering facts through "discovery" and from presenting their case to the jury. Recent amendments and interpretations governing how civil trials work—pleading standards, motions to dismiss, class-action standards, summary judgment, and case management procedures—have also narrowed the gateway to a jury trial. All of these changes are to the benefit of those with money and power who tend to be defendants in civil trials, namely, corporations.

Let's say a consumer believes she was harmed by a chemical and sues the corporation that made the chemical. Before a string of corporate-friendly Supreme Court decisions over the past few decades, the consumer could file a complaint in court and would likely have the opportunity to review any evidence necessary to make her case (that's called "discovery") and then present this case to a jury. After the Supreme Court tilted the playing field in favor of civil defendants— often corporations—it is more likely that the consumer's case would be thrown out before her attorneys ever had a chance to review documents and depose witnesses. If she did make it to that point, her case would be more easily thrown out by a judge for being insufficiently persuasive before it ever reaches a jury of her peers. As Justice Stevens

reminded us in his dissent in one of these decisions, the rules of federal civil procedure were intended "not to keep litigants out of court
but rather to keep them in."[22] More and more, the trend in judicial
interpretation of those rules is to keep litigants out.

Class actions are a key tool for citizens to join together to sue a corporation. Small-denomination, large-scale frauds are the stuff of class
actions. A company cheats a hundred thousand people out of a hundred dollars each, and it makes a bundle. But it's not worth it for the
victims to bring hundred-dollar lawsuits one by one. Hence the class
action, which provides a path to a group remedy for such frauds. The
Roberts Court has made it far more difficult for individual citizens
who had been injured in these low-dollar, large-scale frauds to join
together, bring their case before a jury, and hold corporate wrongdoers
accountable.[23]

Even where a case does get filed and begins to proceed toward a
trial before a jury, a summary judgment can stop it in its tracks. In the
1980s, the Rehnquist Court issued a game-changing trio of decisions
known in legal circles as the "Celotex trilogy."[24] Traditionally, defendants had to meet a high bar to get the case thrown out at this stage,
but the Celotex trilogy shifted that burden toward the plaintiff, making it much more likely that a case would get thrown out by a judge far
before reaching a jury.

Courts took notice. Federal courts have cited this trilogy in astounding numbers: *Anderson* has been cited more than 204,000 times,
Celotex more than 190,000 times, and *Matsushita* more than 98,000
times.[25] Vast numbers of plaintiffs were left unable to reach a jury of
their peers.

Another trend undercutting the civil jury is the addition by big corporations of arbitration clauses into consumer contracts. We consumers never bother to read the fine print, but in the contract you signed
for your cellphone, for your credit card, for your bank account, and
for many other services, you likely gave away your right to a jury trial.
Parallel to this trend has been a series of Supreme Court decisions
through which the five conservative justices approved these contracts,
again and again allowing consumer claims to be forced out of the civil
courts and into arbitration.

Dissenting in the most recent of these anti-consumer Supreme

Court cases, Justice Ruth Bader Ginsburg noted: "These decisions have predictably resulted in the deprivation of consumers' rights to seek redress for losses, and, turning the coin, they have insulated powerful economic interests from liability for violations of consumer-protection laws."[26] She cited a recent series of *New York Times* articles exposing the severity of this problem and the intensity of the corporate effort to keep cases out of the civil court system. As Jessica Silver-Greenberg and Robert Gebeloff reported in the *Times*, "By inserting individual arbitration clauses into a soaring number of consumer and employment contracts, companies [have] devised a way to circumvent the courts and bar people from joining together in class-action lawsuits, realistically the only tool citizens have to fight illegal or deceitful business practices."[27]

There are two big problems with these forced arbitration provisions. First, giving up your jury right is not a fairly bargained choice. Credit cards and cellphones are necessities in our economy, and the contracts for those services are what lawyers would call "contracts of adhesion," contracts in which the weaker party has no real choice—take it or leave it. Second, the arbitration process lends itself to bias: it's always one-sided, big corporation against individual, and the corporation is usually a repeat player in arbitrated disputes, while each individual is usually new to the process, a one-timer. The arbitrators—very often corporate lawyers—will not want to displease the corporation, lest they not be selected for more arbitrations. So a bias emerges. State attorneys general came together and shut down the consumer arbitration work of one firm—the National Arbitration Forum—because it had become such a racket of pro-corporate bias. Before the attorneys general shuttered its practice, the firm had managed more than 214,000 consumer debt-collection claims in 2006 alone.[28]

The corporate lust for arbitration even reaches into our international trade policy. Big corporations and industries have secured "investor-state dispute settlement" (ISDS) provisions in trade deals like NAFTA. These provisions give corporations the ability to sue nations not in court but rather before panels of arbitrators who are mostly corporate lawyers. Multinational corporations use these clauses to fight health, environmental, and safety standards established by sovereign nations that could hurt the corporate bottom line. Big nations such

as the United States and Canada and Australia have all been sued.[29]
Little nations such as tiny Togo, a sliver of a nation on the West African coast, have been threatened—in the case of Togo by the tobacco
industry, whose revenues are more than six times Togo's entire gross
domestic product.[30]

A recent *BuzzFeed* investigation, "The Court That Rules the
World," released August 28, 2016, looked at "the secret operations of
these [ISDS] tribunals, and the ways that business has co-opted them
to bring sovereign nations to heel."[31] "ISDS has morphed . . . into a
powerful tool that corporations brandish ever more frequently, often
against broad public policies that they claim crimp profits." The investigation noted "the potential use of ISDS by corporations to roll
back public-interest laws, such as those banning the use of hazardous chemicals or raising the minimum wage," and as a "shield for the
criminal and the corrupt."[32] There is no similar tribunal in which environmental groups or labor unions can sue when things go the other
way. The revolving door spins freely, as lawyers who negotiate the
ISDS measures in treaties on behalf of the U.S. Trade Representative
then go and practice law as ISDS litigators. One is the head of his
firm's ISDS practice. Why would you cut back on the opportunities for
your future corporate clients, who will pay you to bring the ISDS cases
whose way you paved while in government?

The gradual suffocation of the American civil jury is neither random
nor coincidental. Supreme Court justice Abe Fortas once noted, "Procedure is the bone structure of a democratic society."[33] Corporations
know this. They know that procedure is power. And undermining the
civil jury is a power grab. Blackstone warned that the civil jury would
be a thorn in the side of the wealthy and powerful, and an annoyance to those who are used to special treatment. And it's true. There,
in front of the civil jury, the wealthy and powerful have to stand an-
noyingly equal before the law. Their assiduously acquired influence
breaks, against the hard, square corners of the jury box. As a body that
"prevents the encroachments of the more powerful and wealthy,"[34] the
civil jury inevitably provokes their enmity.

It should be no surprise, then, that corporations spread a mythol-
ogy of greedy trial lawyers, runaway juries, abusive discovery, and

preposterous verdicts, and push for "tort reform" to further insulate corporations from lawsuits for wrongdoing. It should be no surprise that corporations seek the appointment of "business-friendly" judges. And it should thus be no surprise that an already business-friendly Congress and those business-friendly judges steadily whittle away at this vital and historic American institution, the civil jury.

The cost of this institution vanishing is high. Again, you may think this is fine; what the hell, no more jury duty. But remember what we Americans lose if an institution such as this goes away. Juries are a check on political might—they disband after making their decision in a case, and consequently are hard to subject to political pressure. Juries are designed to be indifferent to wealth and power—they are made up of random people with nothing to gain from their decision. Juries are the last hope of lost causes when other elements of government, compromised by influence, become bulwarks of well-kept indifference. Juries can blow the status quo to smithereens if they don't think it's fair. They don't care if some fat ox gets gored; their job is to do justice in the one case before them. Period. That quality is not only important in the particular case the jury is deciding; it also sends a powerful message through the whole rest of the political system.

Think about it from the big special interest's point of view. If the special interest can put the fix in everywhere in government, that offers a big prize, and that prize encourages putting in the fix. But if that prize of control can't be seized because the jury stands out there as a lonely sentinel of resistance, immune to that pressure, then the whole exercise of putting the fix in elsewhere in government becomes less alluring. If a jury can blow up the special-interest fix in government, that dials back the special interests' incentive to fix those other elements of government that yield more readily to power and wealth. It doesn't cure it, but it dials it back.

When we reflect on America and the jury, we should think about the word "corruption." The Founding Fathers thought about it a lot. Noted historian (and fellow Rhode Islander) Gordon Wood has written that, according to the republican ideals of the Founders, corruption was "a technical term of political science" of the Founding era. Americans then saw as corruption things such as "monarchical instruments of personal influence and patronage" and "attempts by great men and their power-hungry minions to promote their private interests at the expense of the public good."[35] Corruption had a broad political meaning to the Founders. "Any loss of independence and virtue was corruption."[36] Corruption was the opposite of virtue, because it yielded to selfishness; it was the opposite of egalitarianism, because it allowed undue influence by some over others; and it was the opposite of independence, because it made government dependent on influence. Political dependency, writes Lawrence Lessig in *Republic, Lost,* was seen by the Framers as "dependence corruption."[37]

Hamilton, writing in the Federalist Papers, discussed the "business of corruption," worried about influences "corrupting the body of the people," and warned of "instruments of foreign corruption."[38] In their writings, the term "corruption" makes sense only if it is read as meaning far more than the simple transaction of a specific bribe. Corruption was a state of political disease; the antithesis of "corruption" was not just an absence of bribery but a "free and independent nation." "By corruption," historian Zephyr Teachout has observed, "the early generations meant excessive private interests influencing the exercise of public power."[39]

This generous meaning has collapsed in our era. The Supreme Court has in recent decades narrowed the meaning of the term down to where "corruption" means only a specific trade of a specific gift or benefit for a specific official favor or service. Now it means only what the Court calls "quid pro quo" corruption: tit for tat, precisely. The rest of the work of influence, the Court pretends, is free speech.[40] It just happens to be the kind of free speech that can be practiced only by the big influencers, who in our day and age tend to be the big politically active corporations, their front groups, and their billionaire owners. And the collapse just happens to be led by the corporatists on the Court.

This is new. Legal historian Bill Novak talks about how the classical tradition running from Aristotle through Montesquieu, the sage of the Founders, had a "preoccupation" with corruption, meaning "the private capture of the public sphere."[41] He reminds us of Socrates's definition of corruption: when "the guardians of the laws and of the government are only seemingly and not real guardians."[42] Teachout, in her book *Corruption in America*, writes of how *any* secret influence was viewed as virtually per se corruption, and how courts once read lobbying contracts with a sharp eye to the health of the public sphere. "Courts routinely held that it was not necessary to find that the parties agreed to some 'corrupt' or 'secret' action. Instead, the question was whether the 'contract tends directly to those results.' A contract was problematic when,'" to quote a decision in a Supreme Court case from 1869, it "'furnishes a temptation to the plaintiff, to resort to corrupt means or improper devices, to influence legislative action.'"[43]

Justice William O. Douglas expressed a similar view, placing corruption squarely in the context of the health of the public sphere, indeed describing it as a form of "pollution" of politics: "Free and honest elections are the very foundation of our republican form of government. . . . The fact that a particular form of pollution has only an indirect effect on the final election is immaterial. . . . [T]he Constitution should be read as to give Congress an expansive implied power to place beyond the pale acts which, in their direct or indirect effects, impair the integrity of Congressional elections. For when corruption enters, the election is no longer free, the choice of the people is affected."[44]

The current Court's dramatic narrowing of the definition of "corruption" has had a number of effects. The Court has stripped Congress of its power to protect elections by narrowing the definition of what it could protect against. That in turn unleashed forces of secret influence to operate with greater impunity. It also stripped prosecutors of their ability to bring corruption before a jury, absent an obvious quid pro quo bribe. Ultimately, the new, narrow definition elevated the private interest of influencers above the public interest in a healthy public sphere.

There is an eternal contest in government, between big, motivated private influencers who want a government that will yield its prizes readily to their influence and, on the other side, the public who want a government that will not yield so readily; between the players and those who just don't want to be played. This is not a new thought. Centuries ago, Niccolò Machiavelli spoke of "two distinct parties" in a governed society: one, "the nobles [who] wish to rule and oppress the people," and two, "the people [who] do not wish to be ruled nor

oppressed by the nobles." The people's object is the more "righteous,"
he said, for they "only desire not to be oppressed."[45] More recently, and
in our land, President Andrew Jackson's veto message regarding the
rechartering of the Bank of the United States distinguished between
"the rich and powerful [who] too often bend the acts of government
to their selfish purposes" and "the humble members of society—the
farmers, mechanics and laborers—who have neither the time nor the
means of securing like favors to themselves."[46] In our times, we see
the contest less colored by class or occupation. The contest is simple:
between those who want to influence, and therefore want a government that will be amenable to influence, and those who just want to
go about their own lives, and would like a government that resists influence on its own so they don't have to defend themselves constantly
against the influencers.

In this contest, the big influencers don't need help. They are fully
motivated by greed and reward. Instead, they need restraining. The
public interest in a government free of their improper influence has no
similarly motivated champion—the public has "neither the time nor
the means" for that. The public interest doesn't need restraint, it needs
protecting. By narrowing the restraint on improper influence down
to its most precise, rash, and solitary transaction—a direct "quid pro
quo" bribe—the Supreme Court took the side of the influencers. They
opened up to the power of influencers space in the political sphere that
was once occupied by that concept of a "free and independent nation."
Indeed, the Court is so blind to this distinction that in a campaign
finance decision it spoke of the importance of "unreserved communication" between a politician and his "constituents"[47]—by which they
meant not the actual constituents in the politician's district, but his donors. As a failure to appreciate the difference between the influencer
class and regular citizens, that's hard to top.

The narrow quid pro quo standard gives a particular boon to those
big influencers who are a constant presence in government. Those
frequent fliers can now create "dependence corruption" within government to advance their interests, so long as they avoid tying any
particular favor at any particular time to any particular vote. Frequent
fliers have to be very stupid if they can't structure their work of influence around the quid pro quo restriction.

The one-time actor coming to Washington seeking to influence a single vote has no such advantage. As a prosecutor who has led political corruption investigations, I know how often it's the stupid, sad-sack defendant who gets clobbered, not the big interests that have learned how to work the system. In the grand scheme of things, these sad sacks are defendants with minuscule political might compared to the big forces exerting their will day to day over government. The public is still humored with the odd corruption prosecution, but the really powerful and constant interests operate undisturbed.

The definition of "corruption" had historically in America been a jury question, and against this background, one can see why. The jury, as the Constitution's watchman against "encroachments of the more powerful and wealthy citizens," is well suited to bring its popular common sense to the definition of corruption. It is the "more powerful and wealthy" who are most likely to be the big influencers, the corrupters. So placing the jury as our public sentinel over corruption sends a powerful signal to the political class. When juries are deciding what sort of influence is honest and acceptable versus what sort of influence is excessive and against the public good, that call is in the hands of regular people. Juries are the arbitrators least likely to be either in the pocket of industry or subject to the worldview of the political class. And that's a good thing, sending a shiver of caution into the influencer class.

The Supreme Court has narrowed the field of vision of civil juries when they do hear cases involving corruption. Back when horses were the common mode of transport, leather pads called "blinkers" were often attached to the bridles beside the horses' eyes, to narrow their field of view to only what was right in front of them. By narrowing the legal definition of corruption to an explicit quid pro quo transaction, the Supreme Court narrowed the role of the jury. If the jury is our constitutional watchman, the Court has in effect blinkered the watchman.

The Court considered one case in which a trade association made a series of gifts to a lawmaker—expensive luggage, tickets to sporting events, and more—during a time when the lawmaker had direct influence over two matters affecting the association. In an opinion by Justice Scalia, the Court held that these gifts were not illegal, even if they were intended to "buy favor or generalized goodwill" and the official was "*in a position to act* favorably to the giver's interests."[48] It's not at all clear that a jury of ordinary people would agree. A jury might well think that buying ongoing influence with a lawmaker through many gifts is just as pernicious as giving one big gift in exchange for one big favor. If the Court hadn't ruled as it did, the influencer class might have to worry a bit about what a group of regular people sitting on a jury might think about a trade association, corporation, or wealthy individual buying the "favor or generalized goodwill" of a politician, and the result might be a good thing for America.

But a jury will no longer make that decision. This decision was made instead by five conservative justices, who seemed much in thrall to business interests, whose lives are remote from the daily cares and struggles of Americans, and who are profoundly ignorant of politics. Their decision has damaged the health of the public sphere in its enduring battle with private influence. I don't think America is a better place because a group of justices gave the influencer class the ability to "buy favor or generalized goodwill" with gifts of expensive luggage and tickets to sporting events.

The Supreme Court did not just narrow corruption to direct quid pro quo exchanges, they also have narrowed what official acts they will deem bribe-worthy. Recently, the Supreme Court unanimously overturned a jury's conviction of Virginia's former governor, Bob Mc-Donnell, who with his family accepted an array of gifts and loans, including a Rolex watch, vacations, and a big payment for his daughter's wedding, from a Richmond businessman. In one instance, the Court reported, the businessman "took Mrs. McDonnell on a shopping trip and bought her $20,000 worth of designer clothing."[49] The *Washington Post*, long a witness to corruption in Washington, D.C., recently described McDonnell's case as "as hackneyed as any in America's lurid history of political graft" and his actions as "what any layman would recognize as bribery."[50]

Beyond the quid pro quo distinction, the Court's McDonnell decision held that certain official acts didn't even count as "quids" or "quos." The businessman had wanted Virginia's state universities to perform tests on a company product. Because the governor did not formally direct such tests, the court held it was not an "official act" for the governor to help the businessman in other ways that signaled gubernatorial favor, such as summoning university executives and researchers for meetings about the product. "In sum," Justice Roberts wrote, "an 'official act' is a decision or action on a 'question, matter, cause, suit, proceeding or controversy.' . . . Setting up a meeting, talking to another official, or organizing an event (or agreeing to do so)—without more—does not fit that definition of 'official act.'"[51] The *Washington Post* described the ruling in plainer terms: "the court's crabbed definition of official corruption . . . provides comfort for future sticky-fingered politicians, who will find it easier to line their pockets while leading supplicants and suitors by the nose."[52] As put by Democracy 21 president Fred Wertheimer, the decision "belies reality. If you show the facts in the case to any citizen, the citizen will conclude that the public official has sold his office for personal, financial gain."[53]

I'm with Wertheimer. In my experience working for a governor (who did not accept Rolexes or shopping sprees), those signals of gubernatorial favor indeed make a difference. Decision makers in state agencies want pictures with the governor, they want face time with the governor, and for sure they want goodwill with the governor at budget time. When the governor's office calls or sets up the meeting, it has impact. When the governor puts people face-to-face and asks them to work something out, it has impact. The idea that you're not selling your services when you're a governor who takes a Rolex for setting up such meetings is just false. It is indeed an "act," the act of showing gubernatorial favor in an arena where gubernatorial favor can be expected to have an impact. Obviously the problem isn't setting up the meeting or exerting the influence, because that's what governors do. It's accepting the damned Rolex and the damned shopping spree. Just accepting the damned Rolex looks reasonably enough like private influence-buying at work, done to acquire and reward the governor's official influence, that a jury ought to be allowed to make the call. Letting the big influencers and those politicians who accept their gifts run right to the chalk line, indeed to a line that looks morally out of bounds to many, is a significant (and in my view wrong) decision about the basic standards of our democracy.

Clearly, the public's trust in a political system where governors can receive Rolexes for setting up meetings, conduct that even the Court said was "tawdry" and "distasteful," was not a priority in this decision.[54] In the age-old political contest between big influencers, who want a system to maneuver in that is amenable to their influence, and the general public, who just want to be left alone in a system they can trust to resist such tawdry influence, yet another blow was struck for the big influencers. As Fred Wertheimer said, "The court forgot about the public."[55] And the jury's authority to draw those lines on behalf of the public was further chopped away.

While the Founders did not foresee the vast wealth, power, and influence of the modern mega-corporation and its armada of influencers, they did foresee dangerous concentrations of wealth, power, and influence. I believe they also foresaw that virtually every element of government could be subject to influence, and even foresaw the possibility that *all* the great powers of government—the presidency, the Senate, and the House of Representatives—could together fall under the sway of a very powerful influence. I am confident that this grim prospect was part of their reason for protecting the jury, that last sentinel, in the Bill of Rights.

If you think this talk about influence is just a lot of political science hooey and doesn't matter in your real life, think about what is happening in Congress. Look first at whose priorities get attention. The things that matter a lot to regular people are pretty clear: student loans and the massive debt that results; getting something done on climate change before it's too late; cleaning up our nasty campaign finance system; stopping jobs going offshore and offshore tax-dodging schemes; fixing a still-broken health care system; getting a handle on the debt; and having a fair tax system where taxes are not just "for the little people." But these things don't matter much to most big corporations—certainly not as their lobbying presence is felt in Congress—and as a result, none of those things is getting done. It's not a coincidence. The big corporate stuff, like defense spending and extending corporate tax benefits, somehow gets done every year. And in any direct conflict between corporate and public interests, in Congress the advantage is almost always with corporations. For instance, almost every measure passed or ventured by Republicans on the House or Senate floor recently on clean air, clean water, and climate change was an effort to roll back public protections. The House has taken more than a hundred runs at the EPA[56]—this in a country where the public water in Flint, Michigan, was unsafe to drink.

In a nutshell: when you shrink the definition of corruption and take it away from the jury, you degrade the health of the public sphere and you empower the big, constant corporate influencers. Power shifts to the influencers and away from the public, and the agenda and possibilities in Congress shift accordingly. People then lose confidence in the health of the public sphere and become disaffected and suspicious, and the great enterprise of American democracy suffers and falters. The only happy customers are the influencers, and we end where we began this chapter—with the "great men and their power-hungry minions who promote their private interests at the expense of the public good."[57] The jury is a small and often overlooked institution, but damaging it—blinkering the watchman—has big consequences.

Of course, juries can be bothersome to some, and can sometimes be inconvenient. They do take effort. They require care and feeding, both figuratively and literally. But the jury is an institution that makes popular sovereignty real; an institution that checks the encroachments of the wealthy and powerful; an institution that will listen when the ears of the other branches of government are deaf to you; and an institution that brings ordinary Americans together to make important decisions in their community. The jury is a little institution with a big, big role.

CHAPTER TEN

The Denial Machine

WE HAVE DISCUSSED VARIOUS WAYS that giant corporations and their minions exert power over our democracy—flooding our elections with cash intended to buy results, pushing the Supreme Court to promote the corporate agenda, capturing administrative agencies, and even trying to undermine the civil jury to meet their needs. But wait, as the TV ads say, there's more.

As we have seen, corporate money and influence are flowing into our politics through secret funding organizations. But it doesn't end there. On major issues where the facts are against them, the corporate lobby has developed a very complex system to do a very simple thing: to lie. To lie so persistently, so smoothly, and with such craft that plain truth is distorted, obscured, and sometimes demonized. This system—call it the "denial machine"—has been carefully built over the past several decades to deceive the public about the scientific facts at the heart of major political debates.

The denial machine fills a useful purpose for its corporate masters. In Edward Bernays's seminal 1928 book *Propaganda*, he wrote of twentieth-century society: "We are governed, our minds are molded, our tastes formed, our ideas suggested, largely by men we have never heard of." After the Nazis gave the word "propaganda" a bad name, Bernays gave a new name to his chosen field: "public relations." He described public relations as the "conscious and intelligent manipulation of the organized habits and opinions of the masses." Bernays described this manipulation as "an important element in democratic society. Those who manipulate this unseen mechanism of society constitute an invisible government which is the true ruling power of our country." The elite can use the power of public relations to steer democracy in ways unseen, or unappreciated, by the general public. "In almost every act of our daily lives, whether in the sphere of politics or business, in our social conduct or our ethical thinking, we are dominated by the relatively small number of persons . . . who understand the mental processes and social patterns of the masses. It is they who pull the wires which control the public mind."[1] What better way to control democracy, if you are a very big industry, than to pull those wires controlling the public mind?

The machine did not spring up at once, full-grown, like Athena from the brow of Zeus. It grew, over time, in industry-fueled campaigns to obscure risks the public faced: the dangers of cigarette smoke, the hazard to children of lead paint, the environmental harm of ozone depletion, and the health effects of chemicals. This machine has as its purpose to deceive the public, to give cover to politicians in the pockets of industry, and to thwart or delay laws and policies that warn or protect people against the dangers. Even in the earliest days of environmental PR crisis management, industry counterattacks "used emotional appeals, scientific misinformation, front groups, extensive mailings to the media and opinion leaders, and the recruitment of doctors and scientists as 'objective' third party defenders."[2]

Built up for the tobacco battles, expanded for the pollution debates of the 1980s and 1990s, and presently at work to fight climate action, the denial machine is big and artfully constructed: organizations designed to look and sound like they're real, messages honed by public relations experts to sound like they're reasonable, compromised scientists whom industry can trot out when they're needed, and the whole organism so vast and multifaceted that when you see its parts you could be fooled into thinking it's not all the same beast. But it is. Just like the mythological Hydra: many heads, same beast.

One of the frustrations of countering this denial apparatus is that over the years it has gotten so clever and so big. Robert Brulle, professor of sociology and environmental science at Drexel University, has tracked well over a hundred entities now engaged in this network.[3] By contrast to what's going on now, the attempts of the tobacco companies to fool everyone about the hazards of their cigarettes feel like the good old days. Yes, they created an entity to be their corporate front and called it the Tobacco Institute—almost quaint. In the realm of corporate subterfuge, the Tobacco Institute is a hallmark of an earlier time, like an old flivver you have to hand-crank to start, or a biplane with stretched-canvas wings. I guess the cigarette industry thought calling it an "institute" would make the Tobacco Institute sound scientific and neutral.

The Tobacco Institute might not have been the zenith of corporate subterfuge, but its work was wicked enough, along with the mischief of the tobacco companies themselves, that it earned them all a verdict in federal court as "racketeers" under the federal Racketeer Influenced and Corrupt Organizations (RICO) Act for their fraudulent misrepresentations of the health risks of tobacco.[4] Back to Bernays again: "Propaganda becomes vicious and reprehensive . . . when its authors consciously and deliberately disseminate what they know to be lies, or when they aim at effects which they know to be prejudicial to the common good."[5] The tobacco industry's propaganda effort was indeed wicked and reprehensible.

The method behind their wicked work, however, did not disappear with the verdict. Big industries regularly face the foreseeable predicament that scientists might someday find hazards in their product. They need a mechanism to deploy when that happens.

And there it is, ready to go: Big Tobacco's strategy, which worked for decades. As Steve Coll reported, the tobacco industry's example showed "how industry funding and purposeful, subtle campaigning could profitably delay a legal reckoning for a dangerous product through the manipulation of public opinion, government policy, and scientific discourse."[6] It wasn't a complicated game plan. It required some money, sure, but when really big money is at stake—selling cigarettes, for instance, or emitting megatons of CO_2—money comes easily. The machinery has gotten much better at obscuring itself, but the game plan is still pretty much the same.

So what is this game plan?

First you create counterfeit science, paid science, "science" that looks like real science but comes to the conclusions that industry wants. The great advantage to industry in this "counterfeit science" game is that the counterfeit scientists don't need to defeat the real scientists; they just need to sow enough doubt about the real science among the uninformed and sometimes gullible public to forestall action. As one tobacco memo said: "Doubt is our product."[7] To manufacture that doubt, you need a stable of agreeable "scientists" at your disposal.

Second, you need a mouthpiece, an entity with a name that sounds more neutral and dispassionate than your corporation. If you say, "This is ExxonMobil, or Peabody Coal, and we're here to tell you climate change isn't real," well, you will probably have a little credibility problem. They do have the American Petroleum Institute out there, but that's not much of an improvement over the Tobacco Institute—it's old-school stuff. If you really want to trick the public today, you've got to do way better than that. And they do.

Third, you need to fund this apparatus. That creates a little problem. Not the money—there's plenty of money available when big money is at stake—but the money *trail*. Since even front organizations often have to reveal their donors, industry money leaves obvious fingerprints that can embarrass a front organization, and that doesn't help create the desired confusion. Thus there has emerged a way to launder the money, to scrub it of its corporate identity, so it doesn't come through with a corporate name on it.

One, two, three: it's not all that complicated, considering the stakes. You might call it Big Tobacco 2.0. As Brulle reports, "Some of the same people and some of the same organizations that were involved in the tobacco issue are also involved in climate change,"[8] with the fossil-fuel industry now waging an extremely well-funded, well-organized effort to "delegitimate the science that supports . . . mandatory limits on carbon emissions."[9]

Let's look at this machinery in its most active modern role, denying the science that shows how carbon emissions are causing climate and ocean changes. First, there is the counterfeit science and the "scientists" who front for the climate denial apparatus. The same names crop up over and over again, a few ubiquitous performers. That's because (here's a good thing) there are not many people who are actually willing to do what these individuals do, even for money. So the fossil-fuel industry has to go repeatedly to their same stable of agreeable climate "scientists."

Many of the "scientists" who front for the climate denial apparatus are hired hands. The funding of one of them was unearthed recently by the *New York Times*, which disclosed that this one scientist had been paid by the fossil-fuel industry to the tune of over a million dollars.[10] According to the *Times*, he also cleared his work in advance with his industry patrons. Obviously, in real science, that would be objectionable. This, however, is public relations in a lab coat. And in public relations, the product is cleared with the client.

One recent academic study of this phenomenon described climate change deniers' reliance on "researchers who are relatively inactive in their field and focus on favorable reports isolated from larger bodies of research in order to justify their positions, clearly contradicting decades of consensus within the climate-science community regarding anthropogenic global warming." As a result, the claims of climate deniers "lack evidence considered acceptable by the standards of the international scientific community," but they do "give insight into the political and rhetorical strategies of organized climate change denial."[11]

Many of the "scientists" who front for the climate denial apparatus are merely talk-show performers. Their work rarely appears in actual scientific journals, where real scientific debate takes place. In those scientific journals, their far-fetched schemes and baloney theories would have to face stiff scientific peer review. As former vice president Al Gore pointed out in his "Inconvenient Truth" presentation, out of more than nine hundred peer-reviewed scientific journal articles addressing climate change, exactly zero deny the science connecting man-made carbon emissions to climate change.[12] (To be exact, Professor Naomi Oreskes's peer-reviewed article in *Science* magazine, titled "The Scientific Consensus on Climate Change," puts the precise score at 928–0.)[13] Peer review is a tough standard for deniers; it requires authors to subject their work to the scrutiny of objective experts in their field.

Anyway, if you're in the counterfeit science business, real scientists are not your target audience. They don't count. You're in the public relations business, and the public is your audience. So instead of wasting time in peer-reviewed academic journals, industry "scientists" are out on Fox News and talk radio, where they don't face peer review and can address their target audience directly. Out there, the listeners are not experts in the science, they're an uninformed public ripe for the counterfeit scientists' mischief.

The "scientists" who front for the climate denial apparatus also tend to be selective. They rarely talk about the warming of the oceans, which you can measure with a thermometer. They rarely talk about the resulting sea level rise, because the law of thermal expansion is a little too obvious to deny, even for a "scientist." They rarely address ocean acidification, because you can put sea water and carbon dioxide together in a high school chemistry lab and watch the pH change. The "scientists" who front for the climate denial apparatus tend to focus on things such as atmospheric modeling, where the complexity of computer projections leaves more room for their mischief. Industries that want to sow doubt focus their efforts on areas where complexity or uncertainty create an atmosphere more conducive to deception.

This focus on creating uncertainty is intentional. Yale professor Justin Farrell describes the climate denial apparatus as "a complex network of think tanks, foundations, public relations firms, trade associations and *ad hoc* groups" that operate "complex counter-movement efforts that foster intractable uncertainty"[14] about real climate science. Their other goal is "to create ideological polarization around climate change."[15] Why polarization? Because it is "well understood that polarization is an effective strategy for creating controversy and delaying policy progress, particularly around environmental issues."[16] You can mask old special-interest special pleading as a partisan or cultural battle, and distract the public and the media from the smelly special interest in the corner.

Of course, it's not enough for the fossil-fuel industry to have its stable of "scientists." It also needs mouthpieces to publish climate denial op-eds, hold climate denial conferences, produce climate denial witnesses for hearings, and release climate denial articles (rarely peer-reviewed ones, of course). The machinery for propagating counterfeit science into public debate has become increasingly sophisticated since the days of the Tobacco Institute or the American Petroleum Institute. Now industry front organizations come with names like the Heartland Institute (they're the ones who notoriously compared scientists who believe in climate change to the Unabomber),[17] the Heritage

Foundation, the Cato Institute, the Mercatus Center, and the Annapolis Council. All take fossil-fuel money; all deny climate change. Most galling, perhaps, are the John Locke Institute for Public Policy (Locke and Montesquieu were the two great social scientists behind the ideals of our American Revolution), the Franklin Center for Government and Public Integrity (with a nice profile of Ben Franklin on its logo), the James Madison Institute for Public Policy (our Founding Father), and the George C. Marshall Institute for Public Policy (George C. Marshall was the architect of our military victory in Europe in World War II, described by British prime minister Winston Churchill as "the organizer of victory"[18]). Co-opting these great names for mouthpieces in this corporate-funded denial operation shows how low these interests will stoop to paste on themselves a veneer of credibility—a veneer that makes the think tank, in Jane Mayer's memorable phrase, a "disguised political weapon."[19]

Brulle describes the purpose of this network of front groups today as "a deliberate and organized effort to misdirect the public discussion and distort the public's understanding of climate change."[20] The coordinated tactics of this network, his report shows, "span a wide range of activities, including political lobbying, contributions to political candidates, and a large number of communication and media efforts that aim at undermining climate science."[21]

In *The War on Science*, Shawn Otto describes a recurring pattern as technologies emerge: discovery and application of the new technology; development of industries to manufacture and sell it; discovery of harmful side effects; battle between industry and science over that harm; crisis when the harm becomes too clear to overlook; and adaptation as society ultimately shifts to mitigate the harm.[22] His description of the "battle" phase is instructive: "vested economic interests sense a potentially lethal blow to their production systems and fight the proposed changes by denying the environmental effects, maligning and impeaching witnesses, questioning the science, attacking or impugning the scientists, and/or arguing that other factors are causing the mounting disaster." In this battle, "science becomes a rhetorical tool and facts are cherry-picked to win arguments, pitting real science against clever public relations campaigns, with the public unsure about what or whom to believe."[23] Otto breaks the industry strategy in this battle phase into seven steps. "Step one . . . starts with phony science,"[24] using scientists "who supply a steady stream of pseudoscience that can be used by foot soldiers to sway the public debate."[25] "Step two follows with slanted press materials spoon-fed to journalists by industry-affiliated nonprofits and bloggers."[26] Then comes "the third step: building and financing industry-aligned front groups (fake public-interest organizations) and astroturf groups (fake grassroots organizations)."[27] "Step four is to proselytize the intelligentsia who fund political campaigns and shape opinions in the press."[28] Step five pushes the materials out to "industry-aligned, or otherwise sympathetic talk-radio and cable-news purveyors, who reference these mainstream sources, react with outrage, and call for policy action."[29] Next is "the sixth stage of the attack: legislative or other policy action by partisan allies in government."[30] Last comes "the seventh and final stage. Now seemingly supported by science, the press, the government, the public, [and] business and professional opinion leaders, . . . industry representatives can step safely out from behind the curtain . . . and plead their case."[31]

Behind the network of climate denial fronts lurks the fossil-fuel industry. It takes big money to fund all these front organizations. And big money is what they've got. Brulle's report chronicles, from 2003 to 2010, "140 foundations making grants totaling $558 million to 91 organizations" that actively oppose climate action—more than half a billion dollars distributed over seven years.[32] Jane Mayer has reported Greenpeace investigators' discovery that the Kochs alone, from 2005 to 2008, "poured almost $25 million into dozens of different organizations fighting climate reform," outspending even ExxonMobil.[33]

The War on Science describes the political logic of this spending. "The shifting—or as economists say, the externalizing—of private costs onto the commons takes from everyone, and in fact reduces wealth throughout the economy."[34] Of course, it "takes from everyone" in order to transfer wealth to the special interest, and it "reduces wealth throughout the economy" in order to increase wealth in that special-interest sector of the economy. This fails a test of civilization quoted by Otto, enunciated by John Hubble (father of Edwin of Hubble Telescope fame): "'The best definition we have found for civilization is that a civilized man does what is best for all, while the savage does what is best for himself.'"[35] By this standard, the fossil-fuel sector behaves as a savage in its climate denial, not as a civilized social force.

Some simple math explains the economic logic of the fossil-fuel sector's creating such a big, expensive machine just to propagate climate denial. The EPA has estimated U.S. combustion of fossil fuels in 2011 to have emitted over 6.8 billion metric tons of carbon dioxide.[36] The federal Office of Management and Budget recently set the social cost of carbon—the economic and health costs of carbon pollution that the polluters inflict on the rest of society—at $45 per metric ton of CO_2 emitted.[37] So do the math: 6.9 billion metric tons of carbon at $45 of social cost per metric ton means that just one year's carbon emissions costs the public over $310 billion. The price would be pretty high for the polluters if they were to be forced by the government to make up for the harm that they're causing.

A properly working market economy would put those "negative externalities," as economists call them, into the price of the product, so that the correct market signal was sent through the price about the true costs. Even very conservative economists agree with that. Our failure to do this amounts to a massive subsidy, worth at least $310 billion per year in the United States alone. The International Monetary Fund's effort to calculate the "effective subsidy" yielded a much higher number: $700 billion, every year, to the benefit of the fossil-fuel industry in the United States.[38] That's a subsidy worth fighting for.

Spending half a billion dollars over seven years to get away with $310 billion (or even $700 billion) of harm every year? It's the best bargain on the planet. It's a better than a thousand-to-one return on investment. We talk in ten-year budget cycles in the Senate; over a ten-year Senate budget cycle the $700 billion IMF number becomes $7 trillion. Can you imagine what mischief people might be willing to make for $7 trillion? So money is not a problem for the polluters.

The last element of paying for this racket is funding the network of climate denial fronts without leaving too many dirty, telltale, fossil-fuel fingerprints. And the industry has set up just the thing: an organization called DonorsTrust and its related Donors Capital Fund. Fossil-fuel corporations can put their money in the front end of DonorsTrust, and out the back end comes laundered, identity-free money that can go exactly where you direct, with no fingerprints. DonorsTrust has no business purpose except to launder the identities of donors who want to fund groups without attribution. It is an identity-laundering machine.

And it's a great big machine. Jane Mayer calculates that as much as $750 million was redistributed through DonorsTrust to various conservative causes.[39] DonorsTrust alone has provided about a quarter of the funding for what Brulle's report calls the "climate change countermovement,"[40] and what I call the climate denial machine or network. More than a third of the organizations examined in the Brulle report get over 90 percent of their money from hidden sources.[41]

DonorsTrust/Donors Capital Fund is by far the biggest source of funding in that climate denial web. These twin entities reported giving a combined $78 million specifically to climate denier groups between 2003 and 2010. According to Brulle's report, the DonorsTrust/ Donors Capital Fund operation does double duty both as the "central component" and "predominant funder" of the denier apparatus and as the "black box that conceals the identity of contributors."[42]

This anonymous funding has grown as disclosed funding from fossil-fuel polluters has declined, with DonorsTrust/Donors Capital Fund donations to the denial network jumping from 3 percent of all foundation funding in 2003 to over 23 percent in 2010.[43] At the same time, disclosed donations from foundations affiliated with the Koch brothers declined from 9 percent of all foundation funding to the climate denier network in 2006 down to 2 percent by 2010, and Exxon-Mobil Foundation wound down its disclosed funding of organizations in the climate denier network, basically zeroing out by 2008, according to Brulle.[44]

It's working. As Professor Farrell at Yale has observed: "Academic researchers have had a very difficult time tracking flows of economic resources between members of this network, especially in recent years because of foundations like DonorsTrust, which enables contributors to give to specific causes while at the same time shielding the identity of the donor. Reliably assessing the influence of corporate benefactors has thus been extremely difficult."[45] Similarly, the Brulle report finds that "most funding for denial efforts is untraceable. Despite extensive data compilation and analyses, only a fraction of the hundreds of millions in contributions to climate change denying organizations can be specifically accounted for from public records. Approximately 75 percent of the income of these organizations comes from unidentifiable sources."[46] All this secrecy helps the string-pullers manipulate public opinion, and in a democracy that's a dangerous place to go.

If the fossil-fuel industry weren't up to something fishy, why all this effort to conceal? Why the commandeering of respected men's names when the people are dead and can't disassociate themselves? Why the identity laundering? And why make the scheme so big and complex?

Perhaps for $7 trillion.

But how could this intricate web of lies get by a free and independent media? Aren't they supposed to blow the whistle on this kind of stuff? Well, some have. Indeed, some have been heroic. But not all. Certain elements of the press have even been complicit—there is no gentler way to put it—in building and running the denial machine. And with corporate ownership of large parts of the media, it's perhaps no surprise that some outlets have gone over to the corporate side.

We count on the press in America to report faithfully and accurately on our changing world, and to alert the public to looming threats. Our Constitution gives the press special, vital rights so that they can perform this special, vital role. But what happens when the press fails in this role? What happens when elements of the press stop being independent, when press outlets climb into bed with special interests? The Latin phrase "Quis custodiet ipsos custodes?"—who will watch the watchmen themselves?—then becomes the question. The press is supposed to scrutinize all of us. Who watches them when they fail at their independent role?

It is assuredly an industry strategy to work the refs, trying to get their message out through legitimate media channels. Otto's *The War on Science* describes this as "[t]he industry and public-relations front, financed by corporations and conducted by PR experts, shills, and front groups, who take advantage of journalists' naiveté about objectivity and truth in order to manipulate the media, thereby shaping public opinion using 'uncertainties,' deception, personal attacks, and outrage to move public policy toward an antiscience position that supports the funders' business objectives."[47] They also seek to control their own outlets, as they have great success with people who "have drifted under the influence of slanted conservative commercial media."[48]

The editorial page of one of our nation's leading publications, the *Wall Street Journal*, is a case study in how complicit parts of the news media can be in the denial network. The *Wall Street Journal* is one of America's great newspapers. It is a paragon in journalism—right up to the editorial page, which opens to a chasm of polluter sludge. When a harmful industrial pollutant is the issue, this editorial page will misleadingly deny the scientific consensus and ignore its own excellent news pages' actual reporting, all helping the industry campaign to manufacture doubt, and delay remedial action.

As outlined in an excellent and far-reaching report by Media Matters, a deniers' playbook is visible in the pattern of the *Wall Street Journal's* commentary on acid rain, on the ozone layer, and now—most pronouncedly—on climate change.[49] The pattern is simple: deny the science, question the motives, and exaggerate the costs. Call it the polluting industries' 1-2-3 step.

Let's start in the 1970s, when chlorofluorocarbons (CFCs) were used in everything from aerosol cans to refrigerators. Scientists warned that CFCs could create a hole in the ozone layer, putting human beings at heightened risk of cancer from exposure to the sun's ultraviolet rays. The *Wall Street Journal's* editorial page for more than twenty-five years doggedly printed editorials devaluing the science and attacking any regulation of CFCs.[50]

As Media Matters lays it out:

A January 1976 editorial said the connection between CFCs and ozone depletion "is only a theory and will remain only that until further efforts are made to test its validity in the atmosphere itself."[51] . . . A May 1979 editorial said that scientists "still don't know to what extent, if any, mankind's activities have altered the ozone barrier or whether the possibly harmful effects of these activities aren't offset by natural processes. . . . Thus, it now appears the excitement over the threat to the ozone layer was founded on scanty scientific evidence."[52] A March 1984 editorial said that concerns about ozone depletion were based on "premature scientific evidence" and claim[ed] that "new evidence shows that the ozone layer isn't vanishing after all; it may even be increasing."[53] . . . A March 1989 editorial called for more research on the "questionable theory that CFCs cause depletion of the ozone layer," calling on scientists to "continue to study the sky until we know enough to make a sound decision regarding the phasing out of our best refrigerants."[54]

Predictably, the page also attacked the motives of reformers. A February 1992 editorial, insinuating other motives, stated: "It is simply not clear to us that real science drives policy in this area."[55]

And—playbook step 3—they warned that action to slow ozone depletion would be costly. Again, from Media Matters:

A March 1984 editorial claimed that banning CFCs "cost the economy some $1.52 billion in forgone profits and product-change expenses" and 8,700 jobs.[56] An August 1990 editorial warned that banning CFCs would lead to "a dramatic increase in air-conditioning and refrigeration costs."[57] It added: The likely substitute for the most popular banned refrigerant costs 30 times as much and will itself be banned by the year 2015. The economy will have to shoulder at least $10 billion to $15 billion a year in added refrigeration costs by the year 2000."[58] A February 1992 editorial warned that accelerating the phaseout of CFCs "almost surely will translate into big price increases on many consumer products."[59]

Despite the protests of the *Wall Street Journal* editorial page, Americans actually listened to the science. Congress took action, banning these refrigerants, protecting the ozone layer and protecting the public's health, and the economy prospered. The ozone hole is healing. What about all those costs that the *Journal* claimed? Looking back, we see that action to slow ozone depletion in fact saved money. According to the EPA's 1999 progress report on the Clean Air Act, "[e]very dollar invested in ozone protection provides $20 of societal health benefits in the United States."[60] One dollar spent, twenty dollars saved. The *Journal*'s response? Silence. They just stopped talking about it.

When scientists began reporting that acid rain was falling on most of the northeastern United States the *Journal* followed a nearly identical pattern. Again, according to the Media Matters report, out came the playbook: saying "data are not conclusive and more studies are needed"; arguing that "nature, not industry, is the primary source of acid rain"; claiming "the scientific case for acid rain is dying"; and charging "that politics, not nature, is the primary force driving the theory's biggest boosters." At the same time, President Reagan's panel on the issue warned that failing to act on acid rain would risk "irreversible damage."[61]

Now, as told by Media Matters, the *Journal* is using the same old polluter playbook against climate change. First, they deny the science:

> 1993—WSJ claims there is "growing evidence that global warming just isn't happening" . . . 1999—WSJ: "Serious scientists" call global warming "one of the greatest hoaxes of all time." . . . 2005—WSJ says the link between fossil fuels and global warming has "become even more doubtful." . . . A December 2011 editorial said that the global warming debate requires "more definitive evidence."[62]

The polluter playbook then produced the usual inflate-the-costs warning that solving climate change would "make the world poorer than it would otherwise be."[63] This "world poorer" piece actually hit the full polluter-playbook trifecta in just one editorial, also questioning motives of the "political actors" they claim are out to gain economic control and denying the science, saying "global surface temperatures have remained essentially flat."[64] If only the editorial page writers at the *Wall Street Journal* would read the actual news their own paper reports on climate change.

Climate Nexus did a more recent analysis of the *Wall Street Journal* editorial page and concluded that the page "overwhelmingly ignores the science, champions doubt and denial of both the science and effectiveness of action, and leaves readers misinformed about the consensus of science and of the risks of the threat . . . consistently ignoring or ridiculing the scientific consensus on the reality and urgency of climate change." Specifically, Climate Nexus found that of 201 editorials relating to climate science or policy "dating back to 1997, none explicitly acknowledges that fossil fuels cause climate change"; out of 279 op-eds published since 1995, a paltry 14 percent "reflect mainstream climate science"; and out of 122 columns published since 1997, just "four accepted as fact that fossil fuels cause climate change, or endorse a policy to reduce emissions." Between April 2015 and May 2016, as global heat records were broken monthly, the *Journal* published one hundred climate-related op-eds, columns, and editorials; ninety-six failed to acknowledge the link between human activity and climate change. The report concluded that the *Wall Street Journal's* posture "consistently highlights voices of those with vested interests in fossil fuels . . . presenting only the dismissive side of the climate discussion," and is "a failure of journalistic responsibility." [65]

"Those who corrupt the public mind are just as evil as those who steal from the public purse," said Adlai Stevenson in a speech on September 12, 1952.[66] The big polluters aren't just polluting our atmosphere and oceans; they are polluting our democracy, with misinformation and money. They are doing it purposely. The *Wall Street Journal* editorial page, and the whole denial apparatus, has been wrong every time they've gone down this road: wrong about tobacco, wrong about lead paint, wrong about acid rain, wrong about mercury, wrong about the ozone layer, and now wrong about climate change. Yet they keep going there. Being wrong over and over doesn't seem to bother them. If being right mattered to them, or to the corporate interests behind them, they'd reassess what they do. So you have to wonder if they don't mind being wrong. Maybe it's not their intention to be right. Maybe it's much more cynical than that. Maybe the point simply is to create doubt, buy time, and maximize profits.

When the inevitable happens and climate change really starts to hit home, people will want to know why we didn't take proper steps in time. It's not as if there isn't enough scientific evidence out there for us to act. This denial machine will likely go down as one of our great American scandals, like Watergate or Teapot Dome—a deliberate, complex scheme of lies and propaganda that caused real harm to the American people, our country, and the world, all so that a small group of powerful corporations could make more money a little longer. Thank God that a small group of dogged investigators, academics and journalists is gradually exposing this rancid network, even if elements of the press have joined the other side.

I will close this chapter with a recent example I ran into of this denial apparatus at work. I had the nerve to write an op-ed piece suggesting a legal investigation into the fossil-fuel industry to look for tobacco-type fraud.[67] That prompted an outburst of dozens of articles from right-wing editorial pages, fossil-fuel front groups, and various climate-denial outfits. The editorials popped up like mushrooms after rain. Later, at a Senate Judiciary hearing,[68] I asked Attorney General Lynch about a civil fraud investigation into the denial operation of the fossil-fuel industry, and in the following days there was another outburst of dozens more articles. These outbursts against any fossil-fuel fraud investigation were notable for the homogeneity of the message. You could mix and match the dozens of articles virtually interchangeably. Some were actually written by the same people. If you looked at the authors and the outlets, and knew the players, you could inevitably find a link back to the fossil-fuel industry.

The core common argument in these two outbursts was that any investigation would be a terrible infringement on corporate free speech rights protected by the First Amendment. Someone very much wanted to protect any fossil-fuel industry misdeeds from investigation, hiding them under the skirts of the First Amendment. So let's take a look at the merits of the "First Amendment" argument that was at the core of this barrage.

Robert Post is the dean of the Yale Law School, arguably America's most renowned and prestigious law school. In response to the barrage of editorial argument I have described, Dean Post wrote an article titled "ExxonMobil Is Abusing the First Amendment," which ran in the *Washington Post* on June 24, 2016.[69] I will quote a full section of his article.

Global warming is perhaps the single most significant threat facing the future of humanity on this planet. It is likely to wreak havoc on the economy, including, most especially, on the stocks of companies that sell hydrocarbon energy products. If large oil companies have deliberately misinformed investors about their knowledge of global warming, they may have committed serious commercial fraud.

A potentially analogous instance of fraud occurred when tobacco companies were found to have deliberately misled their customers about the dangers of smoking. The safety of nicotine was at the time fiercely debated, just as the threat of global warming is now vigorously contested. Because tobacco companies were found to have known about the risks of smoking, even as they sought to convince their customers otherwise, they were held liable for fraud. Despite the efforts of tobacco companies to invoke First Amendment protections for their contributions to public debate, the U.S. Court of Appeals for the D.C. Circuit found: "Of course it is well settled that the First Amendment does not protect fraud."

The point is a simple one. If large corporations were free to mislead deliberately the consuming public, we would live in a jungle rather than in an orderly and stable market.

ExxonMobil and its supporters are now eliding the essential difference between fraud and public debate.

Dean Post's reminder—which most lawyers know—that "'it is well settled that the First Amendment does not protect fraud'" illustrates a big logical flaw in the fossil-fuel front groups' First Amendment argument. It is not logical to presume the propriety of the fossil-fuel industry's climate denial operation, when that would be the very question at issue in an investigation. If in fact there is "serious commercial fraud" at the core of the fossil-fuel industry's climate denial operation, the First Amendment argument evaporates, since fraud is not protected free speech. To assert freedom of speech as the reason there should be no investigations is to prejudge the answer that the investigations would ultimately determine: was there fraud, or was it just public debate? Courts figure that distinction out all the time.

I was the subject of these outbursts, and I couldn't help noticing their very high emotional tone. The insults were bitter ones, with language sometimes veering into hysteria. I was the terrible inquisitor Torquemada, for instance, and mighty ExxonMobil was the lonely Galileo in his cell.[70] The outbursts' high moral dudgeon ran into some ironies, however. The attorney general of Virginia once harassed a climate scientist at the University of Virginia so vilely that the university had to take the attorney general all the way to the Virginia Supreme Court to make the attorney general knock it off.[71] Where was these groups' outrage about the scientist's free speech then? When a U.S. senator called for criminal prosecution of named climate scientists a few years back, where was their outrage over the scientists' freedom of speech? (For whatever it's worth, I had called for a civil investigation of corporate entities, not criminal prosecution of scientists.) Climate scientists are still regularly bombarded with Freedom of Information Act requests for their university emails, and often threatened with physical harm. Where are the outbursts of outrage about such harassment? There is none. The outrage animating these editorial outbursts is an outrage of convenience, appearing only when the target of a proposed investigation is the fossil-fuel industry; when the target of an investigation actually is an individual scientist, not a peep out of them.

These editorial outbursts were presumably intended to shove a phony First Amendment argument into the public debate, to help the fossil-fuel industry defend against any investigation. Ironically, with their nearly identical message, the same logical fallacy, and the falsely histrionic tones, they actually highlighted a network of mouthpieces linked to the fossil-fuel industry. This was no sincere expression of concern about rights of free speech protected by the First Amendment. It was an elaborate sham, an effort in masquerade and misdirection supporting the fossil-fuel interests who erected the front group screen in the first place, to discourage any fair and proper investigation into possible fraud at the heart of the denial machine.

But if you weren't a United States senator who gets a lot of news clips, if you were just an ordinary citizen reading only one or two of these editorials, you might not see the pattern. You might think the argument was honest, or well-founded. You would not notice any links to the fossil-fuel industry. ExxonMobil had its name on none of the editorials in these outbursts.

As we leave the fossil-fuel groups' First Amendment argument, consider what would happen if their argument were actually to succeed. If even fraudulent corporate speech were protected by the First

Amendment, out would go decades of legal precedent allowing regulation of corporate commercial speech to protect consumers and honest markets. Out would go state and federal consumer protection laws protecting individuals from corporate misrepresentations. It would be open season on the consumer. That's a ludicrous world to envision, but it's the world that would result if the First Amendment "outburst" argument actually became the law. It's a world these forces are willing to contemplate, if it would help protect the fossil-fuel industry against the risk that a court might find they crossed the line into fraud.

CHAPTER ELEVEN

Climate Change and the "Flies of Summer"

THE PROBLEM OF CORPORATE CONTROL OF OUR POLITICS is correctable. We can stand up, push back, and make it right. Teddy Roosevelt did; we can, too. However, there is one place where this corporate power can push us over a tipping point that is not correctable. That is climate change.

In a Vatican Radio speech, Pope Francis quoted the old warning "God always forgives, we men forgive sometimes, but Nature never forgives," and added his own admonition: "If you give her a slap, she will give you one."[1] We are giving Nature a hell of a slap. As noted essayist and Kentucky farmer Wendell Berry wrote: "Whether we and our politicians know it or not, Nature is a party to all our deals and decisions, and she has more votes, a longer memory, and a sterner sense of justice than we do."[2]

For as long as our species has been on planet Earth, the amount of carbon dioxide in the atmosphere has fluctuated between 170 and 300 parts per million. In 2015, the amount of carbon dioxide in the earth's atmosphere blew through 400 parts per million, for the first time in human history.[3] That's a measurement, not a theory. There's no dispute.

The science linking carbon pollution to global warming is nothing new. It dates back to the time of President Lincoln, when Irish physicist John Tyndall first measured how different gases in the atmosphere absorbed heat to varying degrees, essentially predicting the atmospheric warming that excess carbon dioxide would cause.[4] In the century and a half since, we have measured changes in the climate and oceans that legitimate scientists conclude, with virtual unanimity, are caused by our burning of fossil fuels.

Our oceans are warming and acidifying. Those are measurements. Every legitimate scientist concurs that the oceans acidify because they absorb carbon dioxide and it changes their chemistry, and they warm because oceans have absorbed so much of the excess heat from global warming—more than 90 percent of it is the prevailing measure.[5] The chemistry change in the oceans is science you can replicate in a high school science lab. The warming of the oceans is something we measure with thermometers.

The rate of the warming and acidifying of the ocean is the fastest in human history.[6] We measure that, too. We are experiencing the warmest years ever recorded.[7] That's more measurement. Measurements show rising seas lapping at our shores. Rhode Island has measured nearly ten inches of sea level rise since the 1930s.[8]

These are all measurements, not projections. These are facts, not theories. They portend dire consequences for coastal flooding, dying timber forests, farmland drought, shifts in fisheries, and weather emergencies.

Unbelievably, scientists for the fossil-fuel industry have known about the threat of global warming for nearly *fifty years*. A 1968 report commissioned by the American Petroleum Institute noted that the "greenhouse effect" was likely due to carbon dioxide emissions and that significant global warming would likely cause "the melting of the Antarctic ice cap, a rise in sea levels, warming of the oceans, and an increase in photosynthesis." They concluded: "Even the remote possibility of such an occurrence justifies concern."[9]

Even scientists within ExxonMobil concurred. As early as 1979, Exxon scientists wrote in an internal memo:

> The CO_2 concentration in the atmosphere has increased since the beginning of the world industrialization. It is now 15% greater than it was in 1850 and the rate of CO_2 release from anthropogenic sources appears to be doubling every 15 years. The most widely held theory is that:

- The increase is due to fossil-fuel combustion
- Increasing CO_2 concentration will cause a warming of the earth's surface
- The present trend of fossil-fuel consumption will cause dramatic environmental effects before the year 2050.

The memo went on to predict "dramatic world climate changes within the next 75 years, according to many present climatic models."[10] That memo was produced thirty-eight years ago. We are halfway there.

In a 1982 internal memo, Exxon scientists wrote again:

Over the past several years a clear scientific consensus has emerged regarding the expected climatic effects of increased atmospheric CO_2. The consensus is that a doubling of atmospheric CO_2 from its pre–industrial revolution value would result in an average global temperature rise of (3.0 ± 1.5) degrees C. . . . There is unanimous agreement in the scientific community that a temperature increase of this magnitude would bring about significant changes in the earth's climate.[11]

Thirty-five years ago they admitted that "a clear scientific consensus has emerged."

Exxon science memos also pointed out the "possibility that an atmospheric CO_2 buildup will cause adverse environmental effects in enough areas of the world to consider limiting the future use of fossil fuels as major energy sources"[12] and that "mitigation of the 'greenhouse effect' would require major reductions in fossil-fuel combustion."[13] For the biggest fossil-fuel company in the world, this was serious.

Instead of going into high gear to try to mitigate or reverse some of the effects of its corporate behavior, Exxon chose to dedicate itself to spouting denial and funding the denial machinery. In 2005 the *Wall Street Journal* reported, "Openly and unapologetically, the world's No. 1 oil company disputes the notion that fossil fuels are the main cause of global warming."[14] Assessing Exxon's track record, Naomi Oreskes, a Harvard professor and author of *Merchants of Doubt*, and Congressman Ted Lieu wrote in an opinion piece in *The Hill*,

"A new word needs to be invented in the English language for what ExxonMobil has done. The level of corporate hypocrisy and the potential consequences are staggering, as is their blatant denial of both the facts of science and of their own shameful history."[15] As Shawn Otto summarizes in *The War on Science*, fossil fuel, "the world's most powerful industry," launched "an industrial war on science the likes of which the world has never seen."[16]

Exxon even went so far as to coach its CEO to cite a bogus "petition" of seventeen thousand scientists asserting, in the CEO's words, that there is "no convincing scientific evidence that any release of carbon dioxide, methane or other greenhouse gases is causing or will in the foreseeable future cause catastrophic heating of the earth's atmosphere and disruption of the earth's climate."[17] The CEO omitted to mention to his shareholders that the "petition" was put together by a climate denier named Fred Seitz, who has worked in Exxon-funded climate denial fronts and whose former job was to refute the criticisms of cigarettes on behalf of tobacco giant R.J. Reynolds.[18] Nor did he mention that signatories on the "petition" included imaginary TV and cartoon characters.[19]

The path Exxon chose was well described by Steve Coll in his prize-winning investigative book *Private Empire: ExxonMobil and American Power*: "a kaleidoscope of overlapping and competing influence campaigns, some open, some conducted by front organizations, and some entirely clandestine. Strategists created layers of disguise, subtlety, and subterfuge—corporate-funded 'grassroots' programs and purpose-built think tanks, as fingerprint-free as possible. In such an opaque and untrustworthy atmosphere, the ultimate advantage lay with any lobbyist whose goal was to manufacture confusion and perpetual controversy. On climate, this happened to be the oil industry's position."[20]

Conservation and stewardship were once fundamental principles of American conservatism. From seminal thinkers of the conservative movement to great Republican leaders of the twentieth century, the conservative ideal included a commitment to the interests of future generations, and the conservation that honored that commitment.

Edmund Burke, an Irish-born member of Britain's Parliament, is considered by many the father of modern conservatism. His 1790 conservative pamphlet, "Reflections on the Revolution in France," cautioned that we are but "temporary possessors" of our society. If individuals are "unmindful of what they have received from their ancestors, or what is due to their posterity," he wrote, "no one generation could link with the other. Men would become little better than the flies of a summer." [21] In our case, flies of a carbon-fueled summer.

A Distinguished Scholar at the Heritage Foundation, Russell Kirk was dubbed by President Ronald Reagan "the prophet of American conservatism." [22] In a 1970 piece in the *Baltimore Sun*, "Conservation Activism Is a Healthy Sign," Kirk wrote, "There is nothing more conservative than conservation." [23]

President Dwight Eisenhower's 1961 farewell address invoked our national legacy: "As we peer into society's future, we—you and I, and our government—must avoid the impulse to live only for today, plundering, for our own ease and convenience, the precious resources of tomorrow. We cannot mortgage the material assets of our grandchildren without risking the loss also of their political and spiritual heritage." [24]

President Gerald Ford, who once worked as a national park ranger, said in 1975: "We have too long treated the natural world as an adversary rather than as a life-sustaining gift from the Almighty. If man has the genius to build, which he has, he must also have the ability and the responsibility to preserve." [25]

In 1984, President Ronald Reagan, perhaps the figure most revered by today's Republican Party, put this question to his fellow Republicans: "What is a conservative after all but one who conserves, one who is committed to protecting and holding close the things by which we live. . . . And we want to protect and conserve the land on which we live—our countryside, our rivers and mountains, our plains and meadows and forests. This is our patrimony. This is what we leave to our children. And our great moral responsibility is to leave it to them either as we found it or better than we found it." [26] President Reagan's conservative credentials are unassailable, and GOP candidates for elected office strive mightily to out-Reagan each other at every turn, but those words would make Reagan a fringe liberal candidate in today's corporate/conservative movement.

Even the National Association of Evangelicals has said: "Christians must care about climate change because we love God the Creator and

Jesus our Lord, through whom and for whom the creation was made. This is God's world, and any damage that we do to God's world is an offense against God Himself."[27]

The long lineage of conservative thinkers and politicians who felt a duty to protect the environment did not end with Reagan. There was a steady, healthy heartbeat of Republican support for major U.S. legislation to address carbon pollution, all the way through the first decade of this century. In 2003, Senator John McCain was the lead Republican co-sponsor of the Climate Stewardship Act, which would have created a market-based emissions cap-and-trade program to reduce carbon dioxide and other heat-trapping pollutants from the biggest U.S. sources. At the time, McCain said: "While we cannot say with 100 percent confidence what will happen in the future, we do know the emission of greenhouse gases is not healthy for the environment. As many of the top scientists through the world have stated, the sooner we start to reduce these emissions, the better off we will be in the future."[28] McCain's Climate Stewardship Act then actually got to a vote. And when it did not prevail, McCain reintroduced the measure himself in the following Congress. Republican senators Olympia Snowe of Maine and Lincoln Chafee of Rhode Island—my predecessor—were among that bill's co-sponsors.

Other Republicans got behind other cap-and-trade proposals: Senator Tom Carper's Clean Air Planning Act at one time or another counted Senator Lamar Alexander of Tennessee, Senator Lindsey Graham of South Carolina, and Senator Susan Collins of Maine among its supporters. In 2007, Republican senator Olympia Snowe was a lead co-sponsor of Senator John Kerry's Global Warming Reduction Act. Senators Lisa Murkowski and Ted Stevens from Alaska, and Senator Arlen Specter of Pennsylvania, then a Republican, were original co-sponsors of the Low Carbon Economy Act. And that same year, Alexander introduced the Clean Air/Climate Change Act. Each of these bills sought to reduce carbon emissions through a cap-and-trade mechanism. Said Alexander in 2007: "It is also time to acknowledge that climate change is real, human activity is a big part of the problem, and it is up to us to act."[29]

That bipartisan heartbeat remained alive in 2009. Senator Mark Kirk of Illinois, while he served in the House of Representatives, was one of eight Republicans to vote for the Waxman-Markey cap-and-trade proposal. In that same year, Senator Jeff Flake of Arizona, then representing Arizona in the House, was an original co-sponsor of the Raise Wages, Cut Carbon Act, to reduce payroll taxes for employers and employees in exchange for equal revenue from a carbon tax. On the House floor, Flake argued the virtues of this approach: "If we want to be honest about helping the environment, then just impose a carbon tax and make it revenue neutral, give commensurate tax relief on the other side. . . . Let's have an honest debate about whether or not we want to help the environment by actually having something that is revenue neutral where you tax consumption as opposed to income."[30]

Those words were echoed in the Senate by Susan Collins, a lead co-sponsor of the Carbon Limits and Energy for America's Renewal Act, a carbon fee bill she sponsored with Senator Maria Cantwell. "In the United States alone," said Collins, "emissions of the primary greenhouse gas, carbon dioxide, have risen more than 20 percent since 1990. Climate change is the most daunting environmental challenge we face and we must develop reasonable solutions to reduce our greenhouse gas emissions."[31]

As recently as 2009, there was clear and forceful acknowledgment from leading Republican voices of the real danger posed by climate change, and of Congress's responsibility to act.

Then came 2010, the year of *Citizens United*.

As *Citizens United* unleashed its torrent of corporate money into our elections, Republicans were the initial targets of the fossil-fuel industry's onslaught, and Republican interest in climate change suddenly disappeared from Congress. One of the lessons learned by the fossil-fuel industry from David Koch's quixotic bid for the vice presidency in 1980 was that third parties are a fool's errand: they tend to steal voters from the party they most resemble, helping the adversary. So instead of running their own candidate, the industry decided it would be more effective to co-opt one of the existing parties. The chief climate deniers are the Koch brothers, and they and the fossil-fuel industry have captured the Republican Party, through *Citizens United* money and the Tea Party apparatus. One of my Republican colleagues said to me after a speech I gave on the Senate floor slamming the Koch brothers: "What are you complaining about? They're spending more against us than they are against you!"

By capturing the Republican Party on climate change, the fossil-fuel industry has been able to disguise what is basically special-interest special pleading as a partisan contest, tangling their pollution up in our culture wars.

As the fossil-fuel industry tightened the screws on the Republican Party after *Citizens United*, the climate evidence only became stronger. NASA and NOAA officially declared 2014 and 2015 the hottest years ever recorded, "easily breaking the previous records."[32] Yet in Washington, no Republican would step forward. *Citizens United* had uncorked all that vicious dark money to cast its shadow of intimidation over our democracy, the industry brought that brute force to bear on the Republican Party, and Republicans had to walk back from any major climate legislation. Even colleagues who know this is real and who privately encourage me to keep fighting went silent after *Citizens United*. I have been told by Republican colleagues, "Keep working on your carbon fee bill; I can't be with you yet but it's the right thing and I'll get there." I've been told, "I know I need to do the right thing on this, but I've got to be *so* deft about how I do it." I've been told, "Let's keep talking—but don't tell my staff. Nobody else can know."

Talking to these Republican senators about climate change is like talking to prisoners about escape. Political attacks funded by *Citizens United* money, and the very real threat of those attacks if you don't behave, loom over Republicans who might work with Democrats on curbing carbon pollution. These threats are particularly concrete and potent when it comes to the primary process: the Koch network has made plain that any Republican lawmaker who goes against the corporate line on climate change will be at a "severe disadvantage in the nominating process."[33] If a Republican in Congress were to publicly acknowledge the reality of climate change and try to do something about it, the fossil-fuel industry could handpick a Tea Party candidate and throw millions of dollars her way from behind innumerable masks to take that Republican out in the next primary.

We have Republican senators who represent historic native villages that are now washing into the sea and need relocation because of climate change and sea level rise. We have Republican senators who represent great American coastal cities now flooded by high tides on sunny days because of climate change. We have Republican senators representing states swept by drought and wildfire. We have Republican senators whose home-state forests are being killed in the hundreds of square miles by the marauding pine beetle, whose range has expanded due to the warming climate.[34] We have Republican senators whose home states' glaciers are disappearing before their very eyes. We have Republican senators whose states are having to raise offshore bridges and coastal highways before rising seas. We have Republican senators whose emblematic home state species are dying off or migrating away. Yet none will work on a major climate bill. None will place a price on carbon. It's simply not safe, not since *Citizens United* allowed special interests to bombard our elections—and threaten and promise to bombard our elections—with their attack ads. *Citizens United* did not enhance speech in our democracy; instead it allowed wealthy special interests to suppress and silence real debate.

Outside the walls of Congress, where *Citizens United* money holds less sway, the situation is very different. Responsible Republican voices outside of Congress more and more acknowledge the threat of climate change and call for responsible solutions. Many want to correct the market failure that aids and abets the fossil-fuel industry's irresponsible practices. These Republicans don't face the political threat of *Citizens United*. They're not prisoners.

Former members of Congress, for example, are free now from the polluters' thrall, and implore their colleagues to take on climate change. Bob Inglis, the former Republican representative from South Carolina, who was bombarded in the primaries by outside money for supporting climate action, invokes the tenets of conservative economics. "If you're a conservative, it is time to step forward and engage in the climate and energy debate because we have the answer—free enterprise," he argues. "Conservatives understand that we must set the correct incentives, and this should include internalizing pollution and other environmental costs in our market system. We tax income but we don't tax emissions. It makes sense to conservatives to take the tax off something you want more of, income, and shift the tax to something you want less of, emissions."[35]

Sherwood Boehlert and Wayne Gilchrest, former Republican

representatives from New York and Maryland, respectively, in a joint February 2012 *Washington Post* op-ed with Representative Henry Waxman and Senator Ed Markey, both Democrats, made the fiscal case for a carbon fee: "The debate over how to reduce our nation's debt has been presented as a dilemma between cutting spending on programs Americans cherish or raising taxes on American job creators. But there is a better way: We could slash our debt by making power plants and oil refineries pay for the carbon emissions that endanger our health and environment. This policy would strengthen our economy, lessen our dependence on foreign oil, keep our skies clean—and raise a lot of revenue. The best approach would be to use a market mechanism such as the sale of carbon allowances or a fee on carbon pollution to lower emissions and increase revenue."[36]

Top advisors to former Republican presidents have joined the chorus. William D. Ruckelshaus, Lee M. Thomas, William K. Reilly, and Christine Todd Whitman wrote in a *New York Times* op-ed: "As administrators of the E.P.A. under Presidents Richard M. Nixon, Ronald Reagan, George Bush and George W. Bush, we held fast to common-sense conservative principles—protecting the health of the American people, working with the best technology available and trusting in the innovation of American business and in the market to find the best solutions for the least cost."[37] These Republican officials recognize that a "market-based approach, like a carbon tax, would be the best path to reducing greenhouse-gas emissions," and urge, "[w]e must continue efforts to reduce the climate-altering pollutants that threaten our planet. The only uncertainty about our warming world is how bad the changes will get, and how soon. What is most clear is that there is no time to waste."[38]

For one former Republican member of the Senate, the threat of climate change had serious professional implications. As secretary of defense, Chuck Hagel was responsible for accounting for all hazards to our national security and our interests in the world. He gave this clear-eyed assessment at the Halifax International Security Forum: "Climate change does not directly cause conflict, but it can significantly add to the challenges of global instability, hunger, poverty, and conflict. Food and water shortages, pandemic disease, disputes over refugees and resources, more severe natural disasters—all place additional burdens on economies, societies, and institutions around the world. . . . The effects of climate change and new energy resources are far-reaching and unpredictable . . . demanding our attention and strategic thinking."[39] Hagel joined twenty-two other Republican former national security officials and Republican former members of Congress, along with ten senior retired military officers, in taking out a full-page ad in the *Wall Street Journal* on October 22, 2015, under the blaring headline "Republicans and Democrats Agree: U.S. Security Demands Global Climate Action."

George Schultz served as secretary of both labor and treasury under President Nixon, and as secretary of state under President Reagan. In a 2013 *Wall Street Journal* op-ed written with Nobel Prize–winning economist Gary Becker, Schultz appealed to our American sense of fairness, writing: "Americans like to compete on a level playing field. All the players should have an equal opportunity to win based on their competitive merits, not on some artificial imbalance that gives someone or some group a special advantage. We think this idea should be applied to energy producers. They all should bear the full costs of the use of the energy they provide. . . . Clearly a revenue-neutral carbon tax would benefit all Americans by eliminating the need for costly energy subsidies while promoting a level playing field for energy producers."[40]

David Frum, speechwriter to George W. Bush, wrote in a December 2012 CNN.com op-ed that a carbon fee could help address a number of pressing national issues: "Take three worrying long-term challenges: climate change, the weak economic recovery, and America's chronic budget deficits. Combine them into one. And suddenly three tough problems become one attractive solution. Tax carbon. . . . The revenues from a carbon tax could be used to reduce the deficit while also extending new forms of payroll tax relief to middle-class families, thus supporting middle-class family incomes."[41] Gregory Mankiw, economic advisor to George W. Bush and Mitt Romney, specifically highlighted a Senate carbon fee proposal in an August 2013 op-ed in the *New York Times*. The bill, he wrote, "is more effective and less invasive than the regulatory approach that the federal government has traditionally pursued. . . . [I]f the Democratic sponsors conceded to using the new revenue to reduce personal and corporate income tax rates, a bipartisan compromise is possible to imagine. Among economists the issue is largely a no-brainer."[42]

Jim Brainard, five-term Republican mayor of Carmel, Indiana, implored in an *Indianapolis Star* op-ed, "This issue isn't just about saving polar bears. It's about saving our cities. No matter your politics, there is overwhelming evidence of climate change and we as a nation have a moral obligation to address these issues."[43]

The contrast is plain. Republican leaders who are not captive to the *Citizens United* threats and bullying of the big polluters are ready to get to work on climate change. The problem is not Republicans, but abuse post–*Citizens United* by the fossil-fuel industry of corporate political power.

How exactly does one narrow slice of the country—namely, the fossil-fuel industry—silence an entire political party in Congress on what is perhaps the single most consequential issue facing Americans today? Much of the action has got to be in behind-the-scenes threats that we can never fully appreciate. But some lobbying groups are bolder, and their boldness gives us a window into what must be taking place behind closed doors.

There's the striking example of the Koch-backed Americans for Prosperity openly promising to wipe out candidates who support any curbs on carbon pollution. The group's president said that if Republicans supported a carbon tax or climate regulations, they'd "be at a severe disadvantage in the Republican nomination process. . . . We would absolutely make that a crucial issue."[44] The threat is plain: step out of line, and here come the attack ads and the primary challengers— all funded by the deep pockets of the fossil-fuel industry, enabled by *Citizens United*, and largely protected from disclosure. It's a modern political version of the ancient threat from Shakespeare's evil Richard III: "I'll make a corpse of him that disobeys."[45]

It worked. And Americans for Prosperity is happy to claim credit. As its president, Tim Phillips, told the *National Journal*, according to author Jane Mayer, "If you look at where the situation was three years ago and where it is today, there's been a dramatic turnaround. . . . We've made great headway. What it means for candidates on the Republican side is, if you buy into green energy or you play footsie on this issue, you do so at your political peril. The vast majority of the people who are involved in the nominating process—the conventions and the primaries—are suspect of the science. And that's our influence. Groups like Americans for Prosperity have done it."[46]

The political primary process is key to understanding how Republicans in Congress are put in "political peril." If you look at who is scared of whom and who is angry at whom in Congress, you will see that most Democrats and Republicans (at least in the Senate) actually get along rather well. We're policy adversaries on many things, but we've been policy adversaries for decades. Democrat versus Republican is old news. It doesn't explain the new weirdness of Congress.

The new factor in this equation is the Tea Party. The real fear and the real anger around Congress, at least from my vantage point in the Senate, has been between the mainstream Republicans and the Tea Party extremists. Where do emotions run the highest? Where are the shouting matches? Where are insults hurled? Where are senators heckled by their colleagues? The worst of it is not between Democrat and Republican; it's between Tea Party Republican and mainstream Republican. Who is being told how they can and cannot vote and what they can and cannot say? Who is being bullied and punished when they don't follow the party line—the Tea Party line? Not Democrats. It is regular Republicans.

But I've got news. It's not the irrefutable logic of Tea Party argument that convinces regular Republicans. Logic is not the Tea Party's strong suit. It's not the clear grasp by the Tea Party of modern economic, cultural, and scientific realities that convinces regular Republicans. The Tea Party exists in an angry, white, elderly, predominantly southern bubble. Extremists everywhere share telltale clues: the phony facts they rely on, the conspiracy theories they believe, their scorn of compromise, their visceral anger and impatient simple-mindedness. They do not seek policy solutions, but instead relish the feverish role of aggrieved victims. They'd rather yell than listen. Anger is not a cure for ignorance, but extremism doesn't know that.

Extreme views are not a new thing in politics, not even in American politics. Ordinarily, though, the political system adapts: a coalition of grown-ups comes together and forms a working majority, the majority rules, and the cranky extremists hoot and holler and jump up and down in the back benches. So why is it in this particular era that Congress has not adapted? The problem of cranks and extremists in a legislative body isn't new with the Tea Party; it's as old as legislative bodies. Back in 1932 Duff Cooper wrote in his biography of Talleyrand that extremists "are the disease germs in the body politic. They can never create, but when the general health of the body is weak, they can bring destruction."[47] So why has a simple political solution to this recurring political problem eluded us in Congress?

The thing that scares regular Republicans about challenging the Tea Party is the big money—the big corporate money, the billionaire money—behind the Tea Party. The Tea Party would ordinarily be a fringe group of outliers in Congress, and a centrist governing coalition of regular Republicans and Democrats would ordinarily have emerged, except for the threat of massive *Citizens United* money.

A lot of the right-wing special-interest money has actually been spent against Republicans. Remember what my Republican friend said to me about the Koch brothers: "What are you complaining about? They're spending more against us than against you!" And when the Koch brothers' big money comes in and bombs you in a small Republican primary election, it's pretty scary. When the paid-for right-wing attack machine turns its chatter-guns on you in your Republican primary, that can be pretty scary.

The gridlock and silence we see on climate change are the result. Republicans won't work with Democrats on serious climate legislation, not because Democrats don't make sense, and not because most Republicans don't want to make sense, but because they're scared of Tea Party attacks funded by *Citizens United* money out of the fossil-fuel industry. That's how they became, in Peggy Noonan's great phrase, "the party of Donor's Policy Preferences."[48] Yes, some senators actually believe that climate change is a liberal fabrication, and some have state industries and state economies so dependent on fossil fuels that they have a real constituent problem if they try to address climate change. But that's not all of them. It's not even most of them.

Think of Republican senators in a corral, fenced in. Think of the fences as high and barbed. Think of gun towers at the corners, and signs on the fence warning "Political Peril." Imagine bullhorn-amplified voices warning, "Nobody leaves the corral. Try to leave and we're going to 'severely disadvantage' you!" That's not a bad analogy. There are mutinous rumblings in the corral—a lot of the inmates are restless. The corral is not a great place to be. Nobody likes to be threatened and bossed around. Nobody likes having to play the fool or cater to someone else's whims. Nobody likes having to go against what so many respected voices, and their own consciences and home state universities, are telling them. NASA is driving a rover around on Mars right now; when NASA warns us about climate change, most colleagues understand that these are scientists who know what they're talking about. But nobody wants to be the first one to take a run at the fence.

Take away *Citizens United*, and the fence loses its barbs. The fossil-fuel guns disappear from the guard tower. Maybe the fence just becomes a chalk line, and all the guards can do is blow whistles when you cross it. They may blow their whistles and be angry, but without *Citizens United*, they neither have the tools to do worse nor a credible threat to do worse.

Look again at Americans for Prosperity, the Koch brothers venture that openly threatened to take out pro-climate Republicans in the primaries and that so publicly threatened to spend $750 million in the 2016 elections. This is the group that rivals or exceeds the Republican National Committee. Small wonder that it is hard to have an honest conversation with Republicans about carbon pollution in the Senate when the anti-climate big spenders have more muscle come election time than their own political party.

Put simply, the U.S. Congress has lost the ability to address climate change in a bipartisan way because of the evils of the Supreme Court's *Citizens United* decision. And the fossil-fuel industry couldn't be happier. *Citizens United* allowed this bullying, wealthy special interest to quash real debate.

In the silence of regular Republican voices in Congress, the voices you hear are the extreme ones; the message you hear is denial. What do Republicans in Congress today have to say to our heirs, to our children and grandchildren, about the looming threat of climate change? "Catastrophic global warming is a hoax," says Republican senator James Inhofe of Oklahoma.[49] (He's so extreme, he's even listed as "extreme" in University of Oklahoma presentations by the state of Oklahoma's own climatologists.)[50] "It's not proven by any stretch of the imagination," says Republican senator Ron Johnson of Wisconsin.[51] He's so extreme, he's been called out by Wisconsin's largest newspaper, which noted that his practice of "stubbornly denying the facts on climate change may be akin to denying the facts on evolution or whether the Earth is flat."[52] "A lot of this is condescending elitism," says Republican senator Pat Roberts of Kansas, while Kansas State University researchers project the effect of climate change on Kansas wheat production as "pretty severe."[53] That's the captive voice of today's Republican Party.

According to one analysis, 56 percent of congressional Republicans in the 113th Congress have denied or questioned the overwhelming scientific consensus that the Earth's oceans and atmosphere are changing in unprecedented ways, driven by carbon pollution. This includes every single Republican member of the Senate Committee on Environment and Public Works.[54]

That is not the message from mainstream Republicans voters. Sixty-one percent of non–Tea Party Republicans say there is "solid evidence the earth is warming."[55] And a survey conducted for the League of Conservation Voters found that more than half of young Republican voters—53 percent of Republicans under the age of thirty-five—describe a politician who denies that climate change is happening as "ignorant," "out-of-touch," or "crazy."[56] Former Republican senator Judd Gregg of New Hampshire, who also served his state as governor, has warned of the political consequences in New Hampshire of ignoring climate change. "Anybody who says science doesn't support it is going to have a hard time making that case in New Hampshire," said Gregg, adding, "That's just not going to fly. Most Republicans in New Hampshire are very environmentally focused."[57]

On climate change, it's not so much Republican Party voters as it is Tea Party voters that are the deniers. Is there "solid evidence the earth is warming"? Only 25 percent of Tea Partiers say yes, while 61 percent of Republicans do—a thirty-six-point swing. And 41 percent of Tea Partiers assert that warming is "just not happening." Not "we don't have enough information yet"—it is "just not happening."[58]

"Just not happening"? Regardless of what you think causes climate change, there are independent measurements from all over the Earth that it is happening. This isn't a theory. We measure the rise in the temperature of the atmosphere and oceans. We measure the rate at which ice caps and glaciers are melting. We measure the rise of the seas. We measure the shifting of the very seasons. It is one thing to be the party that's against scientific modeling, but the Tea Partiers would turn the great and historic Republican Party into a party that is against measurement. The Tea Party wants to lead the Republican Party off the climate cliff. And *Citizens United* money gives them and their corporate industry backers the weaponry to do it. Without *Citizens United*, they would be a crank caucus that responsible members of both parties would simply ignore or work around.

For a country that prides itself on its democracy and offers its example of democracy to the world, this has ramifications beyond climate change.

CHAPTER TWELVE

America's Lamp in Peril

AMERICA HAS LONG STOOD BEFORE THE WORLD as an exceptional country, and deservedly so. We proved the case for popular sovereignty, with no need of kings or crowns. We rode our balanced market capitalism (and the safety of two oceans) to international economic dominance. We have long been the vanguard of civil and human rights for our people and for people around the globe. When we must use our military power, we don't conquer and rule, we come home. Where we have succeeded, we have left freedom in our wake.

Across our small globe dawn sweeps each morning, lighting cities and cottages, farms and barrios and villages. The poorest and most brutalized people can come out of their homes and huts and tenements into each new morning's sun and know from our American example that life does not have to be the way it now is for them. Each can know that an example of liberty and self-government stands free before them as a rebuke to the tyranny, corruption, and injustice they may suffer every day.

This exceptional nature of America confers upon us a responsibility. It also confers on us a gravitational power that allows us influence by our example. That power of example draws people to our country. It draws people to our ideals, and it draws people to free and democratic government. These are tidal forces, pulled by the gravity of our good example, and they have flooded in our favor for generations. They have helped make America "the essential nation." No edict makes that so. Generation by generation, Americans must earn that standing.

Years ago, Daniel Webster described the work of our American

Founders as having "set the world an example."[1] This was not a unique vision of America. From Jonathan Winthrop[2] to Ronald Reagan,[3] we have called ourselves "a city upon a hill," set high for the world to witness. From President John F. Kennedy[4] to President Obama,[5] inaugural addresses have noted that the glow of our ideals "light[s] the world." We Americans see our nation as a beacon of hope, as a light in the darkness. Our lamp is lifted up in welcome and in example. President Bill Clinton has argued that "people the world over have always been more impressed by the power of our example than the example of our power."[6]

Each American generation receives this precious inheritance from generations that fought, bled, and died to put it safely in our hands. When Daniel Webster said that our Founding Fathers had set the world an example, he went on to say this: "The last hopes of mankind, therefore, rest with us; and if it should be proclaimed, that our example had become an argument against the experiment, the knell of popular liberty would be sounded throughout the earth."[7]

It is not ordained that the rest of the world must be proud of us. We have to earn it by our example. In response to the damage done to America's image by the Wall Street bailout, Joseph Stiglitz, Nobel Prize–winning economist and former chief economist of the World Bank, wrote: "In the developing world people look at Washington and see a system of government that allowed Wall Street to write self-serving rules, which put at risk the entire global economy, and then when the day of reckoning came, Washington turned to those from Wall Street and their cronies to manage the recovery—in ways that gave Wall Street amounts of money that would be beyond the wildest dreams of the most corrupt in the developing world. They see corruption American-style as perhaps more sophisticated—bags of money don't change hands in dark corners—but just as nefarious."[8] And the Wall Street meltdown was a lesser day of reckoning than the climate crisis portends.

We are in a period of political crisis at home. It sounds harsh to say these things, but the truth is harsh: corporate money is calling the tune in Congress; Congress is unwilling or unable to stand up to corporate power (indeed, Congress is often its agent); and a massive propaganda effort is churning full steam to deny the facts of major policy issues wherever those facts are contrary to corporate interests. In Federalist No. 63, James Madison (or perhaps Alexander Hamilton; authorship is debated) warned of "moments in public affairs when the people . . . misled by the artful misrepresentations of interested men, may call for measures which they themselves will afterwards be the most ready to lament and condemn."[9] We are aswarm now in "artful misrepresentations" and "misled by interested men" gathered and organized in corporate form; the result has been both action and inaction that our descendants will surely "lament and condemn."

Lord Acton urged historians "to suffer no man and no cause to escape the undying penalty which history has the power to inflict on wrong."[10] Those dishonorable corporations and their allies will be judged harshly by history for what they are doing, as they infiltrate our democracy and exert their wicked influence. Their success, however, is also our failure—a failure to defend the American democracy that we inherited. That failure too will be judged harshly.

My father was a member of the Greatest Generation. He was a Marine in the Pacific Islands campaign in World War II. He lost his only brother in that war, a Navy fighter pilot killed over Legaspi in the Philippines. He dedicated the rest of his life to his country's service, serving in faraway places, often at great personal danger. His last task for his country was to come out of retirement to set up Special Operations Command in the Pentagon for President Reagan. He is representative of thousands and thousands of Americans who went in harm's way against the great Axis powers to protect democracy for us and for people all over the globe, and then went on to build the American Century. American cemeteries in Normandy and Manila tell mutely of that generation's willingness, their bravery, and their sacrifice. In light of that sacrifice, it does not seem too much to ask of this generation that we be willing to stand up to the "resolute enemy within our gates"[11] and win in our time the "trial of strength"[12] that Jefferson foretold.

If you believe that the world needs America, if you believe that America is to be the essential and exceptional nation, then it matters that we do right. It matters that we get these issues, such as climate change, right—even when the conflict pits "We the People" against mighty corporations. A world fouled and impoverished by carbon pollution will want to know why. We will be held to account: a democracy disabled by special interests, a democracy that knew what carbon pollution was doing to our atmosphere and our oceans but could not rouse itself to do what was required. Failing to lead at this moment of necessity will soon and long darken the lamp America holds up to the world, and it will make a powerful argument for our adversaries against our democratic experiment. We must not be the generation that failed at our duty. We can still leave an honorable legacy of our own, one that will echo down the corridors of history and justly earn the wholehearted admiration of future generations.

The historian David McCullough spoke recently to a group of us at the Library of Congress about John Adams and America's Founding generation. He reminded us that when those men pledged their lives, their fortunes, and their sacred honor to this cause, it was not mere words. When they signed the Declaration of Independence, he said, they were signing their own death warrants. Asked how they found the courage to do this, David McCullough explained, "It was a courageous time."[13]

It just takes courage to make this our own courageous time.

Postscript

THE 2016 CAMPAIGN IS OVER. This postscript looks back at the lessons for this book from a boisterous, bizarre, and joyless American election. The focus of the 2016 presidential campaign was on personalities, whether the relentless personal smearing of Hillary Clinton as "Crooked Hillary" who should be "locked up," or the boastful antics and crude personal behavior of Donald Trump. Behind the distracting dazzle of that contest of personalities, however, the constant, intrusive forces I describe in this book remained at play and often showed their heads. The media are easily distracted by a shiny object, and Donald Trump was the ultimate shiny object. As president, he will likely continue to occupy the center of the media's attention. That makes paying attention to these more silent and surreptitious forces all the more important.

One of the major topics of this book has been the underlying problem of secret and unlimited money in our politics. This problem persisted throughout the election, and in one important sense, it worsened: Democrats overcame their distaste for secret money and big donors. This allowed Democrats, particularly Secretary Clinton, to compete more effectively in the new, post–*Citizens United*, political bizarro-world the Supreme Court has made. As the *New York Times* reported, "Democrats have built the largest and best-coordinated apparatus of outside groups operating in the 2016 presidential campaign, defying expectations that conservative and corporate wealth would dominate the race."[1]

This otherwise bad news actually gives me some faint hope that with sufficient public pressure Congress may be able to drain the big-donor, "dark-money" swamp. I remember talking with a Republican colleague on the Senate floor as the 2016 political season was gearing up, seeking some bipartisan support for my campaign spending disclosure bill (requiring transparency for all political spending over $10,000, whether corporate, individual, or union) and telling him, "you guys have got to hate this, too. It's bad for everyone." He replied, "Yeah, but you Democrats have got to start raising some real money of your own this way. Then we might be able to get rid of the stuff. You can't expect us to give it up while so much of it is coming our way."

Well, it sure looks like we Democrats got into the big donor game in this election. In an article titled "How Democrats Stopped Worrying and Learned to Love Big Donor Money," Nicholas Confessore and Rachel Shorey reported that "just 250 donors have accounted for about $44 million in contributions to the Hillary Victory Fund," through a "legal end-run around contribution limits, allowing wealthy donors to give far more."[2] The device for that legal end-run was a one-stop-shopping campaign account that allowed big donors to consolidate into one check donations to Hillary Clinton's campaign and to all the Democratic state party committees around the country, many of which then cycled some or all of the funds back into the account, to go to key battleground states. The result "def[ied] expectations at the beginning of the campaign that Republicans would dominate the money chase."[3] And that didn't count super PACs or dark money.

On the super PAC front, big money continued to rule in 2016, as super PAC donations blew through the billion-dollar mark. And independence of the super PACs was a joke: as the *Washington Post* reported, "personalized super PACs became the norm in a presidential campaign, run by the candidates' close advisers."[4] Over half a billion dollars came in to the super PACs from just sixty-two individuals, corporations, and unions, with the big-money parade led by a few mega-donors.[5] As of the beginning of November, the top ten mega-donors had given a grand total of more than $300 million to super PACs; the number ten donor alone gave $17 million—a retire-in-style, won-the-lottery fortune for most Americans.[6] Put another way, if you had written million-dollar checks to sixteen of your favorite candidates' super PACs in the last election, you wouldn't even have made the Top 10 list! And this sum only counts the disclosed super PAC contributions, not the dark money.

A good deal of this Democratic funding reflected what the *New York Times* described as "Mrs. Clinton's close personal ties to her party's elite donors and her allies' willingness to exploit the 2010 ruling in the *Citizens United* case far more aggressively than President Obama did," but there's also a Trump factor.[7] His "provocations and tirades—along with a loud crusade against his own party's donors—have virtually shut off what once promised to be a half-billion-dollar spigot of outside money."[8] Democrats should not expect this big money shift to persist, however, and Republicans can read the same tea leaves.

All this big money on the Democratic side creates a slim opening for Republicans, without undue political sacrifice, to help us clear mega-donors and dark money out of politics. It was, after all, Republican Teddy Roosevelt who said, "If our political institutions were perfect, they would absolutely prevent the political domination of money in any part of our affairs."[9] Those who profit by the political domination of money in our affairs, however, will vigorously defend the present system. The ability to threaten and promise unlimited political spending is a massive political weapon in the hands of the corporate donor class, a weapon regular people don't enjoy. And the ability to do it anonymously makes it even more formidable.

The machinations to hide identities remained creepy. Here's one example, reported by BNA, Inc.'s *Money and Politics Report* (yes, political spending has gotten so weird there is such a thing): Republican Senate Leader Mitch McConnell has a super PAC called the Senate Leadership Fund. The Senate Leadership Fund shares an address with a 501(c)(4) organization called One Nation. They are run by the same person, who, by the way, also heads American Crossroads and Crossroads GPS, set up by Karl Rove. The 501(c)(4) hides donor identities, so someone gave $11 million to One Nation anonymously, One Nation gave $11 million to McConnell's Senate Leadership Fund, and the Fund spent the $11 million defending GOP Senate seats.[10] Don't tell me Mitch McConnell won't know who's behind the $11 million and all the other dark money that helped save his job as majority leader; we just won't.

Donald Trump's flamboyant personality became a media fixation, allowing Trump to jump the usual fundraising rails and provoke free media attention, where his rivals had to buy airtime for ads. But let's remember how this season started and how it ended. "The hunt for big dollars began in January 2015 outside Palm Springs at a luxury hillside resort," wrote *Washington Post* political correspondent Matea Gold. "There the emerging crop of Republican presidential candidates jockeyed to impress the millionaires and billionaires who make up the Koch political network."[11] Donald Trump ridiculed them as "puppets" of the Kochs and other big donors, and differentiated himself from the Republican pack right away. Sure enough, the other candidates' "all-consuming pursuit of mega-donors . . . drew them away from the campaign trail, leaving them vulnerable to the fiercely populist mood gripping voters—and to a candidate on the GOP side, Donald Trump, uniquely positioned to harness that anger."[12] Trump commanded enough media attention not to need the usual advertising barrage, and enough personal wealth to scorn the big donors for a while.

But at the end, he reverted to form, with "his own billionaire backers," and an "array of superPACs that cropped up to support his campaign."[13] As *The Guardian* reported, "Rich Republicans may have initially balked at Donald Trump, but pro-Trump billionaires [left] the sidelines in the last week of the election to dump cash directly into crucial counties and swing states."[14] The *Wall Street Journal* reported that five billionaires "poured at least $24 million into groups backing Donald Trump."[15] And after the election, the *New York Times* reported, "President-elect Donald J. Trump, who campaigned against the corrupt power of special interests, is filling his transition team with some of the very sort of people who he has complained have too much clout in Washington: corporate consultants and lobbyists."[16] Corporate money is relentless; money still matters, a lot; and the influencers are already crawling in.

One last secret-money consideration from the 2016 presidential scrum was a new rationale for secret political donations: embarrassment. Said one big fundraiser: "There is a substantial appetite for a non-disclosing vehicle [to give money through], because it's embarrassing to support Trump."[17] Indeed, this was the actual fundraising pitch of a pro-Trump super PAC.[18]

Whatever its reason, no good can come from secret money and unlimited money in our elections. It gives too much power to a donor class and the corporate political machine. It lets them hide their hands, and the result is that regular people lose out even more to the big influencers seeking control in our democracy.

Another focus of this book has been the relentless efforts at political manipulation by the Koch brothers on behalf of the fossil-fuel industry their corporation inhabits. One unexpected development in the 2016 race was the Koch brothers' political machine getting thrown off course by the Great Trump Disruption within the Republican Party, and turning its focus away from the presidential race to the 2016 Senate races. It was effective in inundating the Senate races with political spending, mostly on attack ads, limiting Democrats to two gained seats and no majority, in what had been a promising year to take five or more seats and regain a Democratic majority. The Republican Senate majority can be expected to be a bastion of corporate, billionaire influence after this dark-money, big-money deluge.

The Koch machine continued to grow and develop its database, expanding "the vast trove of voter information the Kochs are building. . . . Its database is a vault of voting records, consumer data, census information and social media profiles on more than 250 million adults."[19] (If you're worried about the government knowing too much about you, you might want to expand your orbit of concern.) The Koch machine continues to plan for the future. With the machine having time in this election cycle "to further build up its ground game and data operations" as the Kochs' distaste for Trump kept them largely out of the 2016 presidential race, "the Koch network leaders are focusing on 2020 and 2024."[20]

Secrecy remained the Kochs' political hallmark. "The Kochs have gone to great lengths over the years to conceal the nature of their vast political operations," *Newsweek* reported, and the Kochs' political network "is made up almost entirely of 501(c)(3) and 501(c)(4) nonprofit organizations that can accept unlimited funds and do not have to disclose their donors."[21] That won't change. And Republican bullying of the IRS to keep the agency ineffectual in enforcing the laws against dark money persisted. (Or, as Koch Companies' operative Phillip

Ellender calls enforcing the dark money laws, "targeting of non-profit organizations by the Internal Revenue Service (IRS) to limit free speech."[22] Yeah, right.)

Cut to Florida, where the Kochs were very active, with fourteen field offices in that one state (small wonder that Senator Rubio remains opposed to climate legislation even as his state sinks under sea level rise). The head of the Florida Chamber of Commerce has a close-up view there of the Kochs' methods and aspirations. "They've been very transparent about what they're trying to do," he said, "and I think a lot of people don't believe them. They want to replace political parties."[23]

The muscle and threats that are the Koch brothers' other hallmark also persisted. *USA Today* reported, "Conservative billionaire Charles Koch and his allies celebrated Republicans retaining their grip on Congress this week and signaled that his powerful political network plans to play a larger role in policy as the nation prepares for a GOP-controlled capital."[24] Move aside, Trump. In a rare public letter to his network, Koch touted wins by "pro-freedom" (pro-freedom-to-pollute is what that means) candidates in the Senate and voter anger about a "rigged economy" and urged that his orthodoxies offered "something to unite behind"; that it is his network that "offers that vision," not Donald Trump.[25]

USA Today reported that the Kochs' network "deployed big sums in Senate races" and racked up Republican wins in most targeted states. "In all, the network spent about $250 million on its political and policy programs this year, including $42.1 million in advertising to shape Senate contests in states. Activists and staffers knocked on four million doors, made 33 million calls and sent out 37 million pieces of mail to sway voters in key states. . . . The network regularly touts its standing force of 2.8 million activists who are willing to engage in policy fights even in non-election years."[26]

All that political muscle emboldens the Koch apparatus to make big threats. Koch network officials, *USA Today* reported, "will aggressively fight efforts in Washington to increase government spending, even if the push comes from the nation's most powerful Republican himself, President-elect Donald Trump."[27] James Davis is the spokesman for the Koch brothers' front group Freedom Partners Chamber of Commerce. As *USA Today* reported, "If senators veer 'off course,' Davis said, 'we can hold them accountable and turn up the heat from the people to change the policy.'"[28] It will get interesting if what the Kochs deem "off course" for senators they manipulate is actually something "on course" for President Trump: for instance, things he campaigned on such as infrastructure investments, paid family leave, and closing the carried interest tax loophole.

Another telling comment by a Koch operative helps clarify the control relationship between the Kochs' big money operation and the conservative base it supports and manages. The Kochs' lead front group is Americans for Prosperity. Its president, Tim Phillips, reflected in late 2016 on Donald Trump's success in engaging the Republican base voters' support for Medicare and Social Security (there are many signals that the Republican base's support for Medicare is strong, including anti-Obamacare protesters during the fights over that law telling us to "keep your government hands off our Medicare"). Phillips also spoke of Trump's success in animating the populist Republican voter's distaste for "free trade." Phillips was distressed, because antagonism to Medicare and Social Security and support for free trade are Koch political dogma. "Just when you think you've won an issue within the base, you realize no issue is really ever won," he said. "We thought it was settled orthodoxy; suddenly, it's not anymore."[29]

This is a candid admission that the Koch operation is out to drive its "orthodoxies" into the Republican base to suit the Kochs' agenda, rather than listening to and reflecting what working-class Republicans actually want. The Kochs manufacture and control a big-money, pro-polluter, "settled orthodoxy" to sell to the base like soap. Without Trump coming in and unsettling their orthodoxy, it probably would have worked. Now they may even have to fight President Trump, and they have signaled their willingness to do so.

The anguish of Republicans who expected a Trump defeat opened other telling glimpses of candor. A striking admission of how this big-money fixery works was written by *Business Insider*'s Josh Barro, a Republican who interned for Grover Norquist, worked at the conservative Manhattan Institute for Policy Research, and left the party in disgust over Trump. Just before the election, Barro wrote, "If [conservatives] look honestly enough, they will realize the conservative information sphere has long been full of lies. The reason for this is that lying has been the most effective way to promote many of the policies favored by donor-class conservatives, and so they built an apparatus to invent and spread the best lies."[30] Barro uses as one example that "wealthy conservatives favor lower taxes on themselves for the obvious reason," but since billionaires keeping more money and paying less taxes is, to put it mildly, "not a compelling electoral argument," they have "built a network of think tanks and magazines and pressure groups funded by wealthy donors whose job was to come up with arguments that would sell the donor-class agenda to the masses."[31] Similarly, conservative commentator and author Jamie Weinstein wrote on election day, "As for the Republican primary electorate, we learned that perhaps they don't care so much about conservative principles after all—that the conservative movement may be nothing more than a collection of magazine offices and think tanks in Manhattan and Washington, DC."[32] This collection, I would add, is funded, run, and controlled by big money, not by little voters, so pushing the big-money corporate agenda is easy to do. (Another glimpse of candor came from Romney chief campaign strategist Stuart Stevens, about the role of "angry rich media figures" such as Sean Hannity and Rush Limbaugh in selling nonsense to the Republican base: "they have made fortunes peddling bile and prejudice"; "even if they are wrong, there is a lot of money to be made denying reality."[33])

Much of the fodder that is fed to irate right-wingers by this apparatus is a corporate product designed to trick them. It's an ideological form of consumer fraud on the Republican voter. Other candidates sought the political blessing of the right-wing corporate intermediaries and the political backing of the big-money influencers behind them, and paid the price of signing on to their corporate, big-money agenda. Trump blew all this up by taking his message directly from what he heard in voters' anger, rather than joining in on the corporate intermediaries' plan to fool them. This disruption may explain much of the distaste for Trump in certain Republican establishment quarters, in particular from the Koch brothers.

Although Trump blew up the selfish "settled orthodoxy" the Koch political machine thought it had sold to Republican voters, the Kochs will assuredly be back, with billions in secret money to manipulate the public and press their pro-corporate agenda. The big, behind-the-scenes battle of the Trump presidency will be how—or whether—Trump fends off the billionaire agenda and what the terms are of any quiet reconciliation reached between him and the corporatist Kochs. Clearly, the Koch operation wants to stamp out the populist agenda of Donald Trump and restore the corporate "settled orthodoxy" he disrupted.

The player to watch in this battle is Vice President–elect Mike Pence. Early on in the election cycle, before he disqualified himself as a presidential candidate with his harsh stand against gay rights (before Donald Trump made harsh stands a new political art form), Pence was seen by many Republican colleagues in the Senate as the likeliest candidate to become their nominee, because he was so close to the Koch brothers and their dark money operation. Such is the power of the Kochs: as their guy, he was seen as the likely Republican nominee. He probably still is their guy, so President Trump and his voters need to watch Vice President Pence closely.

This book's point about the power of the fossil-fuel industry over the Republican Party became more and more evident through the election: "an overwhelming 91 percent of fossil fuel industry campaign donations now flow to Republican candidates," one report calculated.[34] The disclosed campaign contributions in this election cycle exceeded $37 million.[35] That does not even count super PAC or dark money. Oklahoma State University sociologist Riley Dunlap reported that the environmental voting record of the Republican Party in Congress has fallen to a nearly exact reciprocal of its fossil-fuel money share. Measured by the League of Conservation Voters' environmental votes tally, Democrats average about 90 percent, and Republicans have fallen into single digits.[36] For me, a senator from Rhode Island, which has a history of environmental Republicans such as Senator John Chafee and his son Lincoln, this is a harsh fact to have to report. The fossil-fuel industry has taken over and now occupies the Republican Party, much as that *Men in Black* alien dressed itself in the clothing and skin of the unfortunate farmer.

My point about this occupation of the party by fossil-fuel interests was underscored by President-elect Trump's appointment of militant climate denier Myron Ebell (who has cycled through several

Koch-funded front groups) to lead his EPA transition team. *Politico* reported that Ebell "has largely been an outside agitator attacking politicians who look like they may be going soft on environmental issues—especially Republicans."[37] Conservative economist Jerry Taylor, who worked with Ebell at the Koch-funded Cato Institute, writes that Ebell was involved in "building a skeptic movement and enforcing that political orthodoxy as best he could in the Republican Party."[38] What one environmentalist gave Ebell credit for was "taking the tobacco playbook and applying it to climate change."[39]

With Trump having reached his new, ill-considered, campaign conclusion that climate change is a "hoax," another Republican obstacle now exists to responsible climate policies. I say "new" because of the full-page ad he signed in the *New York Times* in 2009 calling for strong climate action. "We support your effort," the ad said to the Obama administration, "to ensure meaningful and effective measures to control climate change, an immediate challenge facing the United States and the world today. Please don't postpone the Earth. If we fail to act now, it is scientifically irrefutable that there will be catastrophic and irreversible consequences for humanity and our planet."[40] Signatories were Donald Trump, his son Donald Jr., his son Eric, and his daughter Ivanka. That was then.

We heard in 2016 the oil company CEOs' statements that climate change is real, that fossil fuels are causing most of it, and that they would support a carbon price as a remedy.[41] To be clear, all of that is window dressing. The CEOs may be wildly ignorant of their own lobbying operation, but all their lobbying muscle is still exerted to push Congress in the exact opposite direction. The fossil-fuel machine exerts its own lobbying force through groups such as the American Petroleum Institute, but it also controls the climate agenda of the big business lobbying organizations (notwithstanding the good climate positions of most of those organizations' members), so all that big business lobbying muscle gets added to the fossil-fuel industry's direct lobbying against any climate action. Unless and until the rest of America's corporate community takes an interest in Congress doing something on climate change (which now they do not, I know from firsthand experience[42]), the fossil-fuel machine will continue to bully Republicans, lie to the public, and shut down progress. With Republicans controlling the

House, Senate, and White House, the mainstream American corporate
community can no longer look to those institutions of government for
leadership. The corporate community will need to step up.

The best-case industry scenario is that the fossil-fuel industry
has been dragging its heels to put counterpressure against President
Obama's climate program, and to gain time to figure out how to address the clean power revolution quaking the energy industry, all the
while knowing and accepting that progress was being made and actually needed to be made. In effect, they were braking the carriage so it
didn't careen downhill, but they didn't want the carriage to come to a
halt. The best-case political scenario is that Republican opposition to
clean power and to Obama worked for them politically and kept their
fossil-fuel money flowing. But it worked politically so long as progress
was actually being made anyway—so long as the carriage was moving.
If the carriage were actually to grind to a halt, a whole new array of
forces and consequences could emerge.

Now that Republicans own accountability for what happens and
know they will pay the price of America failing at this, they may decide
they have to figure something out. The Republican Party is nowadays
by its nature happier as an opposition party: complaining rather than
governing, criticizing rather than compromising, and scorning rather
than working. Once you've got all the elements of government under
your control, however, there's no refuge left in complaining, criticizing, and scorning.

It's a hell of a dangerous bet for them and for the industry that
funds them to actually halt the carriage on climate; it's much safer to
drag their heels and complain as the carriage moves. If the fossil-fuel
industry and the Republicans come to this realization, we can do great
things and they will be surprise heroes. Or they can drive us off the
climate cliff. And own that.

This book lays out how the Supreme Court conservative bloc has become a vital political tool for Republican and corporatist forces. This
point was confirmed by the end-of-campaign comments from some
Republican senators that they thought the Senate should block any
Supreme Court appointees of President Hillary Clinton, for her whole
term, if necessary. Political control of the institution is so important to

them that they'd rather break the Court than lose control of it.[43] With control of the presidency and the Senate now in Republican hands, it will be up to the Court itself to assert its independence from the forces that secure conservative justices' nominations, and from the crowded array of corporate-funded courtier groups that pile together to signal the corporate agenda to the conservatives. The decision to step free from their influence is a decision that cannot be made by all the members of the Court. It will take the conservative justices themselves to break the link I have described between their decisions and the wishes of the corporate establishment. It is out of anyone else's hands now. History will be watching. I'm sorry to be pessimistic, but I suspect they'll keep dancing with the guys that brung them.

My point that the tentacles of corporate power reach into government in ways we don't expect was demonstrated by recent reporting about political influence being exerted down into the offices of secretaries of state, the officials who ordinarily manage the election apparatus in the states. You may not even know who your secretary of state is, but they do. As the *New York Times* disclosed, "the targeting of secretaries of state with campaign donations, corporate-funded weekend outings and secret meetings with industry lobbyists reflects an intense focus on often overlooked ballot questions, which the secretaries frequently help write."[44] If corporate forces can get a local secretary of state to put the fix in on the language of a ballot referendum, they can limit the voter's options before he or she ever gets the chance to vote. They win the battle before it even starts. It is just one more example of the ardent pursuit by corporatist forces, at least those that have chosen political influence as a profit-making enterprise, to find new, clever, quiet ways to exert that political influence.

The ultimate goal I have in this book is that you, the reader, consider what role our Founders expected corporations to have in the political operation of our American democracy (no political role at all, I believe); and that you consider the astounding number of ways corporate influence exerts itself today. I say again: it is not always corporations themselves that do this directly. It can be corporate billionaires, or the foundations and front groups they have thrown up to do their dirty work, or the big business lobbies they direct and control. But the corporate political machinery is infiltrating everywhere.

Corporate dark money and corporate billionaire big money dominate our election spending. Behind all that actual corporate political spending lurks its shadow twin: the quiet, private threat or promise to engage in massive election spending. Reported corporate lobbying of Congress dominates by thirty to one all other lobbying of Congress combined. Corporate control and manipulation of regulatory agencies is so pervasive that it has coined the term "regulatory capture." The corporate alternate-reality machine is up and running, prepared to react with calculated misinformation and denial whenever science begins to warn of a danger associated with a profitable corporate product. Its phony alt-science then gets propagated by an array of corporate right-wing media outlets. Corporate power captured the Supreme Court, lost that majority control with Justice Scalia's death, freaked out and caused the Senate to disrupt constitutional norms by refusing to give even a hearing to the sitting president's nominee, and now looks ready (with a sigh of corporate relief) to recapture the Court. The Supreme Court's conservative majority has obediently repaid the corporate powers by changing the basic operating systems of our democracy in ways that consistently give big corporate powers even more power in our process of government, rewiring our democracy to corporate advantage. Corporate power even seeks to crush a constitutional element of our government: the civil jury, which is (not coincidentally) the one element designed to protect us against concentrations of private wealth and power.

We can be dazzled by the outlandish behavior of candidates, or distracted by the personal smears and character assassination that pervade our politics, and never notice the real danger to the republic: the quiet infiltration throughout our government of corporate forces. These forces are only too pleased for us to look elsewhere. They don't want to be the center of attention, and an election that became a soap-opera slugfest was a dazzling distraction. But they are infiltrating everywhere, their tentacles constantly creeping and grasping. They often have virtually unlimited money and usually enjoy the remorseless staying power that comes from this effort being a profitable exercise. They seek power, and they seek power over us. Their behavior on climate change, civil juries, and election corruption shows they are willing to drag America down as long as it helps them get their way. We'd be fools to be distracted by all the dazzle and not see the real menace.

So please, let's wake up and get off the couch. There are plenty of groups out there that want your participation. There are plenty of issues out there that need your voice. There are plenty of tentacles creeping around that need to be spotlighted and driven out. Find the ones that move you, and engage.

Sheldon Whitehouse, Newport, Rhode Island
November 17, 2016

Notes

Introduction

1. William S. White, *Citadel: The Story of the U.S. Senate* (New York: Harper, 1957), 135.

2. "Satisfaction with the United States," Gallup, February 3–7, 2016, www.gallup.com/poll/1669/general-mood-country.aspx.

3. Abraham Lincoln, "Gettysburg Address," November 19, 1863, http://avalon.law.yale.edu/19th_century/gettyb.asp.

4. Lee Drutman, "How Corporate Lobbyists Conquered American Democracy," *The Atlantic*, April 20, 2015.

5. James Madison, *The Debates in the Several State Conventions of the Adoption of the Federal Constitution*, ed. Jonathan Elliot (Virginia: Collected and revised from contemporary publishers, 1836), 3:87.

Chapter One: The Constitution's Blind Spot

1. "Declaration of Independence," www.archives.gov/exhibits/charters/declaration_transcript.html.

2. Naomi Lamoreaux and William J. Novak, "Corporations and American Democracy: An Introduction," in *Corporations and American Democracy*, ed. Naomi Lamoreaux and William J. Novak (Harvard University Press, forthcoming: 2017), available at http://tobinproject.org/books-papers/corporations-american-democracy.

3. 1 *Fletcher Cyc. Corp.* § 2, n. 12.

4. *Encyclopaedia Britannica Online*, s.v. "Massachusetts Bay Colony."

5. Horace Walpole, quoted in William Dalrymple, "The East Indian Company: The Original Corporate Raiders," *The Guardian*, March 4, 2015.

6. John Francis, "Chronicles and Characters of the Stock Exchange" (London: Willoughby, 1849), reprinted in *The Church of England, Quarterly Review* 27 (1850): 142.

7. *Journals of the House of Commons, Volumes 18–34* (reprint; London, 1805), 110.

8. *Encyclopedia Britannica,* s.v. "Bank of the United States."

9. *The Federalist Papers,* www.congress.gov/resources/display/content/The +Federalist+Papers.

10. James Madison, "Detached Memoranda," ca. 1817, http://press-pubs.uchi cago.edu/founders/documents/amendI_religions64.html.

11. Thomas Jefferson, letter to George Logan, November 12, 1816, http://tjrs .monticello.org/letter/1392.

12. Eric Hilt, "Early American Corporations and the State," in *Corporations and American Democracy,* ed. Naomi Lamoreaux and William J. Novak (Harvard University Press, forthcoming: 2017), 5–6, available at http://tobinproject.org /books-papers/corporations-american-democracy.

13. Ibid.

14. *Citizens United v. FEC,* 558 U.S. 310, 430 (2010) (Stevens, J., dissenting).

15. Ibid., 479 (Stevens, J., dissenting).

16. Rick Unger, "The Founding Fathers and Occupy Wall Street," *Washington Monthly,* October 28, 2011.

17. William Novak, email message to the author, March 9, 2016.

18. See Robert C. Hinkley, "How Corporate Law Inhibits Social Responsibility," *CommonDreams,* January 29, 2002.

19. *In re Indiana Brewing Co.'s License,* 75 A. 29, 30.

20. *Peasley v. Producers' Market Co.,* 261 P. 733, 736 (1927).

21. *Hannibal Inv. Co. v. Schmidt,* 113 S.W.2d 1048, 1052 (Mo. App. 1938).

22. 1 *Fletcher Cyc. Corp.* § 7.

23. Lee R. Raymond, quoted in Steve Coll, *Private Empire: ExxonMobil and American Power* (New York: Penguin, 2012), 71.

24. 1 *Fletcher Cyc. Corp.* § 6, citing *Gast Monuments, Inc. v. Rosehill Cemetery Co.,* 207 Ill. App. 3d 901 (1st Dist. 1990).

25. 18 C.J.S. Corporations § 2, "Corporation as person" (2015), citing *Matter of Estate of Cooper,* 1992 OK CIV APP 90, 838 P.2d 40 (Ct. App. Div. 2 1992).

26. Jesse Unruh, quoted in Mark A. Uhlig, "Jesse Unruh, A California Political Power, Dies," *New York Times,* August 6, 1987.

27. *Bank of the United States v. Deveaux,* 9 U.S. 61, 86 (1809), cited in "Brief of Amici Curiae Historians and Legal Scholars Supporting Neither Party," Jonathan Massey, in the Supreme Court of the United States in *Hobby Lobby,* January 28, 2014.

28. Burt Neuborne, *Madison's Music: On Reading the First Amendment* (New York: The New Press, 2015), 70.

29. *Citizens United,* 558 U.S. at 465–6 (Stevens, J., dissenting).

30. Ibid.

31. *The Voice of Madison* (from "The Nationalist," Boston, August 1889), www .slp.org/pdf/de_leon/eds1889/1889_aug.pdf.

32. See David Michaels, *Doubt Is Their Product: How Industry's Assault on Science Threatens Your Health* (New York: Oxford University Press, 2006).

33. Catherine Greene, "Consumer Demand Bolstering Organic Production and Markets in the U.S.," *USDA Blog*, February 26, 2016.

34. Franklin Roosevelt's Address at Madison Square Garden, New York City, October 31, 1936, American Presidency Project, www.presidency.ucsb.edu/ws/?pid =15219.

35. Franklin Delano Roosevelt, "Acceptance Speech for the Re-nomination for the Presidency," June 27, 1936, American Presidency Project, www.presidency .ucsb.edu/ws/?pid=15314.

36. Franklin Roosevelt's Address at Madison Square Garden.

37. This language appears in Theodore Roosevelt's Progressive Party Platform of 1912, available at www.pbs.org/wgbh/americanexperience/features/primary -resources/tr-progressive.

38. Theodore Roosevelt, speech delivered at Osawatomic, KS, August 31, 1910, www.whitehouse.gov/blog/2011/12/06/archives-president-teddy-roosevelts-new-na tionalism-speech.

39. Ibid.

Chapter Two: The Growth of Corporate Power

1. "What Is the Greatest Collaboration of All Time?" *The Atlantic*, Jan./Feb. 2016.

2. 1 *Fletcher Cyc. Corp.* § 1.

3. Ibid.

4. Ibid.

5. 1 *Fletcher Cyc. Corp.* § 2.

6. *Trustees of Dartmouth College v. Woodward*, 17 U.S. 518 (1819).

7. Ibid., 636.

8. *Bank of the United States v. Deveaux*, 9 U.S. 61, 88 (1809).

9. *People v. Knapp*, 206 N.Y. 373, 381 (N.Y. 1912).

10. *Matter of American Fibre Chair Seat Corporation*, 265 N.Y. 416, 420 (N.Y. 1934).

11. *Fairhope Single Tax Corporation v. Melville*, 69 South. 466, 471 (1915).

12. *Dartmouth College*, 17 U.S. at 650.

13. "Appendix: Speech of Charles J. Ingersoll," *United States Democratic Review* 5, no. 13 (January 1839): 99–144.

14. Eric Hilt, "Early American Corporations and the State," in *Corporations and American Democracy*, ed. Naomi Lamoreaux and William J. Novak (Harvard University Press, forthcoming: 2017), available at http://tobinproject.org/books-pa pers/corporations-american-democracy, 25–26.

15. "Appendix: Speech of Charles J. Ingersoll."

16. Thomas Jefferson, letter to George Logan, November 12, 1816, http://tjrs .monticello.org/letter/1392.

17. Charles Perrow, *Organizing America: Wealth, Power, and the Origins of Corporate Capitalism* (Princeton, NJ: Princeton University Press, 2001), 217.

18. Jessica Hennessey and John Wallis, "Corporations and Organizations in the U S After 1840," in *Corporations and American Democracy*, 23.

19. Perrow, *Organizing America*, 217.

20. Hennessey and Wallis, "Corporations and Organizations in the U.S. After 1840," 2.

21. Hilt, "Early American Corporations and the State," 5.

22. H.W. Brands, *American Colossus: The Triumph of Capitalism (1865–1900)* (New York: Anchor Doubleday, 2011), 7.

23. Daniel A. Crane, "The Dissociation of Corporation and Regulation in the Progressive Era and the New Deal," in *Corporations and American Democracy*, 3.

24. Robert C. Post, *Citizens Divided: Campaign Finance Reform and the Constitution* (Cambridge, MA: Harvard University Press, 2014), 28.

25. Doris Kearns Goodwin, *The Bully Pulpit: Theodore Roosevelt, William Howard Taft, and the Golden Age of Journalism* (New York: Simon & Schuster, 2013), 324.

26. Ibid., 338.

27. William J. Novak, "A Revisionist History of Regulatory Capture," in *Preventing Regulatory Capture: Special Interest Influence and How to Limit It*, ed. Daniel Carpenter and David Moss (New York: Cambridge University Press, 2014), 41 (italics added).

28. 1 *Fletcher Cyc. Corp.* § 2.

29. Ibid.

30. *Del Monte Light and Power Co. v. Jordan*, 196 Cal. 488, 495 (Cal. 1925).

31. 1 *Fletcher Cyc. Corp.* § 2.

32. *Louis K. Liggett Co. v. Lee*, 288 U.S. 517, 555 (1933) (Brandeis, J., dissenting).

33. Ibid., 557.

34. Crane, "Dissociation," 4.

35. Ibid.

36. Ibid.

37. *Standard Oil Company of New Jersey v. United States*, 221 U.S. 1, 83 (1901) (Harlan, J., concurring in part and dissenting in part).

38. *Louis K. Liggett Co. v. Lee*, 288 U.S. 517, 549 (1933) (Brandeis, J., dissenting).

39. Crane, "Dissociation," 4, citing Thomas Cooley, *A Treatise on the Constitutional Limitations Which Rest upon the Legislative Power of the United States of the American Union*, 279 n. 2 (3rd ed., 1874).

40. Jacob S. Hacker and Paul Pierson, *Winner-Take-All Politics: How Washington Made the Rich Richer and Turned Its Back on the Middle Class* (New York: Simon & Schuster, 2011), 79.

41. Charles Francis Adams Jr., "The Railroad System," 427, cited in Novak, "Revisionist History."

42. Larry Lessig, *Republic, Lost: How Money Corrupts Congress—and a Plan to Stop It* (New York: Twelve Books, 2011), 5.

43. Goodwin, *Bully Pulpit*, 372.

44. Post, *Citizens Divided*, 28.

45. Goodwin, *Bully Pulpit*, 467.

46. Grover Cleveland, State of the Union address, 1888, American Presidency Project, www.presidency.ucsb.edu/ws/index.php?pid=29529.

47. Adam Winkler, "*Citizens United*, Personhood, and the Corporation in Politics," *Corporations and American Democracy* (Cambridge, MA: Harvard University Press, forthcoming), 7–8.

48. Ibid., 8.

49. Post, *Citizens Divided*, 28, quoting Elihu Root.

50. Ibid.

51. Zephyr Teachout, *Corruption in America* (Cambridge, MA: Harvard University Press, 2014), 181.

52. Ibid., 182.

53. Theodore Roosevelt, speech delivered at the dedication of the John Brown Memorial Park in Osawatomie, Kansas, August 31, 1910, www.whitehouse.gov /blog/2011/12/06/archives-president-teddy-roosevelts-new-nationalism-speech.

54. Post, *Citizens Divided*, 28–29.

55. Theodore Roosevelt, "Nationalism and Popular Rule," *The Outlook*, January 21, 1911, 96, available at http://www.unz.org/Pub/Outlook-1911jan21-00096.

56. A Charter of Democracy speech before the Ohio Constitutional Convention, February 1912, Theodore Roosevelt Collection, MS Am 1454.50 (139), Harvard College Library, www.theodorerooseveltcenter.org/Research/Digital-Library /Record.aspx?libID=0285145.

57. Goodwin, *Bully Pulpit*, 298, quoting Mark Sullivan.

58. Theodore Roosevelt, speech on August 31, 1910.

59. Theodore Roosevelt, State of the Union address, December 3, 1906, www .let.rug.nl/usa/presidents/theodore-roosevelt/state-of-the-union-1906.php.

60 Trevor Potter, "Introduction," January 21, 2016, www.brookings.edu/wp-con tent/uploads/2016/01/20160121_campaign_finance_summit_transcript.pdf.

61. Franklin Delano Roosevelt, "Acceptance Speech for the Re-nomination for the Presidency," June 27, 1936, American Presidency Project, www.presidency .ucsb.edu/ws/?pid=15314.

62. "The Annual Message of the President Transmitted to Congress, December 3, 1907," *Papers Relating to the Foreign Relations of the United States*, congressional ed. (Washington, DC: Government Printing Office, 1910), vol. 5270, issue 1, ix.

63. S. Rep. No. 3056, 59th Cong., 1st Sess., 2 (1906), cited in *Citizens United v. Fed. Election Comm'n*, 558 U.S. 310, 433 (2010) (Stevens, J., dissenting).

64. Teachout, *Corruption*, 188.

65. Post, *Citizens Divided*, 28–29.

Chapter Three: Where We Are Now

1. Zephyr Teachout, *Corruption in America* (Cambridge, MA: Harvard University Press, 2014), 311–12.

2. Federal Election Commission, "The Federal Election Campaign Laws: A Short History," www.fec.gov/info/appfour.htm.

3. Teachout, *Corruption*, 206–7.

4. Lee Drutman, *The Business of America Is Lobbying: How Corporations Became Politicized and Politics Became More Corporate* (New York: Oxford University Press, 2015), 3.

5. Lewis F. Powell Jr., "Confidential Memorandum: Attack on American Free Enterprise System," August 23, 1971, available at http://law2.wlu.edu/deplimages/Powell%20Archives/PowellMemorandumTypescript.pdf.

6. Elizabeth Drew, *Citizen McCain* (New York: Simon & Schuster, 2002), 13.

7. Ibid., 3.

8. Ibid., 34.

9. David Rothkopf, *Power, Inc.: The Epic Rivalry Between Big Business and Government—and the Reckoning That Lies Ahead* (New York: Farrar, Straus, & Giroux, 2013), 201.

10. Ibid.

11. Ibid., 311.

12. Ibid.

13. James Kirkup, "Sony vs North Korea: Some Companies Are Bigger than Countries. So What?" *The Telegraph*, December 18, 2014.

14. Rothkopf, *Power Inc.*, 314.

15. Ibid., 315.

16. "Super PACs, Nonprofits Favored Romney over Obama: Citizens United Decision Helped Romney Neutralize Obama's Fundraising Advantage," Center for Responsive Politics, October 30, 2012

17. Ibid.

18. Michael Beckel and Russ Choma, "Super PACs, Nonprofits Favored Romney over Obama," Center for Responsive Politics, October 30, 2012.

19. Nicholas Confessore, "Koch Brothers' Budget of $889 Million for 2016 Is on Par with Both Parties' Spending," *New York Times*, January 26, 2015.

20. Michael Beckel, "Super PAC Doppelgangers Eclipse Candidates in Campaign Money Chase," Center for Public Integrity, August 1, 2015.

21. Kenneth Vogel, "Democrats Win PACs, Lose Money War," *Politico*, December 6, 2014.

22. Kenneth Vogel, "Koch brothers' Americans for Prosperity plans $125 million spending spree," *Politico*, May 9, 2014.

23. Rebecca Ballhaus, "Koch Brothers Nonprofits' Spending Surged in 2014," *Wall Street Journal*, November 18, 2015.

24. "Koch Industries," Center for Responsive Politics, www.opensecrets.org/lobby/clientsum.php?id=D000000186.

25. Confessore, "Koch Brothers' Budget."

26. Nicholas Confessore, "Koch Political Group Spent $400 Million in 2015, Officials Say," *New York Times*, January 31, 2016.

27. Kenneth P. Vogel, "How the Koch Network Rivals the GOP," *Politico*, December 30, 2015.

28. Riley E. Dunlap, Aaron M. McCright, and Jerrod H. Yarosh, "The Political

NOTES   211

Divide on Climate Change: Partisan Polarization Widens in the U.S.," *Environment* 58 no. 5.

29. Mike Allen and Kenneth P. Vogel, "Inside the Koch Data Mine," *Politico*, December 8, 2014; Kenneth P. Vogel, "The Koch Intelligence Agency," *Politico*, November 18, 2015.

30. Kenneth P. Vogel, "How the Kochs Launched Joni Ernst," *Politico*, November 12, 2015.

31. Claire Moser and Matt Lee-Ashley, "The Fossil-Fuel Industry Spent Big to Set the Anti-Environment Agenda of the Next Congress," Center for American Progress, December 22, 2014.

32. Ibid.

33. Nicholas Confessore, "Charles Koch Defends Big-Money Campaign Contributions," *New York Times*, November 3, 2015.

34. Zephyr Teachout, *Corruption in America: From Benjamin Franklin's Snuff Box to Citizens United* (Cambridge, MA: Harvard University Press, 2014), 246.

35. Lee Drutman, "How Corporate Lobbyists Conquered American Democracy," *The Atlantic*, April 20, 2015. For those interested further I recommend Lee Drutman's excellent *The Business of America Is Lobbying: How Corporations Became Politicized and Politics Became More Corporate* (New York: Oxford University Press, 2015).

36. "Money in Politics Factsheet," Issue One, www.issueone.org/wp-content/uploads/2016/03/gee-whiz-factsheet-sources.pdf.

37. Ibid.

38. "Contribution Limits for 2009–2010," Federal Election Commission, www.fec.gov/info/contriblimits0910.pdf.

39. "The Soaring Price of Political Access," editorial, *New York Times*, September 26, 2015, citing Matea Gold and Tom Hamburger, "Political Parties Go After Million-Dollar Donors in Wake of Looser Rules," *Washington Post*, September 19, 2015.

40. Peter Olsen-Phillips, Russ Choma, Sarah Bryner, and Doug Weber, "The Political One Percent of the One Percent in 2014: Mega Donors Fuel Rising Cost of Elections," Center for Responsive Politics, April 30, 2015.

41. Kenneth P. Vogel and Isaac Arnsdorf, "The Politico 100: Billionaires Dominate 2016," *Politico*, February 8, 2016.

42. "The Soaring Price of Political Access."

43. Nicholas Confessore, Sarah Cohen, and Karen Yourish, "The Families Funding the 2016 Presidential Election," *New York Times*, October 10, 2015.

44. "The Legacy of 'Citizens United' Strays from the Supreme Court's Vision," editorial, *Washington Post*, January 20, 2015.

45. "Policy Basics: Where Do Federal Tax Revenues Come From?", Center on Budget and Policy Priorities, http://www.cbpp.org/research/policy-basics-where-do-federal-tax-revenues-come-from.

46. Ibid.

47. Editorial, "Apple, Congress and the Missing Taxes," *New York Times*, August 30, 2016.

48. Mike McIntire and Nicholas Confessore, "Tax-Exempt Groups Shield Political Gifts of Businesses," *New York Times*, July 7, 2012.

49. Kennedy Elliot, Matea Gold, and Tim Farnam, "Dark Money in the Midterm Elections," *Washington Post*, November 29, 2014.

50. "Money in Politics Factsheet."

51. Paul Blumenthal, "Yes, Citizens United And Other Court Rulings Led To A Rise In Dark Money," *Huffington Post*, August 26, 2016.

52. Ibid.

53. "Why Senator McConnell Is So Nervous," editorial, *New York Times*, July 7, 2012.

54. Anna Palmer and Abby Phillip, "Corporations Not Funding Super PACS," *Politico*, March 8, 2012.

55. Burt Neuborne, *Madison's Music: On Reading the First Amendment* (New York: The New Press, 2015), 22.

56. Rebecca Ballhaus, "New Path for Masking Super PAC Donors," *Wall Street Journal*, February 3, 2016.

57. Joe Hagan, "The Coming Tsunami of Slime," *New York Magazine*, January 22, 2012.

58. "Presidential Ads 70% Negative in 2012, Up from 9% in 2008," Wesleyan Media Project Advertising Analysis press release, May 2, 2012, http://mediaproject.wesleyan.edu/releases/jump-in-negativity-2.

59. E.J. Dionne Jr., "'Citizens United' Is Turning More Americans into Bystanders," *Washington Post*, October 12, 2014.

60. Alex Seitz-Wald, "Huckabee: Super PACs Are 'One of the Worst Things That Ever Happened in American Politics,'" *ThinkProgress*, January 3, 2012.

61. "Annenberg Public Policy Center Calculates Dollars Spent by Third-Party Groups on Deceptive TV Ads Attacking or Supporting the Presidential Candidates," Annenberg Public Policy Center, University of Pennsylvania, September 25, 2012.

62. Benjamin H. Barton, "An Empirical Study of Supreme Court Justice Pre-Appointment Experience," *Florida Law Review* 64 (2012): 1155.

63. Jonathan Weisman, "Tax-Exempt Group's Election Activity Highlights Limits of Campaign Finance Rules," *New York Times*, July 16, 2012.

64. Peter Overby and Andrea Seabrook, "Question Marks Surround Key Election Advertiser," *All Things Considered*, NPR, October 27, 2010.

65. "Hit And Run: How One Supposed Non-Profit Spent Millions On Campaign Ads, Broke The Law, Then Disappeared," *Center for Responsibility and Ethics in Washington*, July 17, 2012, available at http://s3.amazonaws.com/storage.citizensforethics.org/wp-content/uploads/2016/07/20022714/CHGO%20Final%20Report%207%2013%2012.pdf.

66. Weisman, "Tax-Exempt."

67. Trip Gabriel and Ashley Parker, "Republican 'Super PACs' Turn to TV Ads for High-Stakes Primaries," *New York Times*, September 24, 2015.

68. Ibid.

69. Ibid.

70. Ibid.

71. Eric Lichtblau, "Reclusive Media Mogul Stands Firmly in Carly Fiorina's Corner," *New York Times*, October, 8, 2015.

72. Beth Rienhard, "Hank Greenberg Gives $10 Million to Super PAC Backing Jeb Bush," *Wall Street Journal*, January 7, 2016.

73. Julie Bykowicz and Jack Gillum, "Data: Nearly 5 Dozen Give a Third of All '16 Campaign Cash," Associated Press, August 1, 2015.

74. Ibid.

75. Ibid.

76. See *Citizens United*, 558 U.S. at 360.

77. Beth Reinhard and Christopher S. Stewart, "Some Candidates, Super PACs Draw Closer," *Wall Street Journal*, October 25, 2015.

78. Nick Gass, "Jeb Bush Recounts Conversation with Mitt Romney," *Politico*, January 5, 2016.

79. Seth McLaughlin, "Candidates' Super PAC Footage Tests Spirit of Campaign Finance Laws," *Washington Times*, September 21, 2015.

80. Reinhard and Stewart, "Some Candidates."

81. Ibid.

82. Nick Corasaniti, "Carly Fiorina's 'Super PAC' Aids Her Campaign, in Plain Sight," *New York Times*, September 30, 2015.

83. Eric Lichtblau, "Reclusive Media Mogul Stands Firmly in Carly Fiorina's Corner," *New York Times*, October, 8, 2015.

84. Corasaniti, "Carly Fiorina's 'Super PAC.'"

85. Ibid.

86. Julie Bykowicz, "Rubio's Presidential Bid Boosted by Secret-Money Commercials," Associated Press, October 8, 2015.

87. Ibid.

88. Jonathan Martin and Nicholas Confessore, "Nonprofit Masks Source of Ads Backing Rubio," *New York Times*, October 11, 2015.

89. Ibid.

90. Ibid.

91. Ibid.

92. Ibid.

93. Ibid.

94. Bykowicz and Gillum, "Data."

95. Trevor Potter, "A Republic If You Can Keep It," presented July 4, 2016, to The Chautauqua Institution, http://www.campaignlegalcenter.org/sites/default/files/Chautauqua%202016%20Final.pdf.

96. Marc Caputo and Kenneth P. Vogel, "Pro-Rubio super PAC raised $14.4 million in second half of 2015," *Politico*, January 31, 2016; Will Tucker, "Super PACs allow Wall Street to dominate presidential giving in 2015," OpenSecrets .org, February 2, 2016.

97. Josh Barro, "Rubio's Call for No Capital Gains Tax Is a Break with the G.O.P.," *New York Times*, February 4, 2016.

98. Ben Jacobs and David Smith, "'Politics Are Corrupt': Fears About Money and Its Influence on Elections Loom Large," *The Guardian*, July 8, 2016.

99. Kenneth P. Vogel, "The Koch ATM," *Politico*, November 17, 2015.

100. Brendan Fischer, "Kochs' Freedom Partners Spent $129M in 2014, Invested Massively in Voter Data Lists," *PR Watch*, Center for Media and Democracy, November 18, 2015.

101. "Trees of Liberty," Conservative Transparency, accessed January 4, 2016, http://conservativetransparency.org/org/trees-of-liberty.

102. Vogel, "Koch ATM."

103. Vogel, "How the Kochs Launched."

104. Vogel, "Koch ATM."

105. Vogel, "How the Kochs Launched."

106. Ibid.

107. Vogel, "Koch ATM."

108. Vogel, "How the Kochs Launched."

109. Matea Gold and Anu Narayanswamy, "How 'Ghost Corporations' Are Funding the 2016 Election," *Washington Post*, March 28, 2016.

110. Alex Isenstadt and Kenneth P. Vogel, "Trump blesses major super PAC effort," *Politico*, July 20, 2016.

111. Shane Goldmacher, "Trump's economic advisors are also his biggest donors," *Politico*, August 7, 2016.

112. Ibid.

113. Ibid.

114. Peggy Noonan, "America Is So in Play," *Wall Street Journal*, August 27, 2015 (80 percent of Americans think the system is rigged for the wealthy); "Super PACs Having Negative Impact, Say Voters Aware of 'Citizens United' Ruling," Pew Research Center, January 17, 2012 (60 percent of Republicans, 63 percent of Democrats, and 67 percent of independents who had heard of the decision believed *Citizens United* had a negative effect on the campaigns); "Bloomberg Politics National Poll," *Bloomberg BusinessWeek*, September 18–21, 2015 (78 percent of voters say *Citizens United* should be overturned and 87 percent say campaign finance rules should be reformed so the rich don't outinfluence the poor); "National Survey: Super PACs, Corruption, and Democracy," Brennan Center for Justice, April 24, 2012 (one in four Americans less likely to vote because super PACs have so much influence).

115. Martin Gilens and Benjamin I. Page, "Testing Theories of American Politics: Elites, Interest Groups, and Average Citizens" (abstract), *Perspectives on Politics* 12, no. 3 (September 2014): 564.

116. Ibid., 564.

117. Ibid., 565.

118. Ibid., 563.

119. Ibid., 576.

120. Ibid., 577.

121. Geoffrey Wood, "Business and Politics in a Criminal State: The Case of Equatorial Guinea," *African Affairs* 103, no. 413 (2004): 547–67, quoting J.-F.

Bayart, S. Ellis, and B. Hibou, *The Criminalization of the State in Africa* (Bloomington, IN: James Currey, 1999), 25–26.

122. Ken Silverstein, *The Secret World of Oil* (London: Verso, 2014), 107.

123. Ibid., at 119.

124. Ibid., at 175.

Chapter Four: What the Machine Wants

1. "Opportunity Denied: How Overregulation Harms Minorities," Subcommittee on Oversight, Agency Action, Federal Rights and Federal Courts, U.S. Senate, October 6, 2015, www.judiciary.senate.gov/meetings/opportunity-denied_how-overregulation-harms-minorities.

2. Per review on file with author, conducted November 3, 2015.

3. Rebecca Leber and Adam Peck, "House Republicans Voted Against the Environment More Than 500 Times in the Past Four Years," *The New Republic*, December 10, 2014.

4. See, generally, Kevin Cerilli and Christina Marcos, "House Passes Dodd-Frank Changes," *The Hill*, January 14, 2015; Simon Johnson, "The Republican Strategy to Repeal Dodd-Frank," *Baseline Scenario* (blog), January 7, 2015.

5. "Red Tape, Hidden Taxes and Regulation," FreedomWorks, accessed January 5, 2016, www.freedomworks.org/issue/red-tape-hidden-taxes-regulation.

6. "Overregulation," Libre Initiative, accessed January 5, 2016, http://thelibre initiative.com/issue/overregulation.

7. Burgess Everett and Seung Min Kim, "GOP Readying for End-of-Year Spending Fights," *Politico*, November 5, 2015.

8. Tyson Slocum, "Electric Utility Deregulation and the Myths of the Energy Crisis," *Bulletin of Science, Technology and Society* 21, no. 6 (December 2001) .

9. See Marc Gunther, "With Rooftop Solar on the Rise, U.S. Utilities Are Striking Back," *Yale Environment 360*, September 3, 2013; Joby Warrick, "Utilities Fight Rise in Home Solar Power," *Boston Globe*, March 15, 2015.

10. Carolyn Korman, "Greening the Tea Party," *New Yorker*, February 17, 2015; Edward Humes, "Throwing Shade: How the Nation's Investor-Owned Utilities Are Moving to Blot Out the Solar Revolution," *Sierra Magazine*, May/June 2014.

11. Chye-Ching Huang and Brandon Debot, "Ten Facts You Should Know About the Federal Estate Tax," Center on Budget and Policy Priorities, March 25, 2015.

12. For background on "carried interest," see "Business Taxation: What Is Carried Interest and How Should It Be Taxed?" Tax Policy Center, Urban Institute and Brookings Institution, www.taxpolicycenter.org/briefing-book/key-elements/business/carried-interest.cfm.

13. See Paul Solman, "Is Carried Interest Simply a Tax Break for the Ultra-Rich?" *PBS NewsHour*, October 29, 2015.

14. Catherine Rampell, "The Little People Pay Taxes," *New York Times*, Economix blog, February 23, 2011.

15. Ibid.

16. Associated Press, "Maid Testifies Helmsley Denied Paying Taxes," *New York Times*, July 12, 1989.

17. Jane Mayer, *Dark Money: The Hidden History of the Billionaires Behind the Rise of the Radical Right* (New York: Knopf Doubleday, 2016), 57.

18. "What Do the Koch Brothers Want?" Sen. Bernie Sanders website, www .sanders.senate.gov/koch-brothers, accessed January 5, 2016; "1980 Libertarian Party Platform," *LPedia: A Collaborative History of the Libertarian Party*, www .lpedia.org/1980_Libertarian_Party_Platform#2._Taxation, accessed January 5, 2016.

19. Jane Mayer, "New Koch," *New Yorker*, January 25, 2016.

20. See, e.g., Sari Horwitz, "Unlikely Allies," *Washington Post*, August 15, 2015.

21. See, e.g., "Not So Guilty as Charged," editorial, *Wall Street Journal*, December 4, 2015.

22. *People v. Roby*, 52 Mich. 577, 579 (1884).

23. Mayer, "New Koch."

24. Danny Hakim, "U.S. Chamber Out of Step with Its Board, Report Finds," *New York Times*, June 14, 2016; Sheldon Whitehouse, Elizabeth Warren, Barbara Boxer, Bernard Sanders, Sherrod Brown, Jeff Merkley, Richard Blumenthal, and Edward Markey, "The U.S. Chamber of Commerce: Out of Step with the American People and Its Members," June 14, 2016, available at www.whitehouse.senate .gov/news/release/senators-issue-report-on-us-chamber-of-commerce-lobbying.

25. Whitehouse, Warren, et al., "U.S. Chamber of Commerce," 13.

26. Paul Hodgson, "Top CEOs Make More than 300 Times the Average Worker," *Fortune*, June 22, 2015.

27. Benjamin I. Page, Larry M. Bartels, and Jason Seawright, "Democracy and the Policy Preferences of Wealthy Americans," *Perspectives on Politics* 11, no. 1 (March 2013): 51.

28. David Callahan and J. Mijin Cha, "Stacked Deck: How the Dominance of Politics by the Affluent and Business Undermines Economic Mobility in America," *Dēmos*, February 2013, 5–6, table 1.

29. Page, Bartels, and Seawright, "Democracy."

30. Ibid.

31. Ibid.

32. Ibid.

33. Peggy Noonan, "A Party Divided, and None Too Soon," *Wall Street Journal*, June 2, 2016.

Chapter Five: The Powell Memo and the Corporate Strategy

1. S. Rep. No. 3056, 59th Cong., 1st Sess., 2 (1906), cited in *Citizens United v. Fed. Election Comm'n*, 558 U.S. 310, 433 (2010) (Stevens, J., dissenting).

2. Lewis F. Powell Jr., "Confidential Memorandum: Attack on American Free Enterprise System," August 23, 1971, available at http://law2.wlu.edu/deptimages /Powell%20Archives/PowellMemorandumTypescript.pdf.

3. Joan Biskupic and Fred Barbash, "Retired Justice Lewis Powell Dies at 90," *New York Times*, August 26, 1998.

4. Jane Mayer, *Dark Money: The Hidden History of the Billionaires Behind the Rise of the Radical Right* (New York: Knopf Doubleday, 2016), 61.

5. Powell, "Confidential Memorandum."

6. Ryan Grim and Lucia Graves, "GOP, U.S. Chamber of Commerce Beat Back Bill to Combat Outsourcing," *Huffington Post*, September 28, 2010 .

7. Eric Lipton, Mike McIntire, and Don Van Natta Jr., "Top Corporations Aid U.S. Chamber of Commerce Campaign," *New York Times*, October 21, 2010.

8. Lee Drutman, *The Business of America Is Lobbying: How Corporations Became Politicized and Politics Became More Corporate* (New York: Oxford University Press, 2015), 3.

9. Powell, "Confidential Memorandum."

10. Ibid.

11. Ibid.

12. Ibid.

13. See "Public Comment to the Advisory Committee on the Civil Rules," U.S. Chamber Institute for Legal Reform, November 7, 2013, www.instituteforlegalreform.com/uploads/sites/1/FRCP_Submission_Nov.7.2013.pdf.

14. Richard Nixon, "Address to the Nation Announcing Intention to Nominate Lewis F. Powell, Jr., and William H. Rehnquist to be Associate Justices of the Supreme Court of the United States," October 21, 2971, American Presidency Project, www.presidency.ucsb.edu/ws/?pid=3196.

15. John Calvin Jeffries, *Justice Lewis F. Powell, Jr.* (New York: Fordham University Press, 2001), 1.

16. Jacob S. Hacker and Paul Pierson, *Winner-Take-All Politics: How Washington Made the Rich Richer and Turned Its Back on the Middle Class* (New York: Simon & Schuster, 2011), 118.

17. Ibid., 119–20.

18. Ibid., 121.

19. *First National Bank of Boston v. Bellotti*, 435 US 765 (1978).

20. Steven M. Teles, *The Rise of the Conservative Legal Movement: The Battle for Control of the Law* (Princeton, NJ: Princeton University Press, 2008), 142 (internal citation omitted).

21. *Palazzolo v. Rhode Island*, 533 U.S. 606 (2001).

22. Ibid.

23. Adam Liptak, "With Subtle Signals, Supreme Court Justices Request the Cases They Want to Hear," *New York Times*, July 6, 2015.

24. Adam Liptak, "Victory for Unions as Supreme Court, Scalia Gone, Ties 4–4," *New York Times*, March 29, 2016.

25. Jess Bravin, "Supreme Court's Term Disappoints Conservatives and Businesses," *Wall Street Journal*, June 28, 2016, quoting Florida State University law professor Mary Ziegler.

26. Ibid.

27. Robert Barnes, "For Conservatives, High Court's Term Was a Letdown," *Washington Post*, June 28, 2016, quoting Stanford Law Professor Pamela S. Karlan.

28. Adam Liptak, "The Right-Wing Supreme Court That Wasn't," *New York Times*, June 28, 2016.

29. Ibid.

30. Ibid.

31. Barnes, "For Conservatives."

32. Bravin, "Supreme Court's Term."

33. Community Rights Counsel, "Nothing for Free," July 24, 2000, 94, http://communityrights.org/NothingForFREE/NFFmain.php.

34. Ibid., 20.

35. Ibid., 14.

36. Ibid., 12.

37. Bob Sloan, "ALEC's Koch Funded Cabal 'Educating' Our State and Federal Judges," *Daily Kos*, August 20, 2012.

38. Community Rights Counsel, "Nothing for Free," 12.

39. Ibid.; Mayer, *Dark Money*, 110.

40. Chris Young, Reity O'Brien, and Andrea Fuller, "Corporations, pro-business nonprofits foot bill for judicial seminars," *Center for Public Integrity*, March 28, 2013.

41. Ibid., 15.

42. Ibid., 17.

43. Ibid., 79.

44. Ibid., 9.

45. Ibid., 29.

46. Ibid., 31.

47. Sloan, "ALEC's Koch Funded Cabal."

48. Community Rights Counsel, "Nothing for Free," 34.

49. Ibid., 37.

50. Ibid., 39.

51. Ibid., 54 n. 68.

52. Ibid., 62.

53. Ibid., 62.

54. Ibid., 79.

55. Sloan, "ALEC's Koch Funded Cabal."

56. Community Rights Counsel, "Nothing for Free," 8, citing *Ft. Lauderdale Sun-Sentinel*, April 18, 1998, 18A.

57. Ibid., citing *Louisville Courier Journal*, June 19, 1998.

58. Ibid., citing *San Antonio Express-News*, April 19, 1998, 9.

59. Mayer, *Dark Money*, 110.

60. *State of Rhode Island v. Lead Industries Association, et al.*, Civil Action No: PB/99-5226, Superior Court, State of Rhode Island and Providence Plantations Providence, Sc., (2002/09/17, 5:23-6:12).

61. *State of Rhode Island v. Lead Paint Assoc. et al.*, 951 A.2d 428, 443, 444, 448, 449, 450, 454 (R.I. 2008), citing Donald G. Gifford, "Public Nuisance as a Mass Products Liability," *University of Cincinnati Law Review* 71 (2003): 790–91, 794. See also Fidelma Fitzpatrick, "Painting over Long-Standing Precedent: How the

Rhode Island Supreme Court Misapplied Public Nuisance Law in *State v. Lead Industries Association,*" *Roger Williams University Law Review* 15 (2010): 448 n. 32 (describing the court's citations of Gifford).

62. Powell, "Confidential Memorandum."

Chapter Six: Capture of the Court

1. I have previously published on the ideas presented here in Sheldon White-house, "Conservative Judicial Activism: The Politicization of the Court Under Justice John Roberts," *Harvard Law and Policy Review* 9 (Winter 2015): 195.

2. "Transcript: Day One of the Roberts Hearings," *Washington Post*, September 13, 2005.

3. Adam Liptak, "Corporations Find a Friend in the Supreme Court," *New York Times*, May 4, 2013, citing Lee Epstein, William M. Landes, and Richard A. Posner, "How Business Fares in the Supreme Court," *Minnesota Law Review* 97 (2013): 1434.

4. Liptak, "Corporations.".

5. Jeffrey Toobin, "No More Mr. Nice Guy: The Supreme Court's Stealth Hard-liner," *New Yorker*, May 25, 2009.

6. *Trop v. Dulles*, 356 U.S. 86, 120 (1958) (J. Frankfurter, dissenting).

7. Adam Liptak, "Chief Justice John Roberts Amasses a Conservative Record, and Wrath from the Right," *New York Times*, September 18, 2015, citing Lee Epstein, William M. Landes, and Richard A. Posner, "Revisiting the Ideology Rankings of Supreme Court Justices," *Journal of Legal Studies* 44 (2015): S295–S317.

8. Epstein, Landes, and Posner, "Revisiting."

9. Jeffrey M. Jones, "Confidence in U.S. Institutions Still Below Historical Norms," Gallup, June 15, 2015, www.gallup.com/poll/183593/confidence-institu tions-below-historical-norms.aspx.

10. Greenberg Quinlan Rosner Research, "Democracy Corps Supreme Court Project: Frequency Questionnaire," April 16–21, 2014, www.democracycorps.com /attachments/article/979/042214%20DCORPS%20SCOTUS%20FQ.pdf.

11. Ibid.

12. The Mellman Group, "Findings From Recent Polling On The Supreme Court," May 19, 2014, https://perma.cc/X2HA-BCXT.

13. Linda Greenhouse, "Polar Vision," *New York Times*, May 28, 2014.

14. Norm Ornstein, "Why the Supreme Court Needs Term Limits," *The Atlantic*, May 22, 2014; Jeffrey Toobin, "Five to Four," *New Yorker*, June 25, 2007.

15. Dana Milbank, "The Roberts Court Finds a New Way to Stack the Deck in Favor of the Rich," *Washington Post*, January 11, 2016.

16. *National Federation of Independent Business v. Sebelius*, 567 U.S. ___ (2012).

17. Ibid., 39.

18. Ibid., 20.

19. Ibid., 52.

20. "Republican Party Platform of 2000," July 31, 2000, American Presidency Project, /www.presidency.ucsb.edu/ws/?pid=25849.

21. "No More Souters," editorial, *Wall Street Journal*, July 19, 2005.

22. *Brown v. Board of Education of Topeka*, 347 U.S. 483 (1954); Harry Flood Byrd, 1954, quoted in "Brown at 60: The Southern Manifesto and 'Massive Resistance' to Brown," NAACP Legal Defense and Educational Fund, www.naacpldf .org/brown-at-60-southern-manifesto-and-massive-resistance-brown.

23. *Roe v. Wade*, 410 U.S. 113 (1973).

24. *Miranda v. Arizona*, 384 U.S. 436, 468 (1966).

25. *Texas v. Johnson*, 491 U.S. 397 (1989).

26. In a March 22, 2016, CBS/*New York Times* poll, when asked "How important to you is who sits on the Supreme Court?," 49 percent of Republicans answered "Very important," while only 34 percent of Democrats gave the same answer; www .scribd.com/doc/305599300/NYT-CBS-poll-on-Supreme-Court-Mar16d-scotus.

27. Akhil Amar, "Should We Trust Judges?", *Los Angeles Times*, December 17, 2000.

28. *Shelby County v. Holder*, 133 S. Ct. 2612 (2013).

29. Tomas Lopez, "Shelby County: One Year Later," Brennan Center for Justice, June 24, 2014.

30. "North Carolina's Voter ID Shenanigans," editorial, *Washington Post*, January 31, 2016.

31. Anne Blythe, "4th U.S. Circuit Judges Overturn North Carolina's Voter ID Law," *Charlotte Observer*, July 29, 2016.

32. Fifteenth Amendment, United States Constitution.

33. Oral Argument at 16:14–17:7, *Shelby County v. Holder*.

34. *Northwest Austin Municipal Utility District No. 1 v. Holder*, 557 U.S. 193, 203 (2009).

35 *Shelby County*, 133 S. Ct. at 2621.

36. "Transcript: Day One of the Roberts Hearings," *Washington Post*, September 13, 2005.

37. Richard A. Posner, "The Voter Rights Act Ruling Is About the Conservative Imagination," *Slate*, June 26, 2013.

38. See Christopher Klein, "'A New Species of Monster': How Massachusetts Spawned the Gerrymander," *Boston Globe*, September 11, 2011.

39. Christopher Ingraham, "This Is the Best Explanation of Gerrymandering You Will Ever See," *Washington Post*, *Wonkblog*, March 1, 2015.

40. Olga Pierce, Justin Elliott, and Theodoric Meyer, "How Dark Money Helped Republicans Hold the House and Hurt Voters," ProPublica, December 21, 2012.

41. "2012 REDMAP Summary Report," The Redistricting Majority Project, January 4, 2013, www.redistrictingmajorityproject.com/?p=646.

42. Karen L. Haas, Clerk of the House of Representatives, "Statistics of the Presidential and Congressional Election of November 6, 2012," February 28, 2013, http://clerk.house.gov/member_info/electionInfo/2012election.pdf.

43. Ibid.

44. "2012 REDMAP Summary Report."

45. Ibid.

46. Sam Wang, "Let Math Save Our Democracy," *New York Times*, December 5, 2015.

47. "2012 REDMAP Summary Report."

48. Karen L. Haas, Clerk of the House of Representatives, "Statistics of the Presidential and Congressional Election of November 6, 2012," February 28, 2013, http://clerk.house.gov/member_info/electionInfo/2012election.pdf.

49. Ibid.

50. "2012 REDMAP Summary Report."

51. Ibid.

52. *Vieth v. Jubelirer*, 541 U.S. 267 (2004).

53. J. Gerald Hebert, Paul M. Smith, Martina E. Vandenberg, and Michael B. DeSanctis, *The Realist's Guide to Redistricting: Avoiding the Legal Pitfalls*, 2nd ed. (Chicago: American Bar Association, 2011).

54. *First National Bank of Boston v. Bellotti*, 435 U.S. 765 (1978).

55. Joe Hagan, "The Coming Tsunami of Slime," *New York*, January 22, 2012.

56. William F. Buckley Jr., "Our Mission Statement," *National Review*, November 19, 1955.

57. *District of Columbia v. Heller*, 554 U.S. 570 (2008).

58. Interview by Charlayne Hunter-Gault with Warren Burger, *MacNeil/Lehrer NewsHour*, PBS, December 16, 1991 (Monday transcript # 4226), cited in Joan Biskupic, "Guns: A Second (Amendment) Look," *Washington Post*, May 10, 1995.

59. Richard A. Posner, "In Defense of Looseness," *New Republic*, August 27, 2008.

60. Amanda Hollis-Brusky, *Ideas with Consequences: The Federalist Society and the Conservative Counterrevolution* (New York: Oxford University Press, 2015), 148.

61. Adam Liptak, "Supreme Court Prepares to Take On Politically Charged Cases," *New York Times*, October 4, 2015.

62. *Citizens United*, 558 U.S. at 379.

63. Ibid. at 380.

64. "A Corporate Court? Tracking the U.S. Chamber of Commerce and the Roberts Court: Current Term (OT 2015)," Constitutional Accountability Center, accessed March 31, 2016, http://theusconstitution.org/corporate-court.

65. Ibid.

66. *Ledbetter v. Goodyear Tire and Rubber Company*, 550 U.S. 618 (2007).

67. *Leegin Creative Leather Products, Inc. v. PSKS, Inc.*, 551 U.S. 877 (2007).

68. *Janus Capital Group, Inc. v. First Derivative Traders*, 564 U.S. ___ (2011).

69. *Gross v. FBL Financial Services, Inc.*, 557 U.S. ___ (2009).

70. *Ashcroft v. Iqbal*, 556 U.S. 662 (2009); *Bell Atlantic Corp. v. Twombly*, 550 U.S. 544 (2007).

71. *Rent-A-Center West, Inc. v. Jackson*, 561 U.S. 63 (2010).

72. *Wal-Mart Stores, Inc. v. Dukes*, 564 U.S. ___ (2011); *AT&T Mobility LLC v. Concepcion*, 563 U.S. 333 (2011).

73. *DirecTV Inc. v. Imburgia*, 577 U.S. ___ (2015).

74. *Vance v. Ball State University*, 570 U.S. __ (2013); *Mutual Pharmaceutical Co. v. Bartlett*, 570 U.S. ___ (2013); *Comcast v. Behrend*, 569 U.S. ___ (2013).

75. *Burwell v. Hobby Lobby Stores* 573 U.S. ___ (2014); *Harris v. Quinn*, 573 U.S. ___ (2014).

76. "Transcript: Day One of the Roberts Hearings," *Washington Post*, September 13, 2005.

Chapter Seven: Capture of Elections: *Citizens United*

1. *Marshall v. Baltimore & Ohio Railroad Company*, 57 U.S. 314, 335 (1853).

2. I have previously published on the ideas presented here in: Sheldon Whitehouse, "Conservative Judicial Activism: The Politicization of the Court Under Justice John Roberts," *Harvard Law and Policy Review* 9 (Winter 2015): 195.

3. "McCain: Supreme Court Ignorant on Politics," CBS News, January 5, 2012.

4. Fred Wertheimer, "How Chief Justice Roberts and Four Supreme Court Colleagues Gave the Nation a System of Legalized Bribery," *Huffington Post*, October 6, 2015, citing Nina Totenberg, "Federal Judge Richard Posner: The GOP Has Made Me Less Conservative," NPR, June 5, 2012.

5. James Vicini, "Landmark Supreme Court Ruling Allows Corporate Political Cash," Reuters, January 21, 2010.

6. Alan Simpson, Bill Bradley, and Bob Kerrey, "How to Make Our Democracy Work for Everyone," *Roll Call*, January 21, 2015.

7. Connie Morella and Dan Glickman, "We Are Gyrocopter," *Roll Call*, May 22, 2015.

8. Mark McKinnon, "Why We Won't Stop Fighting Corruption," *Daily Beast*, November 11, 2014.

9. *Citizens United*, 558 U.S. at 428–29 (Stevens, J., dissenting), citing *Trustees of Dartmouth College v. Woodward*, 4 Wheat. 518, 636, 4 L.Ed. 629 (1819) (Marshall, C.J.)

10. Ibid. at 466.

11. Burt Neuborne, *Madison's Music: On Reading the First Amendment* (New York: The New Press, 2015), 79–80.

12. See "Warren Buffett: Citizens United Pushes U.S. Toward a Plutocracy," People for the American Way, quoting CNN:Money interview with Buffett, April 3, 2015, http://blog.pfaw.org/content/warren-buffett-citizens-united-pushes-us-toward-plutocracy.

13. Adam Liptak, "Justices, 5–4, Reject Corporate Spending Limit," *New York Times*, January 21, 2010.

14. Jane Mayer, *Dark Money: The Hidden History of the Billionaires Behind the Rise of the Radical Right* (New York: Knopf Doubleday, 2016), 252.

15. *Citizens United*, 558 U.S. at 354–5.

16. Neuborne, *Madison's Music*, 102.

17 Robert Barnes and Dan Eggen, "Supreme Court Rejects Limits on Corporate Spending on Political Campaigns," *Washington Post*, January 22, 2010.

18. Sam Jewler, "The Dark Side of Citizens United," Public Citizen Report,

October 29, 2014, www.citizen.org/documents/us-chamber-of-commerce-dark
-money-spending-report.pdf.

19. Robert Barnes and Dan Eggen, "Supreme Court Rejects Limits on Corporate Spending on Political Campaigns," *Washington Post*, January 22, 2010.

20. Tilman Klumpp, Hugo M. Mialon, and Michael A. Williams, "Yes, 'Citizens United' Gives Republicans an Electoral Edge. Here's Proof," *Washington
Post*, April 7, 2016.

21. See *Citizens United*, 558 U.S. at 358.

22. Voltaire, *Candide*, trans. Lowell Bair (New York: Bantam Books, 1959), 87.

23. Nicholas Confessore, "Koch Brothers' Budget of $889 Million for 2016 Is
on Par with Both Parties' Spending," *New York Times*, January 26, 2015; Matea
Gold, "Charles Koch Downgrades His Political Network's Projected 2016 Spend-
ing from $889 Million to $750 Million," *Washington Post*, October 21, 2015; Coral
Davenport, "Why Republicans Keep Telling Everyone They're Not Scientists,"
New York Times, October 30, 2014.

24. Coral Davenport, "Many Conservative Republicans Believe Climate
Change Is a Real Threat," *New York Times*, September 28, 2015.

25. Kenneth P. Vogel and Burgess Everett, "How the Koch Network Created
the Ex-Im Fight," *Politico*, December 3, 2015.

26. Sarah Karlin-Smith, "Drug lobby plans counterattack on prices," *Politico*,
August 4, 2016.

27. Alex Altman, "Silent Partners," *Time*, October 10, 2016.

28. *Caperton v. A.T. Massey Coal Co*, 556 U.S. 868 (2009).

29. Ibid. at 868, 884.

30. Trevor Potter, "The Supreme Court Needs to Get Smarter About Politics,"
Washington Post, October 11, 2013.

31. Kenneth P. Vogel, "Undisclosed Dollars Dominate Campaign Spending,"
Politico, January 12, 2016.

32. *Citizens United v. FEC*, 558 U.S. 310, 358 (2010).

33. Ibid. at 360.

34. *Marbury v. Madison*, 5 U.S. 137, 177 (1803).

35. Benjamin Cardozo, *The Nature of the Judicial Process* (New Haven, CT:
Yale University Press, 1921), 141.

36. *Citizens United*, 558 U.S. at 400 (Stevens, J., dissenting).

37. See "08-205 Citizens United v. Federal Election Commission," Supreme
Court Docket, accessed March 2, 2016, www.supremecourt.gov/qp/08-00205qp.pdf.

38. See ibid., order of June 29, 2009; see generally *Citizens United*, 558 U.S. at
396-98 (Stevens, J., dissenting).

39. *Citizens United*, 538 U.S. at 398 (Stevens, J., dissenting).

40. *Citizens United*, 558 U.S. at 345 (slip op at 40), citing *Buckley v. Valeo*, 424
U.S. 1, 25 (1976).

41. Ibid.

42. *Citizens United*, 558 U.S. at 358.

43. "National Survey: Super PACs, Corruption, and Democracy," Brennan
Center for Justice, April 24, 2012.

44. Ibid.

45. "Americans' Views on Money in Politics," *New York Times*, June 2, 2015.

46. Harold Meyerson, "Americans See a Government of, by and for the Rich," *Washington Post*, November 18, 2015, citing "Survey: Anxiety, Nostalgia, and Mistrust: Findings from the 2015 American Values Survey," Public Religion Research Institute, November 17, 2015.

47. Patrick O'Connor and Janet Hook, "WSJ/NBC Poll Finds Anger at Political System," *Wall Street Journal*, November 3, 2015.

48. Greg Stohr, "Bloomberg Poll: Americans Want Supreme Court to Turn Off Political Spending Spigot," *Bloomberg Politics*, September 28, 2015.

49. *Citizens United*, 558 U.S. at 425–30 (Stevens, J. dissenting).

50. Ibid. at 429.

51. *Citizens United*, 558 U.S. at 319.

52. *Citizens United*, 558 U.S. at 414 (Stevens, J., dissenting) (quoting *Vasquez v. Hillery*, 474 U.S. 254, 265 [1986]).

53. Ibid. at 414 (Stevens, J., dissenting).

54. "2012 Presidential Race: Candidates Opposed/Supported by Outside Groups and Party Committees," OpenSecrets.org, https://www.opensecrets.org/pres12/indexp.php.

55. WSJ News Graphics, "Super PAC Contributions for the 2016 Presidential Campaign," *Wall Street Journal*, July 31, 2015, http://graphics.wsj.com/elections/2016/campaign-super-pacs/.

56. The Mellman Group, "Findings From Recent Polling On The Supreme Court."

57. *Citizens United*, 558 U.S. at 370–71.

58. *American Tradition Partnership v Bullock*, 567 U.S. ___ (2012).

59. *Western Tradition Partn. v. Attorney General*, 2011 MT 328 (2011).

60. *Western Tradition Partn. v. Attorney General*, 363 Mont. 220, 230–33 (2011).

61. Ibid.

62. Matt Schudel, "Huguette Clark, Copper Heiress and Recluse, Dies at 104," *Washington Post*, May 24, 2011.

63. *Western Tradition Partn. v. Attorney General*, 363 Mont. at 228.

64. Brief of United States Senators Sheldon Whitehouse and John McCain as Amici Curiae in Support of Respondents, *American Tradition Partnership, Inc. v. Bullock*, No. 11-1179, May 2012.

65. See generally *Western Tradition Partn. v. Attorney General*, 363 Mont. 220 (2011).

66. *American Tradition Partnership v. Bullock*, 567 U.S. ___ (2012).

67. *McCutcheon v. FEC*, 572 U.S. ___ (2014).

68. Ibid.

69. Marcia Coyle, "Justice Anthony Kennedy Loathes the Term 'Swing-Vote,'" *National Law Journal*, October 27, 2015.

70. "Scalia on Unlimited Political Ads: Turn Off TV," CBS News, January 21, 2012.

Chapter Eight: Capture of Regulatory Agencies

1. Shawn Otto, *The War on Science* (Milkweed Editions, 2016), 350.

2. See, e.g., Daniel Carpenter and David Moss, eds., *Preventing Regulatory Capture: Special Interest Influence and How to Limit It* (New York: Cambridge University Press, 2014).

3. Charlie Savage, "Sex, Drugs, and Graft Cited in Interior Department," *New York Times*, September 10, 2008.

4. "Gulf Oil Industry, Government Ties Persist," *USA Today*, July 26, 2011.

5. "Investigative Report: Island Operating Company et al.," Inspector General, Department of the Interior, March 31, 2010, 3, http://www.govexec.com/pdfs/052510ts1.pdf.

6. Savage, "Sex, Drugs, and Graft Cited in Interior Department."

7. Ibid., 7.

8. Ibid.

9. Gerald P. O'Driscoll Jr., "The Gulf Spill, the Financial Crisis and Government Failure," *Wall Street Journal*, June 12, 2010.

10. "Editorial: The mess at MMS," *Providence Journal*, May 30, 2010.

11. Stephen Labton, "Agency's '04 Rule Let Banks Pile Up New Debt," *New York Times*, October 2, 2008.

12. Thomas Frank, "Obama and 'Regulatory Capture,'" *Wall Street Journal*, June 24, 2009.

13. Woodrow Wilson, *The New Freedom* (New York: Doubleday, Page, 1913).

14. Marver H. Bernstein, *Regulating Business by Independent Commission* (Princeton, NJ: Princeton University Press, 1955), 87, 90.

15. Ibid., 88.

16. Ibid., 88–89.

17. See "Legislation," U.S. Food and Drug Administration, last updated July 2, 2015, at www.fda.gov/RegulatoryInformation/Legislation.

18. "Famous Cases and Criminals: Willie Sutton," Federal Bureau of Investigation, accessed January 26, 2016, www.fbi.gov/history/famous-cases/willie-sutton.

19. "GDP (Current US$)," World Bank, accessed July 30, 2016, http://data.worldbank.org/indicator/NY.GDP.MKTP.CD; "OTC Derivatives Statistics at End-June 2015," Bank for International Settlements, accessed July 30, 2016, www.bis.org/publ/otc_hy1511.htm.

20. Russell Baker, "Dirksen, Reagan and Real Money," *Chicago Tribune*, October 5, 1985.

21. James Kwak, "Cultural Capture and the Financial Crisis," in *Preventing Regulatory Capture: Special Interest Influence and How to Limit It*, ed. Daniel Carpenter and David Moss (New York: Cambridge University Press, 2014), 92.

22. Luigi Zingales, "Preventing Economists' Capture," in *Preventing Regulatory Capture: Special Interest Influence and How to Limit It*, ed. Daniel Carpenter and David Moss (New York: Cambridge University Press, 2014), 127.

23. Ibid.

24. "BP Found 'Grossly Negligent' in Gulf of Mexico Oil Spill," *New Orleans Sun*, September 5, 2014.

25. Michael Cooper, Gardiner Harris, and Eric Lipton, "In Mine Safety, a Meek Watchdog," *New York Times*, April 10, 2010.

26. "Protecting the Public Interest: Understanding the Threat of Agency Capture," Hearing Before the Subcommittee on Administrative Oversight and the Courts of the Committee on the Judiciary, United States Senate, August 3, 2010.

27. Ibid., statement of Nicholas Bagley.

28. Barbara W. Tuchman, *The March of Folly: From Troy to Vietnam* (New York: Random House, 1985), 382.

29. James Madison, "The Same Subject Continued: The Union as a Safeguard Against Domestic Faction and Insurrection," Federalist No. 10, November 23, 1787, www.congress.gov/resources/display/content/The+Federalist+Papers#The FederalistPapers-10.

30. Kie Relyea, "Ten Years After Pipeline Explosion, Kings Learn to Feel Joy Again," *Bellingham Herald*, June 7, 2009.

31. "Pipeline Accident Report: Pipeline Rupture and Subsequent Fire in Bellingham, Washington," National Transportation Safety Board, June 10, 1999, 11.

32. Ibid., 8.

33. Ibid.

34. Ibid., 11.

35. Keiko Morris, Janet Burkitt, Jim Brunner, and Jack Broom, "Fire Takes Young Lives—Cause Investigated; Pipeline Has Anacortes Refinery Tie," *Seattle Times*, June 11, 1999.

36. "Pipeline Accident Report," 11.

37. Ibid.

38. Ibid.

39. Morris et al., "Fire"; "Pipeline Accident Report," 11.

40. Andrew Restuccia and Elana Schorr, "Pipelines Blow Up and People Die," *Politico*, April 21, 2015.

41. "Pipeline Accident Report," v.

42. Restuccia and Schorr, "Pipelines."

43. Ibid.

44. Ibid.

45. Ibid.

46. Ibid.

47. Ibid.

48. Ibid.

49. A bill I have proposed to create a "regulatory capture cop" has consistently gone nowhere. Maybe it will take yet another disaster to pass it.

50. Restuccia and Schorr, "Pipelines."

51. Relyea, "Ten Years."

52. Ibid.

53. "About the FEC," Federal Election Commission, accessed March 6, 2016, www.fec.gov/about.shtml.

54. 52 U.S.C. Section 301, Federal Election Campaign Act.

55. Mike McIntire and Michael Luo, "Fine Line Between 'Super PACs' and Campaigns," *New York Times*, February 25, 2012.

56. Statement of Reasons Of Chair Ellen L. Weintraub and Commissioners Cynthia L. Bauerly and Steven T. Walther, Before the Federal Election Commission, *In the Matter of Friends of Laura Ruderman, et al.*, MUR 6611, at 3, available at http://eqs.fec.gov/eqsdocsMUR/13044330712.pdf.

57. Statement of Lawrence M. Noble, President and CEO, Americans for Campaign Reform, Before the Subcommittee on Crime and Terrorism Senate Committee on the Judiciary, "Current Issues in Campaign Finance Law Enforcement," April 9, 2013, www.judiciary.senate.gov/imo/media/doc/4-09-13NobleTesti mony.pdf.

58. Paul Blumenthal, "How SuperPACs and Campaigns Are Coordinating in 2016," *Huffington Post*, November 14, 2015.

59. *Citizens United*, 558 U.S. at 370–71.

60. 52 U.S.C. Section 30104.

61. Statement of Lawrence M. Noble; see generally, "The Federal Election Commission Is Worse than Useless," editorial, *Los Angeles Times*, March 31, 2016. See also T.W. Farnam, "Despite Supreme Court support, disclosure of funding for 'issue ads' has decreased," *Washington Post*, September 15, 2010.

62. Statement of Lawrence M. Noble.

63. 2 U.S.C. Section 441f.

64. Statement of Lawrence M. Noble.

65. Ibid., 3.

66. Ellen Killoran, "Phantom Company Donates $1 Million to Romney Group," *International Business Times*, August 4, 2011.

67. See generally Internal Revenue Service, "Social Welfare Organizations," www.irs.gov/Charities-&-Non-Profits/Other-Non-Profits/Social-Welfare-Organi zations, accessed March 6, 2016.

68. Internal Revenue Code 501(c)(4).

69. See Internal Revenue Service, "Social Welfare Organizations."

70. Kim Barker, "How Nonprofits Spend Millions on Elections and Call it Public Welfare," ProPublica, August 18, 2012.

71. Ibid.

72. See generally ibid.

73. Internal Revenue Service, "Social Welfare Organizations."

74. Americans for Prosperity, IRS Form 1024, Question 15, Page 4, filed August 4, 2004; Americans for Prosperity, IRS Form 990, November 8, 2013, see Question 3, page 3, and see page 59.

75. Barker, "How Nonprofits Spend."

76. Ibid.

77. Ibid.

78. Ibid.

79. Ibid.

80. Ibid.

81. Justin Elliot, "Watchdogs to IRS: Reject Rove Group's Tax Application," ProPublica, January 2, 2013.

82. Barker, "How Nonprofits Spend."

83. Ibid.

84. Kim Barker, "Controversial Dark Money Group Among Five That Told IRS They Would Stay Out of Politics, Then Didn't," ProPublica, January 2, 2013.

85. Eric Lichtblau, "FEC Can't Curb 2016 Election Abuse, Commission Chief Says," *New York Times*, May 3, 2015.

86. Matea Gold and Anu Narayanswamy, "How 'Ghost Corporations' Are Funding the 2016 Election," *Washington Post*, March 18, 2016.

87. "The Federal Election Commission Is Worse than Useless," editorial, *Los Angeles Times*, March 31, 2016.

88. See generally Statement of Lawrence M. Noble.

Chapter Nine: Capture of the Civil Jury

1. I have previously published on the ideas presented in this chapter in: Sheldon Whitehouse, "Restoring the Civil Jury's Role in the Structure of Our Government," *William and Mary Law Review* 55 (2014): 1241; Sheldon Whitehouse, "Opening Address," *University of Pennsylvania Law Review* 162 (2013–2014): 1517.

2. Alexis de Tocqueville, *Democracy in America*, trans. Arthur Goldhammer (New York: Penguin Putnam, 2004) , 283.

3. There are some social ills that juries can't cure, as the injustices wrought by all-white juries in the South remind us. There are some conditions that some medicines just can't cure. But they are still good medicine for what they can cure.

4. John H. Langbein et al., *History of the Common Law: The Development of Anglo-American Legal Institutions* (New York: Aspen, 2009), 100 (alteration in original), quoting F.W. Maitland, *The Forms of Action at Common Law*, ed. A.H. Chaytor and W. Whittaker (1909), 22 (internal quotation marks omitted).

5. Ibid., 100, 244–45.

6. Stephan Landsman, "The Civil Jury in America: Scenes from an Underappreciated History," *Hastings Law Journal* 44 (1993): 592 (footnotes omitted), citing Harold M. Hyman and Catherine M. Tarrant, "Aspects of American Trial Jury History," in *The Jury System in America*, ed. Rita J. Simon (Beverly Hills, CA: Sage, 1975), 24–25; Massachusetts Body of Liberties para. 29 (1641), reprinted in *Sources of Our Liberties*, ed. Richard L. Perry and John C. Cooper (Chicago: American Bar Foundation, 1952), 151.

7. Akhil Reed Amar, *America's Constitution: A Biography* (New York: Random House, 2005), 233.

8. Landsman, "Civil Jury," 595.

9. Declaration of Independence.

10. U.S. Constitution, Amendment VII.

11. Alexander Hamilton, "The Judiciary Continued in Relation to Trial by

Jury," Federalist No. 83, www.congress.gov/resources/display/content/The+Feder
alist+Papers#TheFederalistPapers-83.

12. See Thomas J. Methvin, Alabama—The Arbitration State, 62 ALA. LAW.
48, 49 (2001) ("In 1774, John Adams stated: 'Representative government and trial
by jury are the heart and lungs of liberty. Without them, we have no other fortifi-
cation against being ridden like horses, fleeced like sheep, worked like cattle, and
fed and clothed like swines and hounds.'").

13. William Blackstone, *Commentaries* (London: Collins and Hannay, 1832),
vol. 2, book 3, 380.

14. Ibid.

15. Ibid.

16. Nathan S. Chapman, "The Jury's Constitutional Judgment," *Alabama Law
Review* 67 (2015): 207.

17. 18 U.S.C. Section 1503 (influencing or injuring officer or juror generally); 18
U.S.C. Section 1504 (influencing juror by writing).

18. Blackstone, *Commentaries*, 294.

19. David Marcus, "Finding the Civil Trial's Democratic Future After Its De-
mise," *Nevada Law Journal* 15 (2015): 1524.

20. John H. Langbein, "The Disappearance of Civil Trial in the United States,"
Yale Law Journal 122 (2012): 524 (arguing that an increase in pretrial discovery has
eliminated the need for a fact-finding jury).

21. Ibid.

22. *Bell Atl. Corp. v. Twombly*, 550 U.S. 544, 575 (2007) (Stevens, J., dissenting).

23. See, e.g., *Comcast v. Behrend*, 569 U.S. ___ (2013).

24. *Celotex Corp. v. Catrett*, 477 U.S. 317 (1986); *Anderson v. Liberty Lobby,
Inc.*, 477 U.S. 242 (1986); *Matsushita Elec. Indus. Co. v. Zenith Radio Corp.*, 475
U.S. 574 (1986).

25. Per Westlaw search, March 7, 2016, conducted by Rachel Craft, student,
Harvard Law School.

26. *DirecTV v. Imburgio*, 577 U.S. ___ (2015) (Ginsburg, J., dissenting.).

27. Jessica Silver-Greenberg and Robert Gebeloff, "Arbitration Everywhere,
Stacking the Deck of Justice," *New York Times*, October 31, 2015.

28. Associated Press, "Firm Agrees to End Role in Arbitrating Credit Card
Debt," *New York Times*, April 19, 2009.

29. Henry Farrell, "People Are Freaking Out About the Trans Pacific Partnership's Investor Dispute Settlement System. Why Should You Care?" *Washington
Post*, March 26, 2015.

30. Jackie Calmes and Sabrina Tavernise, "U.S. Proposes Provision on Tobacco in Trade Pact," *New York Times*, October 1, 2015 (Philip Morris International
net revenues for 2015: $74 billion; Togo GDP [PPP]: $11 billion).

31. Christ Hamby, "The Court That Rules The World," *BuzzFeed*, August 28,
2016.

32. Ibid.

33. Abe Fortas, *Concerning Dissent and Disobedience* (New York: New American Library, 1968), 60.

34. Blackstone, *Commentaries*, 380.

35. Gordon Wood, *The Radicalism of the American Revolution* (New York: Knopf Doubleday, 2011), 174–75.

36. Ibid.

37. Larry Lessig, *Republic, Lost: How Money Corrupts Congress—and a Plan to Stop It* (New York: Twelve Books, 2011).

38. Alexander Hamilton, "Objections to the Power of the Senate to Set as a Court for Impeachments Further Considered," Federalist No. 66, https://www.congress.gov/resources/display/content/The+Federalist+Papers#TheFederalist Papers-66, and "The Mode of Electing the President," Federalist No. 68, https://www.congress.gov/resources/display/content/The+Federalist+Papers#TheFederalist Papers-68.

39. Zephyr Teachout, *Corruption in America* (Cambridge, MA: Harvard University Press, 2014), 38.

40. Ibid., 7.

41. William Novak, "A Revisionist History of Regulatory Capture," in *Preventing Regulatory Capture: Special Interest Influence and How to Limit It*, ed. Daniel Carpenter and David Moss (New York: Cambridge University Press, 2014), 39.

42. Ibid.

43. Teachout, *Corruption*, 167, citing *Mills v. Mills*, 40 N.Y. 543, 546.

44. Teachout, *Corruption*, 191–92, *citing United States v. Classic*, 313 U.S. 299 (1941) (Douglas, J., dissenting).

45. Niccolò Machiavelli, *The Prince*, ch. IX: "Concerning a Civil Principality" (1513).

46. Andrew Jackson, "President Jackson's Veto Message Regarding the Bank of the United States," July 10, 1832, available at http://avalon.law.yale.edu/19th_century/ajveto01.asp.

47. *McCutcheon v. Federal Election Commission*, 572 U.S. ___ (2014), slip op. at 39, quoting *The Speeches of the Right Hon. Edmund Burke*, 129–130 (J. Burke ed. 1867).

48. *United States v. Sun-Diamond Growers of Cal.*, 526 U.S. 398 (1999) (quoting, and rejecting, an argument made by the Independent Counsel on behalf of the United States) (emphasis added by Justice Scalia).

49. *McDonnell v. United States*, 579 U.S. __ (2016), slip op at 4.

50. Editorial, "Robert McDonnell gets freedom from jail—but not from disgrace," *The Washington Post*, September 9, 2016.

51. *McDonnell*, slip op. at 21–22.

52. Editorial, "Robert McDonnell gets freedom from jail—but not from disgrace."

53. Robert Barnes, "Supreme Court Overturns Corruption Conviction of Former Va. Governor McDonnell," *Washington Post*, June 27, 2016.

54. *McDonnell*, slip op at 28.

55. Carl Hulse, "Is the Supreme Court Clueless About Corruption? Ask Jack Abramoff," *New York Times*, July 5, 2016.

56. Rebecca Leber and Adam Peck, "House Republicans Voted Against the

Environment More Than 500 Times in the Past Four Years," *The New Republic*, December 10, 2014.

57. Gordon Wood, *The Radicalism of the American Revolution* (New York: Knopf Doubleday, 2011), 174–75.

Chapter Ten: The Denial Machine

1. Edward L. Bernays, *Propaganda* (Brooklyn, New York: Ig Publishing, 1928).

2. John Stauber, quoted in Shawn Otto, *The War on Science* (Milkweed Editions, 2016), 264–5.

3. Robert J. Brulle, "Institutionalizing Delay: Foundation Funding and the Creation of U.S. Climate Change Counter-Movement Organizations," *Springer Science and Business Media Dordrecht 2013*, November 19, 2013, 2, citing National Research Council, *America's Climate Choices* (Washington, DC: National Academies Press, 2011).

4. *United States v. Philip Morris USA Inc.*, 449 F. Supp. 2d 1 (D.D.C. 2006), *aff'd in part & vacated in part*, 566 F. 3d 1095 (D.C. Cir. 2009 (*per curiam*), *cert. denied*, 561 U.S. ___, 130 S. Ct. 3501 (2010).

5. Bernays, *Propaganda*, 50.

6. Steve Coll, *Private Empire: ExxonMobil and American Power* (New York: Penguin, 2012), 134.

7. Brown and Williamson, *Smoking and Health Proposal*, Brown and Williamson document no. 680561778-1786, 1969, https://industrydocuments.library.ucsf.edu/tobacco/docs/#id=jryfo138, cited in David Michael, *Doubt Is Their Product: How Industry's Assault on Science Threatens Your Health* (New York: Oxford University Press, 2008), x.

8. Jason M. Breslow, "Robert Brulle: Inside the Climate Change 'Counter-movement,'" *PBS Frontline*, October 23, 2012.

9. Brulle, "Institutionalizing Delay."

10. Justin Gillis and John Schwartz, "Deeper Ties to Corporate Cash for Doubtful Climate Researcher," *New York Times*, February 21, 2015.

11. Jeremiah Bohr, "The 'climatism' cartel: why climate change deniers oppose market-based mitigation policy," *Environmental Politics* 25, no. 5 (2016), 813.

12. David Edelstein, "Devastating in Its Implications," *New York Magazine*, June 5, 2006.

13. Naomi Oreskes, "Beyond the Ivory Tower: The Scientific Consensus on Climate Change," *Science* 306, no. 5702 (2004): 1686.

14. Justin Farrell, "Network Structure and Influence of the Climate Change Counter-Movement," *Nature Climate Change*, November 30, 2015, doi: 10.1038/NCLIMATE2875.

15. Justin Farrell, "Corporate Funding and Ideological Polarization About Climate Change," *PNAS* 113, no. 1 (January 5, 2016): 92.

16. Ibid., 95–96.

17. Leo Hickman, "Heartland Institute Compares Belief in Global Warming to Mass Murder," *The Guardian*, May 4, 2012.

18. John M. Carroll, "Review: Marshall and Military Victory, 1943–1945," *The Review of Politics* 35, no. 4 (October 1973): 585.

19. Jane Mayer, *Dark Money: The Hidden History of the Billionaires Behind the Rise of the Radical Right* (New York: Knopf Doubleday, 2016), 79.

20. Brulle, "Institutionalizing Delay."

21. Ibid.

22. Otto, *The War on Science*, 130.

23. Ibid.

24. Ibid. at 292.

25. Ibid. at 232.

26. Ibid. at 292.

27. Ibid.

28. Ibid. at 293.

29. Ibid.

30. Ibid.

31. Ibid. at 293–4.

32. Brulle, "Institutionalizing Delay."

33. Mayer, *Dark Money*, 204.

34. Otto, *The War on Science*, 350.

35. Ibid., 352.

36. "Sources of Greenhouse Gas Emissions," EPA, www.epa.gov/ghgemissions /sources-greenhouse-gas-emissions.

37. The Office of Management and Budget provides a range of Social Cost of Carbon estimates, which vary based on the assumed discount rates used to monetize future harms. The central range price, which uses a 3 percent discount rate, is $38 in 2016 in 2007 dollars, which equals $45 in inflation-adjusted nominal dollars (rounded up to the nearest dollar). See Appendix A in "Technical Support Document: Technical Update of the Social Cost of Carbon for Regulatory Impact Analysis—Under Executive Order 12866," May 2013, Revised July 2015, https://www.whitehouse.gov/sites/default/files/omb/inforeg/scc-tsd-final-july -2015.pdf.

38. "Counting the Cost of Energy Subsidies, IMF Survey," International Monetary Fund, July 17, 2015, www.imf.org/external/pubs/ft/survey/so/2015/new 070215a.htm.

39. Mayer, *Dark Money*, 206.

40. Ibid.

41. Brulle, "Institutionalizing Delay," 8, fig. 2.

42. Ibid., 10.

43. Ibid.

44. Ibid.

45. Farrell, "Corporate Funding," 92.

46. Alex McKechnie, "Not Just the Koch Brothers: New Drexel Study Reveals Funders Behind the Climate Change Denial Effort," *DrexelNOW*, December 20, 2013, http://drexel.edu/now/archive/2013/December/Climate-Change.

47. Otto, *The War on Science*, 342.

48. Ibid., 152.

49. Jill Fitzsimmons and Jocelyn Fong, *"The Wall Street Journal*: Dismissing Environmental Threats Since 1976," Media Matters for America, August 2, 2012.

50. Ibid.

51. Ibid., quoting *Wall Street Journal*, "A Bit of Prudence at the CPSC," January 6, 1976, via Factiva.

52. Ibid., quoting *Wall Street Journal*, "Ozone Re-Examined," May 15, 1979, via Factiva.

53. Ibid., quoting *Wall Street Journal*, "Heads in the Ozone," March 5, 1984, via Factiva.

54. Ibid., quoting *Wall Street Journal*, "Ozone Chicken Littles Are at It Again," March 23, 1989, via Factiva.

55. Ibid., quoting *Wall Street Journal*, "Press-Release Ozone Hole," February 28, 1992, via Factiva.

56. Ibid., quoting *Wall Street Journal*, "Heads in the Ozone."

57. Ibid., quoting *Wall Street Journal*, "Clean Air Revisited," August 29, 1990, via Factiva.

58. Ibid.

59. Ibid., quoting *Wall Street Journal*, "Asides: Middle-Class Payments," February 14, 1992, via Factiva.

60. Environmental Protection Agency, "Progress Cleaning the Air and Improving People's Health," citing "The Benefits and Costs of the Clean Air Act 190 to 2010," November 1999, www.epa.gov/clean-air-act-overview/progress-cleaning -air-and-improving-peoples-health.

61. Fitzsimmons and Fong, *"The Wall Street Journal."*

62. Ibid.

63. "Climate of Uncertainty," editorial, *Wall Street Journal*, October 1, 2013.

64. Ibid.

65. "Analysis: How the *Wall Street Journal* Opinion Section Presents Climate Change," Climate Nexus, 2016, available at http://static1.squarespace.com /static/534ec657e4b03c887dde2641/t/575f6edd20c647ff95c170a0/1465872094069 /FINAL_CN_WSJ_white_paper-0613.pdf.

66. *Major Campaign Speeches of Adlai E. Stevenson* (New York: Random House, 1952), 130.

67. Sheldon Whitehouse, "The Fossil-Fuel Industry's Campaign to Mislead the American People," *Washington Post*, May 29, 2015.

68. Oversight of the U.S. Department of Justice, Senate Judiciary Committee, March 9, 2016.

69. Robert Post, "Exxon-Mobil is abusing the first amendment," *The Washington Post*, June 24, 2016.

70. See, e.g., Paul Dresser, "RICO for Government Climate Deniers?" *Townhall*, April 16, 2016, http://townhall.com/columnists/pauldriessen/2016/04/16/rico -for-government-climate-deniers-n2149120.

71. See generally, "Timeline: Legal Harassment of Climate Scientist Michael Mann," Union of Concerned Scientists, http://www.ucsusa.org/our-work/center

-science-and-democracy/protecting-scientists-harassment/va-ag-timeline.html#.WA
fuhvkrIdU.

Chapter Eleven: Climate Change and the "Flies of Summer"

1. "Pope Francis Says There Are Limits to Freedom of Expression," Vatican Radio, January 16, 2015.

2. Wendell Berry, "Praise for *The Dying of the Trees: The Pandemic of America's Forests* by Charles E. Little," 1997, available at www.ecobooks.com/books/dying .htm.

3. Brian Kahn, "The World Passes 400 PPM Threshold. Permanently," *Climate Central*, September 27, 2016, http://www.climatecentral.org/news/world-passes -400-ppm-threshold-permanently-20738.

4. Steve Graham, "John Tyndall (1820–1893)," *NASA: Earth Observatory*, October 8, 1999, http://earthobservatory.nasa.gov/Features/Tyndall.

5. "Climate Change Indicators: Ocean Heat," US Environmental Protection Agency, https://www.epa.gov/climate-indicators/climate-change-indicators-ocean -heat.

6. Brad Plumer, "The Oceans Are Acidifying at the Fastest Rate in 300 Million Years. How Worried Should We Be?" *Washington Post*, August 31, 2013; Oliver Milman, "World's Oceans Warming at Increasingly Faster Rate, New Study Find," *The Guardian*, January 18, 2016.

7. National Centers for Environmental Information, "Global Analysis— Annual 2015," National Oceanic and Atmospheric Administration, January 2016, https://www.ncdc.noaa.gov/sotc/global/201513.

8. James Boyd, "CRMC Climate Change Adaptation Actions," Rhode Island Coastal Resources Management Council, http://www.crmc.ri.gov/news /2013_0201_climate.html.

9. Benjamin Hulac, "Tobacco and Oil Industries Used Same Researchers to Sway Public," *Scientific American: ClimateWire*, July 20, 2016.

10. Steve Knisely, Planning Engineering Division, "Controlling the CO_2 Concentration in the Atmosphere," October 16, 1979, with memo to R.L. Hirsch, accessed January 16, 2016, http://insideclimatenews.org/sites/default/files/docu ments/CO2%20and%20Fuel%20Use%20Projections.pdf.

11. Roger W. Cohen, Director, Theoretical and Mathematical Sciences Laboratory, Exxon, "Memo to: Mr. A.M. Natkin, Office of Science and Technology, Exxon Corporation," September 2, 1982, accessed January 16, 2016, http://inside climatenews.org/sites/default/files/documents/%2522Consensus%2522%20on%20 CO2%20Impacts%20%281982%29.pdf.

12. Knisely, "Controlling."

13. M.B. Glaser, Manager, Environmental Affairs Program, "CO2 'Greenhouse Effect,'" November 12, 1982, http://insideclimatenews.org/sites/default/files /documents/1982%20Exxon%20Primer%20on%20CO2%20Greenhouse%20Effect .pdf#page=5.

14. Jeffrey Ball, "Exxon Chief Makes a Cold Calculation on Global Warming," *Wall Street Journal*, June 14, 2005.

15. Naomi Oreskes and Ted Lieu, "The Harm Exxon Mobil Has Done," *The Hill*, November 4, 2015.

16. Shawn Otto, *The War on Science* (Milkweed Editions, 2016), 269.

17. Steve Coll, *Private Empire: ExxonMobil and American Power* (New York: Penguin, 2012), 88.

18. George Monbiot, "The Denial Industry," *The Guardian*, September 19, 2006; Dennis Hevesi, "Frederick Seitz, Physicist Who Led Skeptics of Global Warming, Dies at 96," *New York Times*, March 6, 2008. Whether Exxon paid for this "petition" is unknown.

19. Coll, *Private Empire*.

20. Ibid., 96.

21. Edmund Burke, "Reflections on the Revolution in France," in *The British Prose Writers* (London: Piccadilly, 1819–21), 21:132–33.

22. Peter Schweizer, "Introduction," *Landmark Speeches of the American Conservative Movement* (College Station: Texas A&M University Press, 2007), 3.

23. "Conservation Activism Is a Healthy Sign," *The Sun* (Baltimore), May 4, 1970, A17, cited in James E. Person Jr., *Russell Kirk: A Critical Biography of a Conservative Mind* (Lanham, MD: Madison Books, 1999), 27.

24. Dwight D. Eisenhower, "Transcript of President Dwight D. Eisenhower's Farewell Address, 1961," www.ourdocuments.gov/doc.php?flash=false&doc=90&page=transcript.

25. Gerald Ford, "Remarks at Dedication Ceremonies for the National Environmental Research Center, Cincinnati, Ohio, July 3, 1975," American Presidency Project, www.presidency.ucsb.edu/ws/?pid=5042.

26. Ronald Reagan, "Remarks at Dedication Ceremonies for the New Building of the National Geographic Society," June 19, 1984, https://reaganlibrary.archives.gov/archives/speeches/1984/61984a.htm.

27. Mitch Hescox and Paul Douglas, *Caring for Creation: The Evangelical's Guide to Climate Change and a Healthy Environment* (Ada, MI: Baker Publishing Group, 2016), 51.

28. *Congressional Record*, vol. 149, part 1, January 9, 2003, 379.

29. Ibid., vol. 153, part 7, April 19, 2007, 9342.

30. Ibid., vol. 155, no. 82, June 3, 2009, H6088.

31. Ibid., vol. 154, no. 91, June 4, 2008, S5019.

32. "Global Analysis—Annual 2014," National Centers for Environmental Information, National Oceanic and Atmospheric Administration, www.ncdc.noaa.gov/sotc/global/201413.

33. Coral Davenport, "Why Republicans Keep Telling Everyone They're Not Scientists," *New York Times*, October 30, 2014.

34. Andrew Nikiforuk, "Bark Beetles, Aided by Climate Change, Are Devastating U.S. Pine Forests," *Washington Post*, December 5, 2011.

35. Bob Inglis, "Putting Free Enterprise to Work: A Conservative Vision of

312.........................

Our Environmental Future," *Duke Environmental Law and Policy Forum* 23 (Spring 2013): 248–249.

36. Henry A. Waxman, Sherwood Boehlert, Wedward J. Markey, and Wayne Gilchrest, "Carbon Emission Policy Could Slash Debt, Improve Environment," *Washington Post*, February 23, 2012.

37. William D. Ruckelshaus, Lee M. Thomas, William K. Reilly, and Christine Todd Whitman, "A Republican Case for Climate Action," *New York Times*, August 1, 2013.

38. Ibid.

39. Chuck Hagel, "Secretary of Defense Speech," Halifax International Security Forum, November 22, 2013, http://archive.defense.gov/speeches/speech.aspx?speechid=1821.

40. George P. Shultz and Gary S. Becker, "Why We Support a Revenue-Neutral Carbon Tax," *Wall Street Journal*, April 7, 2013.

41. David Frum, "A Tax We Could Learn to Love," CNN, December 3, 2012.

42. N. Gregory Mankiw, "A Carbon Tax That America Could Live With," *New York Times*, August 31, 2013.

43. Jim Brainard, "Cities Must Take Action on Global Warming," *Indystar*, December 11, 2013.

44. Davenport, "Why Republicans Keep Telling."

45. William Shakespeare, *Richard III*, Act 1, Scene 2.

46. Jane Mayer, *Dark Money: The Hidden History of the Billionaires Behind the Rise of the Radical Right* (New York: Knopf Doubleday, 2016), 278.

47. Duff Cooper, *Talleyrand* (New York: Grove Press, 2010 [1932]), 313.

48. Peggy Noonan, "A Party Divided, and None Too Soon," *Wall Street Journal*, June 2, 2016.

49. "Sen. Inhofe Delivers Major Speech on the Science of Climate Change," July 29, 2003, www.inhofe.senate.gov/epw-archive/press/bsen-inhofe-delivers-major-speech-on-the-science-of-climate-change/b-icatastrophic-global-warming-alarmism-not-based-on-objective-sciencei-ipart-2/i; see also James Inhofe, *The Greatest Hoax: How the Global Warming Conspiracy Threatens Your Future* (Washington, DC: WND Books, 2012).

50. Gary McManus, "Global Climate Change and the Implications for Oklahoma," Oklahoma Climatological Survey, April 2010.

51. "Study Finds Climate Change May Dramatically Reduce Wheat Production," Kansas State University News and Communications Service, February 18, 2015, www.k-state.edu/media/newsreleases/feb15/climatewheat21815.html.

52. "Ron Johnson's Climate Change Denials May Not Fly with Voters," editorial, *Milwaukee Journal Sentinel*, October 22, 2013.

53. Tim Carpenter, "Oil, Gas Industry: It's not our fault," *Topeka Capital-Journal*, August 24, 2010.

54. Tiffany Germain, Ryan Koronowski, and Jeff Spross, "The Anti-Science Climate Denier Caucus: 113th Congress Edition," *ThinkProgress*, June 26, 2013.

55. "GOP Deeply Divided over Climate Change," Pew Research Center, No-

vember 1, 2013, www.people-press.org/2013/11/01/gop-deeply-divided-over-climate
-change.

56. Amy Levin and Greg Strimple, "Recent Polling on Youth Voters," Memo
to League of Conservative Voters, July 24, 2013, http://www.lcv.org/issues/polling
/recent-polling-on-youth.pdf.

57. Matt Viser, "GOP Hopefuls Not Embracing Climate Change," *Boston
Globe*, August 1, 2015.

58. "GOP Deeply Divided over Climate Change."

Chapter Twelve: America's Lamp in Peril

1. Daniel Webster, "The Bunker Hill Monument," address delivered at the
laying of the cornerstone of the Bunker Hill Monument in Charlestown, MA,
June 16, 1825, in *The Writings and Speeches of Daniel Webster* (Boston: Little,
Brown, 1903), 1:235.

2. John Winthrop, "A Model of Christian Charity," 1630, in *Collections of the
Massachusetts Historical Society*, 3rd series, 7 (1838), 31–48.

3. Ronald Reagan, "Reagan's Farewell Speech," 1988, www.pbs.org/wgbh
/americanexperience/features/primary-resources/reagan-farewell.

4. John F. Kennedy, "Inaugural Address of President John F. Kennedy," January 20, 1961, www.jfklibrary.org/Research/Research-Aids/Ready-Reference/JFK
-Quotations/Inaugural-Address.aspx.

5. Barack Obama, "President Barack Obama's Inaugural Address," January 21,
2009, www.whitehouse.gov/blog/2009/01/21/president-barack-obamas-inaugural
-address.

6. William Clinton, "Bill Clinton's Prime-Time Speech," Democratic National Convention, August 27, 2008, www.npr.org/templates/story/story.php?story
Id=94045962.

7. Webster, "Bunker Hill Monument."

8. Joseph E. Stiglitz, *Freefall: America, Free Markets, and the Sinking of the
World Economy* (New York: W.W. Norton, 2010), 225–26.

9. Alexander Hamilton or James Madison, "The Senate Continued," Federalist No. 63, www.congress.gov/resources/display/content/The+Federalist+Papers
#TheFederalistPapers-63.

10. Right Hon. John Edward Emerich, First Baron Acton, "Inaugural Lec-
ture," in *Lectures on Modern History*, ed. John Neville Figgis and Reginald Vere
Laurence (London: Macmillan, 1906), 24.

11. Franklin Delano Roosevelt, "Acceptance Speech for the Renomination
for the Presidency," American Presidency Project, www.presidency.ucsb.edu/ws
/?pid=15314_.

12. Thomas Jefferson, letter to George Logan, November 12, 1816, http://tjrs
.monticello.org/letter/1392.

13. David McCullough, "On John Adams" (notes on file with author from
Q&A session), Library of Congress, February 14, 2014, www.loc.gov/today/cyberlc
/transcripts/2014/140212lib1200.txt.

Postscript

1. Nicholas Confessore and Rachel Shorey, "Outside Money Favors Hillary Clinton at a 2-to-1 Rate Over Donald Trump," *New York Times*, October 22, 2016.

2. Nicholas Confessore and Rachel Shorey, "How Democrats Stopped Worrying and Learned to Love Big Donor Money," *New York Times*, September 30, 2016.

3. Ibid.

4. Matea Gold, "How the Stampede for Big Money Enabled Donald Trump's Rise," *Washington Post*, November 8, 2016.

5. Fredreka Schouten and Christopher Schnaars, "Super PAC Donations Surge Past $1 Billion," *USA Today*, September 21, 2016.

6. Matea Gold and Anu Narayanswamy, "How 10 Mega-donors Already Helped Pour a Record $1.1 Billion into Super PACs," *Washington Post*, October 15, 2016, updated November 2, 2016.

7. Confessore and Shorey, "Outside Money Favors Hillary Clinton at a 2-to-1 Rate Over Donald Trump."

8. Ibid.

9. Theodore Roosevelt, speech delivered at the dedication of the John Brown Memorial Park in Osawatomie, Kansas, August 31, 1910, www.whitehouse.gov /blog/2011/12/06/archives-president-teddy-roosevelts-new-nationalism-speech.

10. "Senate GOP Super PAC Gets $11M from Undisclosed Donors," *BNA, Inc. Money and Politics Report*, October 28, 2016.

11. Gold, "How the Stampede for Big Money Enabled Donald Trump's Rise."

12. Ibid.

13. Ibid.

14. Sam Thielman, "Pro-Trump Billionaires Pour Money into Last-Minute Bid for Swing States," *The Guardian*, November 4, 2016.

15. Rebecca Ballhaus, "Five Big GOP Donors Added at Least $24 Million to Trump Groups in Recent Months," *Wall Street Journal*, October 16, 2016.

16. Eric Lipton, "Trump Campaigned Against Lobbyists, but Now They're on His Transition Team," *New York Times*, November 11, 2016.

17. Kenneth Vogel and Alex Isenstadt, "Secret Money to Boost Trump," *Politico*, September 28, 2016.

18. Ibid.

19. Emily Cadei, "How Charles and David Koch Plan to Remake the Republican Party," *Newsweek*, September 28, 2016.

20. Ibid.

21. Ibid.

22. "Koch Brothers Push Forward Efforts to Hide Nonprofit Donors' Identities," *CBS SF Bay Area*, April 29, 2016.

23. Cadei, "How Charles and David Koch Plan to Remake the Republican Party."

24. Fredreka Schouten, "Charles Koch Say His Network Offers 'Vision' for a Divided Nation," *USA Today*, November 11, 2016.

25. Ibid.

26. Ibid.

27. Ibid.

28. Ibid.

29. Cadei, "How Charles and David Koch Plan to Remake the Republican Party."

30. Josh Barro, "Fact-Free Conservative Media Is a Symptom of GOP Troubles, Not a Cause," *Business Insider*, October 24, 2016.

31. Ibid.

32. Jamie Weinstein, "This Election Was a Great Opportunity for Republicans. Instead, the GOP Lies Broken," *The Guardian*, November 8, 2016.

33. Stuart Stevens, "The Flat-Earth Set Helped Donald Trump Hijack the GOP and Crash It into the Ground," *The Daily Beast*, November 7, 2016.

34. Marianne Lavelle, "Fossil Fuel Money to GOP Grows, and So Does Climate Divide," *Inside Climate News*, September 15, 2016.

35. Ibid.

36. Ibid.

37. Danny Vinik, "Trump's Attack Dog on Climate," *Politico*, November 14, 2016.

38. Ibid.

39. Ibid.

40. For an image of the advertisement, see Ben Adler and Rebecca Leber, "Donald Trump Once Backed Urgent Climate Action. Wait, What?" *Grist*, June 8, 2016.

41. See Andrew Ward, "Exxon Backs 'Serious Action' on Climate Change," *Financial Times*, October 19, 2016; Stanley Reed, "Oil and Gas Companies Make Statement in Support of U.N. Climate Goals," *New York Times*, October 16, 2015.

42. See Sheldon Whitehouse, "Why Isn't Anyone Lobbying For Climate Change?" *Forbes*, June 7, 2016; Sheldon Whitehouse, "The Climate Movement Needs More Corporate Lobbyists," *Harvard Business Review*, February 25, 2016.

43. Carl Hulse, "Supreme Court Stonewall May Not Crumble Anytime Soon," *New York Times*, November 3, 2016.

44. Eric Lipton and Robert Faturechi, "These Officials Help Write Ballot Questions. Companies Write Them Checks," *New York Times*, November 4, 2016.

Index

Center for Public Integrity, 73
CEOs
  American public compared to,
    60–61
  Citizens United and, 101–2
  corporations compared to, 58–59
CFCs. *See* chlorofluorocarbons
Chafee, Lincoln, 174
Chamber of Commerce
  *Austin v. Michigan Chamber of
    Commerce*, 111
  Citizens United for, 98
  Congress compared to, 59
  corporate influence in, 64–66
  dark money for, 98
  Freedom Partners Chamber of
    Commerce, 42
  Institute for Legal Reform for, 65
  as lobbying group, 34
  Republican Party and, 91
  Roberts support of, 91
  for Wall Street, 64
Chapman, Nathan, 135
charters, 12–13
Cheney, Dick, 51
chlorofluorocarbons (CFCs), 161–62
Christie, Chris, 38–39
citizens. *See* American public
Citizens for Responsibility and Ethics,
  37
*Citizens United v. Federal Election
  Commission*
  American public against, 78–79,
    97–98
  in campaign finance, 22, 26, 28,
    30–31, 36–38, 127
  CEOs and, 101–2
  for Chamber of Commerce, 98
  climate change and, 175–77
  in Congress, 182–83
  for corporate agendas, 94, 108–9
  for corporate influence, 22, 26, 28,
    30–31, 110–11
  for corporations, 87–88
  for deceptive advertising, 36–37

for donor class, 87–88
in electioneering, 98–99
free speech and, 107–8, 110
history of, 93–94, 104–9
McCain against, 112
McCain-Feingold Act in, 106
in Montana, 112–13
for negative advertising, 35
against originalism, 109–10
in politics, 95–96, 100–101
for pollution, 98
against popular democracy, 95–97
Posner discussing, 95
Powell and, 66
against precedent, 110–11
Republican Party and, 180
Scalia and, 110, 113
Stevens, J., discussing, 106–7, 110
for Tea Party, 185
Trump and, 44–45
for Wall Street, 98
civil juries, 215n12
  American public for, 133
  corporate influence in, 135–36
  corporations against, 140–41
  against corruption, 145–46
  failures of, 214n3
  Founding Fathers for, 133–35
  history of, 133–35
  in politics, 136–38, 141
  as regulation, 141, 149
  as weak, xviii
Civil Rules of Procedure, 136–37
Clark, William Andrews, 112
class actions, 138
Clean Air Act, 9, 57, 162–63
Clean Water Act, 9
Cleveland, Grover, 19
climate change. *See also* pollution
  Americans for Prosperity in, 180–81,
    183
  Carbon Limits and Energy for
    America's Renewal Act, 175
  Citizens United and, 175–77
  Climate Nexus in, 163–64

DE First Holdings, 43
deceptive advertising
  Citizens United for, 36–37
  in electioneering, 35–36
Declaration of Independence, U.S., 2,
  134, 189
Deepwater Horizon oil spill, 117–18, 122
DeFazio, Peter, 102, 125–26
democracy. See popular democracy
Democracy in America (Tocqueville),
  133
the denial machine
  American Petroleum Institute for,
    153
  CFCs in, 161–62
  for climate change, 153–55, 183–85
  for fossil fuels, 157–60
  free speech and, 165–68
  history of, 150–51
  for lobbying groups, 155–57
  media for, 160–65
  Media Matters discussing, 161–63
  for Tobacco Institute, 151–52
Department of Justice, U.S. (DOJ),
  46, 131–32
Department of Transportation, U.S.,
  64
Dionne, E. J., 35
Dirksen, Everett, 121
DISCLOSE Act, 36–37
District of Columbia v. Heller, 89–90
Dodd-Frank bill, 49–50
DOJ. See Department of Justice
donor class
  American public and, 60–62,
    143–44
  Citizens United for, 87–88
  corporate influence for, 62
Donors Capital Fund, 158–59
DonorsTrust, 158–59
Douglas, William O., 143
Drew, Elizabeth, 25
"Drug Lobby Plans Counterattack on
  Prices" (Politico), 101
Drutman, Lee, 25, 30, 64–66

Earth Day, 9
education
  Abood v. Detroit Board of
    Education, 70–71
  Brown v. Board of Education, 81
  corporate influence in, 75–76
  Friedrichs v. California Education
    Association, 71
Eisenhower, Dwight, 173
electioneering. See also campaign
  finance; Federal Election
  Commission
  American public and, 31–32
  Americans for Prosperity in, 29
  for Bush, J., 39
  Citizens for Responsibility and
    Ethics ion, 37
  Citizens United in, 98–99
  Commission on Hope, Growth, and
    Opportunity in, 36–37
  corporate influence in, 41–42,
    94–97, 99–101, 110
  corporations in, 8, 20–22
  corruption in, 143
  courts in, 81–82
  dark money in, 84–85
  deceptive advertising in, 35–36
  Ernst in, 42–43
  FECA for, 24–25, 126–27
  "The Federal Election Commission
    Is Worse than Useless," 131
  for Fiorina, 39–40
  Freedom Partners in, 29
  Government Integrity Fund in, 37
  Kasich in, 39
  Koch brothers in, 29–30, 42–43
  lobbying groups in, 36–37
  McConnell v. Federal Election
    Commission, 111
  negative advertising in, 35
  Trees of Liberty in, 42–43
  Voting Rights Act, 82–83
Environmental Protection Agency
  (EPA), 64, 148, 178
Epstein, Lee, 77

Trees of Liberty, 42–43
Trump, Donald
  Citizens United and, 44–45
  Republican Party and, 44
  super PACs and, 44–45
Tsiorvas, Stephen, 124
Twombly decision, 92
Tyndall, John, 169

Union Pacific Railway System,
  18
unions, 70
*United States Magazine and
  Democratic Review*, 13
utilities
  as corporations, 50
  *Northwest Austin Municipal Utility
    District*, 83
  Olympic Pipeline Company, 124,
    126
  PHMSA, 125–26

Van Buren, Martin, 13
Vance v. Ball State University, 92
Vieth v. Jubelirer, 86
Voltaire, 99
Voters Legislative Transparency
  Project, 73–74
Voting Rights Act, 82–83

Walker, Scott, 39
Wall Street
  Chamber of Commerce for, 64
  Citizens United for, 98
  corporate influence for, 61
  corruption in, 41, 49–50
  regulation of, 117–19, 122, 187

Wall Street Journal, 179
  corporate influence in, 56, 71–72,
    118
  corruption in, 161–64
Wallis, John, 14
Walmart
  as corporation, 27
  Wal-Mart v. Dukes, 92
The War on Science (Otto), 116–17,
  156–57, 160–61, 172
Warren, Elizabeth, 59
Washington (state), 124–26
Washington Post
  on campaign finance, 31–33
  discussing corruption, 146
  discussing courts, 71–72
  discussing *Shelby County*, 82
Watergate scandal, 24–25
Waxman, Henry, 178
Webster, Daniel, 12, 186–87
welfare, for corporations, 51–52,
  55–56
Wertheimer, Fred, 41, 42,
  147–48
West Inc. v. Jackson, 92
West Virginia, 102–3
White, William Allen, 18
White, William S., xv
Whitman, Christine Todd, 178
Wilson, Woodrow, 120
Winkler, Adam, 19
Winthrop, Jonathan, 187
Wonder Bread, 9
Wood, Gordon, 141
Wood, Liam, 124

Zingales, Luigi, 122

About the Authors

Senator Sheldon Whitehouse represents Rhode Island in the U.S. Senate. He has served as his state's United States Attorney and as the state Attorney General, as well as its top business regulator. He is the author of *On Virtues: Quotations and Insight to Live a Full, Honorable, and Truly American Life,* and has written opinion pieces for the *New York Times,* the *Columbia Journalism Review,* and *U.S. News & World Report,* among other outlets. He lives in Newport, Rhode Island, with his wife, a marine scientist, and his grown children when they visit.

Melanie Wachtell Stinnett is a Boston-based writer and former Director of Policy and Communications at the Tobin Project. She has previously published on regulatory policy and Supreme Court litigation trends.

Celebrating 25 Years of Independent Publishing